WHAT
TO
EAT
WHEN

WHAT
TO EAT
WHEN

A Strategic Plan to Improve Your Health & Life Through Food

Michael F. Roizen, M.D., and
Michael Crupain, M.D., M.P.H.,
with Ted Spiker

Illustrations by Michael Shen, M.D.

NATIONAL
GEOGRAPHIC

Washington, D.C.

Published by National Geographic Partners, LLC

1145 17th Street NW Washington, DC 20036

Library of Congress Cataloging-in-Publication Data

Names: Roizen, Michael F., author. | Crupain, Michael, author.
Title: What to eat when : a strategic plan to improve your health and life
   through food / Michael Roizen, M.D. and Michael Crupain, M.D., M.P.H. with
   Ted Spiker ; illustrations by Michael Shen.
Description: Washington, DC : National Geographic, [2019] | Includes
   bibliographical references and index.
Identifiers: LCCN 2018040549 (print) | LCCN 2018044319 (ebook) | ISBN
   9781426220128 (ebook) | ISBN 9781426220111 (hardback)
Subjects: LCSH: Longevity--Nutritional aspects--Popular works. |
   Aging--Prevention--Popular works. | Self-care, Health--Popular works. |
   BISAC: HEALTH & FITNESS / Nutrition.
Classification: LCC RA776.75 (ebook) | LCC RA776.75 .R658 2019 (print) | DDC
   613--dc23
LC record available at https://lccn.loc.gov_2018040549

Since 1888, the National Geographic Society has funded more than 13,000 research, exploration, and preservation projects around the world. National Geographic Partners distributes a portion of the funds it receives from your purchase to National Geographic Society to support programs including the conservation of animals and their habitats.

Get closer to National Geographic explorers and photographers, and connect with our global community. Join us today at nationalgeographic.com/join

For information about special discounts for bulk purchases, please contact National Geographic Books Special Sales: specialsales@natgeo.com

For rights or permissions inquiries, please contact National Geographic Books Subsidiary Rights: bookrights@natgeo.com

Interior design: Melissa Farris

Printed in the United States of America

19/ BVG-CG/2

CONTENTS

Preface 9

Introduction: What to Eat When 13

PART 1: HOW FOOD WORKS

1. The Science of When 23

2. A Nutritious Breakdown 37

PART 2: THE WHEN WAY

3. Time to Eat! 53

4. The When Way: A 31-Day Plan 69

5. Food for Thought 101

PART 3: WHAT TO EAT WHEN

Section 1: At Odds

6. When You're Stressed and Hangry 113

7. When You're Fighting Fatigue 119

8. When You're Bummed 123

9. When You're Experiencing Grief 127

Section 2: At Home

10. When You Cannot Sleep 131

11. When You Get a Lot of Headaches 137

12. When You're Sick 143

13. When You're in Pain 149

14. When You Have Digestive Problems 155

Section 3: At Work

15. When You're Being Tested 163

16. When You Have a Job Interview 167

17. When You Have to Make a Big Decision..................... 171

18. When You're on the Go 175

19. When You Have an Event 179

Section 4: At Play
20. When You're on Vacation..183
21. When It's the Holiday Season 189
22. When You're at the Stadium 195
23. When You're on a First Date 199
24. When You Exercise 203

Section 5: For Women
25. When You're Trying to Get Pregnant (or Already Are) 211
26. When You're Nursing 217
27. When You Have PMS or Period Pain..........................223
28. When You Have Hot Flashes 227

Section 6: For Men
29. When You Need a Testosterone Boost.........................231
30. When You Want to Improve Fertility 235
31. When You Need to Shrink Your Prostate 239

Section 7: At Risk
32. When You Have a Family History of Cancer 243
33. When You Want to Protect Your Heart 251
34. When You Need to Fortify Your Skeleton..................259
35. When You Don't Want to Lose Your Mind...................265
36. When You Want to Prevent Type 2 Diabetes................271
37. When You Want Healthy Lungs.....................................277
38. When You Want to Reduce Inflammation 281
39. When You Have Hormonal Issues 287
40. When You Have Other Health Issues 293

PART 4: THE FINAL WORD: WHAT TO EAT WHEN
41. How to Win the When Way..303
Conclusion: The 10 Commandments of the When Way.............311

Acknowledgments..313
Glossary 319
Sources...321
Index...345

PREFACE

From Michael Roizen, M.D. (Dr. R)

Chief Wellness Officer, Cleveland Clinic

Food is powerfully evocative and has the ability to convey some of our sturdiest memories. I vividly recall, for example, the first time that five-cent hamburgers were sold in fast food joints. I also think fondly of the early advertising campaign claiming that CorningWare plates and serving dishes were indestructible. (My father promptly tried to show us how permanent it was by dropping one to the ground; it shattered, and I learned that there are exceptions to all science.)

As I embarked on my career as a doctor, I also learned about the medicinal power of food and the secrets behind proper cooking techniques. When I became dean of the College of Medicine at State University of New York Upstate Medical University, I quickly developed a curriculum that taught students how to cook healthy meals in an elective class called Culinary Medicine. We limited the class to 20 students, but 63 tried to register that first year. That was about the time I was developing my cooking expertise as part of *RealAge* (a system that calculates your true biological age versus your calendar age based on your lifestyle and other risk factors). I made 10 recipes a day, five days a week, for 50 weeks with a cooking partner, Donna Szymanski, and my nutritional partner, Dr. John La Puma.

I had always eaten food, of course. But that was the moment when I really *found* food. Through *RealAge,* I learned that eating well is more than just ingredients; it is also, just as crucially, about preparation and technique. You can help your body by learning to make foods you love that are also loaded with health benefits.

In my work as the chief wellness officer of the Cleveland Clinic, as well as my work with Dr. Mehmet Oz, food and food preparation have always been the foundations for giving people the power to change their lives. Jim Perko, our executive chef and culinary medicine master at the clinic, says you should never eat food that doesn't love you back. In this book, we're taking it one step further by adding in the variable of time.

I'm privileged to work with Dr. Michael Crupain on this methodology. Through my work as chief medical consultant to *The Dr. Oz Show* and his role as medical director of that program, I quickly realized that both our approaches were rooted in science—and we had the same goals of helping people better understand food. It was a match made in the kitchen!

Now, we've put together the plan that combines the what and the when—all with the goal of getting your body synchronized like a world-class orchestra so that your life can hit all the notes you want it to.

From Michael Crupain, M.D., M.P.H. (Dr. C)
Medical Unit Chief of Staff, The Dr. Oz Show
If you can still remember the time you were three, you may recollect a favorite toy or singing songs with your parents. For me, those memories revolve around food. I remember making

cookies with my mother, and how delicious lobster tasted. Because I was introduced to cooking at a young age, I've always loved the process more than my peers do. I baked pies and bread in elementary school, and I grilled pizzas (before it was fashionable to do so) when I was in high school.

As the years passed, I found myself returning again and again to the experimentation of cooking. It was one of my favorite activities the year I moved home to New York City as I prepared to apply to medical school. We lived across the street from the World Trade Center; when the towers collapsed in 2001, we had to leave our apartment for months, and found ourselves eating out a lot as a result. It was then that I got really excited about good food. I remember a time we were waiting at a restaurant that had really bad service—we had been there forever and they hadn't even delivered a morsel of bread. All of a sudden, when a man in a chef's uniform walked in carrying a loaf, we jokingly asked him for some. The next thing you know, he invited me into the kitchen. I ended up working weekends there for the year, and later in other kitchens.

In medical school, I started a pastry club and taught other students how to cook. Then, during a month off of my neurosurgery residency, I went to cooking school in Italy. Each morning, we went to the market and prepared the traditional Mediterranean diet dishes of the Apulia (Puglia) region. The teacher, who was American and has since become a good friend, told us that his cooking school and its students allowed him to live the life he dreamed of. That stuck with me.

I ended my neurosurgery residency after two years because it took me away from some of my most important passions: food and cooking. That's when I discovered the field of preventive medicine. Most people have never heard of it (and neither had I); it's a specialty that takes care of populations and tries to keep them healthy, rather than treating patients only after they've been stricken by disease. I was drawn to this area of concentration because it allowed me to combine my interests by focusing on the intersection of food, agriculture, and health.

I always knew food was an important part of medicine; I witnessed this firsthand after a close family member changed his health post–heart attack by adjusting his diet and lifestyle habits. But up until this time in my training, I never saw a way to actually specialize in this branch of medicine.

The Johns Hopkins Bloomberg School of Public Health, where I did my residency, helped me find a way. Its motto is "Protecting Health, Saving Lives Millions at a Time." There was no better way to achieve this than working in the media. After completing my residency program, I went to work at *Consumer Reports,* where I ran the food safety testing program. There, I was able to dig deep into the science of food and agriculture, leveraging the power of the most trusted brand in America to educate consumers and advocate for meaningful food safety and sustainability changes.

Now, at *The Dr. Oz Show,* I help shape the content of a program that millions of Americans welcome into their homes every day. Each week, we are shifting the culture of our country to one of health, where people are focusing more and more on what they eat (who had heard of kale or flax seeds before Dr. Oz?). I'm excited to collaborate in these pages with Dr. Roizen as we zoom in on the next phase of improving our diets— and ultimately our health: the when.

INTRODUCTION

What time is it?

Chances are it took you 0.047 second to answer that question. That's because you're never more than a few inches from a timepiece. Clocks in the car and on your phone. Clocks on your computers and on the wall. Clocks on your wrist and in the corner of the TV screen. Clocks on your nightstand and along city blocks.

Tick tock, the world doesn't stop.

With some exceptions, many of us revolve our entire lives—both work and play—around schedules, appointments, calendars, and the rhythm of minutes, hours, and days. Time is the universal metronome of our lives.

The funny thing is that our bodies work in the same way. They operate with a strong desire to sync *what* you do with *when* you do it.

But instead of a grandfather clock on your colon, a pocket watch dangling from your liver, and a smartphone attached to your meniscus, your body works with an internal rhythm that allows it to function optimally for survival.

The collective diet industry has spent a lot of time addressing the "what" part of eating: Fruit is better than fries, nuts are better than chips, and bears may be onto something because salmon may just be the most perfect food in the world. But we have spent little time on, well, time—the "when" part of the equation.

As it turns out, major scientific breakthroughs have begun to prove that when it comes to nutrition, **timing *is* everything.** The research is so new that it's literally changed the way we eat (and we thought we knew everything about food!). As it turns out, *when* you eat is as essential as *what* you eat for maintaining a good weight, preventing and curing some diseases, and living a long, energetic, and happy life.

This book is about exploring the intersection between the "what" and the "when." We've pulled together all the latest research so you can learn when to eat for optimal health, to minimize stress, and to deal with just about every situation you may encounter over the course of a day. This information just may change your life—and allow you to be your best self.

Now, we're not going to be so strict that you have to chow down on blueberries at 10:23 a.m. every day or eat a bowl of spinach at 4:07 p.m. every afternoon. But we are going to explain the science of how your body's circadian rhythms are programmed to best metabolize and use food for your own benefits—and how you can tap into those rhythms through your eating habits. By the time you're finished reading, you'll understand how the "When Way" will help you achieve all of your health goals—whether losing 10 or 50 pounds, helping you decrease your blood pressure, reducing the pain in your knees, or providing the day-to-day energy you need.

We have spent our medical careers working on the integration of food and medicine (albeit in different ways) and share at least one guiding principle: Food matters. A lot. It matters medically, it matters biologically, it matters physically, it matters emotionally, and it matters socially. It matters in every sphere of life.

There is no question that food has an impact on your health; science has proven it over and over again. But the only "magic pill" we believe in is how—and when—you decide to approach every day and every meal.

As you prepare to launch into the guts of the book, we want you to keep a few of our other guiding principles in mind; they serve as background for what we believe about food and how it can work to improve your health. We'll make references to these principles throughout these pages, but understanding them from the start will help you digest (sorry!) the material a bit more easily:

1. *Food Is Medicine.* Since the time of Hippocrates, physicians have used the power of food to treat disease.[1] Unfortunately, though, our medical system has evolved to alleviate illness, rather than keep you healthy. Instead of developing the tools to prevent disease, we wait for the disease to arrive, and *then* treat it.

Although we spend more money on health care than any other country in the world, the expected life span in the United States has steadily decreased over the past two years. And we are outlived by people of dozens of other countries.[2,3]

Health should be about more than just the absence of disease. It should be about living longer, having high energy, experiencing peak performance for a long time, keeping your immune system sharp, avoiding chronic disease, and strengthening your body to fight off problems and the effects of aging.

That power comes from food.

Although many variables play a role in your health (activity, exposure to toxins, genes), the single most important decision you make every day is what you choose to put in your mouth. In fact, what you eat actually influences whether your genes are expressed—meaning that as much as we like to chalk up our circumstances to genetics, we can actually help shape how our genes function with what we eat.[4]

Scientifically, we have seen the food-as-medicine answer play out time and time again. In a recent study that examined more than 700,000 people who had died from cardiovascular diseases (the leading cause of death in the world) as well as diabetes, more than half were associated with dietary factors like eating too much processed and red meat, unhealthy fat, and simple carbohydrates and sugar.[5]

Or how about cancer? Approximately one in five people will die from the growth of these abnormal cells, and a third of us will discover a cancer in our lifetime.[6] But research suggests that only 5 percent of cancers are unavoidable. The rest—*the 95 percent*—are the result of lifestyle and environmental choices. This, in turn, means they can be prevented. Experts estimate that about a third of cancer cases are linked to what you eat.[7] From brain dysfunction to stroke and arthritis, your food choices are a major determinant of not only your rate of aging, but also the quality of your life.

(Note: Food isn't the solution to every health issue; as much as we'd like it to be so, simply eating an apple will not alleviate an arterial blockage. The truth is that medical interventions are necessary and are sometimes the frontline answer. But food is our number one disease preventer, energy provider, strength giver, and life sustainer, and should be treated as such.)

2. *Timing Matters.* Yes, you will achieve wonders if you can change *what* you eat by consuming more healthy nutrients and less unhealthy ones. But the *when* part? That's the unsung hero of the diet narrative. By syncing up our food habits with our subconscious bodily preferences, we'll have created the proverbial well-oiled machine (extra-virgin olive oil, please).

The skinny on timing, which we will outline in Chapter 1, comes down to just two simple shifts. Make these changes and eat foods that are loaded with good-for-you macronutrients, vitamins, minerals, and other compounds, and you'll have set yourself up to build a body that lasts a long, long time. We'll outline how you can get there. And we'll even teach you one of the best techniques: stopping the stereotyping of foods (page 63).

3. *Give Taste a Chance.* One of the most frustrating pieces of health dogma is that healthy food has to taste like dog food. Not true! Healthy eating does not mean meals that come in cardboard boxes or taste like cardboard boxes. Healthy eating does not mean boiled chicken every day of the week. Healthy eating does not mean you get so bored of the blandness that you feel the urge to dive tongue-first into a bag of M&Ms.

Healthy eating is about experimenting with new things, like spices, to augment flavors and find new definitions of sweet, spicy, and umami.

Healthy eating is about learning to cook with techniques that foster health, not because you have to, but because you want to.

Healthy eating is about simplifying your meals so that you spend less time preparing and more time savoring.

Healthy eating is about the joy of taste—and the joy of knowing that the investment you just made in your meal will pay dividends today, tomorrow, and decades from now.

To get there, we've broken down "when" into two types of timing:

When to Eat What—Your daily routine. We will explore how the most healthful foods interact with your body depending on when you eat them, yielding a smart blueprint for the very best way to eat each day.

What to Eat When—Your best choices for specific situations. We will also explore a variety of common life scenarios so that you can adjust your food choices to prevent and cure ailments, live optimally, and find success. For instance, what do you eat when you're at risk of heart disease or cancer? Or when you're hangry or stressed? Or when you just finished a great workout or are preparing for an interview? You see, our body's internal environment is always changing—and how you feed it during those changes matters. Our goal is to tell you what to eat to best help your body, no matter what situation you're in. *When* isn't just about time of day; *when* is the ever evolving ecosystem that is the human body.

As you go through this book—and ease into a new way of eating with our simple 31-day plan—we promise that you'll never look at food the same way again. Or clocks, for that matter. Tick tock, we don't want your body to stop!

In these pages, we will bring you everything you need to know to help align your food choices with your body's rhythms. You'll find that it's easy to nudge your lifestyle and your eating patterns in this direction. To that end, we'll provide you with the following:

- **A 31-day program:** This month-long plan of action will help you slowly adjust to a new way of eating by adapting your meal choices—and timing—to your lifestyle and preferences. We'll use tips, tricks, quizzes, and simple customized eating strategies to get you there.

- **Surprising new science:** For so many years, we've put so much emphasis on what goes into our mouths, rather than looking at the transit schedule—when it enters, when it exits, when it makes a pit stop in your intestine. The When Way will show you how and why *when* matters.

- **More than 30 customized scenarios:** There are different ways to eat, depending on what you and your body are experiencing. In the second half of the book, we'll take you through dozens of common situations and reveal the best thing to eat at certain times in your day—or in your life. What you eat when you're stressed is different than what you eat when you're trying to have a baby or getting rid of the flu or experiencing low libido.

- **The Sub Shop:** Throughout the book, we'll offer a variety of ideas for substitutions you can make for better eating. These swaps will make it easier for you to change unhealthy habits into healthy ones.

So as you embark on your journey of exploring the *when* and the *what,* how about we get started with *how?*

| PART 1 |

How Food Works

CHAPTER 1

THE SCIENCE OF WHEN

When You Eat Is as Important as What You Eat

I n many aspects of life, we all know that *when* matters as much as *what*. A marriage proposal can be a wonderful thing—but not in the middle of a fight about dried toothpaste in the sink. Asking for a raise is a necessary part of work life—but not right after you spilled coffee on a client. Cheering for your favorite team is one of life's joys—but not if you're checking the score on your phone during your kid's school concert.

The same applies to how you should think about food as it relates to your overall health, longevity, and weight: *When* matters.

That principle, of course, is the entire foundation of this book. You absolutely need to think about what you're eating, which is what we'll cover in Chapter 2. But a number of other factors dictate how food functions. Therefore, the ideal approach is combining *what* you eat with *when* you eat it.

Your body is a dynamic ecosystem of organs, tissues, genes, and chemicals that change from day to day and during the course of each day. That means you cannot just treat it like a vehicle that requires the same gas and oil to run smoothly in every situation. To best fuel your biological ecosystem, you need to think about the nuances of timing, not just the dangers of Alfredo sauce. The tricky part is that timing happens on two different levels, both equally important.

On one hand, you have to consider your body's specific circumstances. Your body ebbs and flows through various emotions, hormone levels, and health situations, meaning that any number of environmental stresses affect the way your insides are working. Because food adds another variable to these scenarios, what you eat during these periods plays a role in how your body reacts. Your ecosystem changes as your fuel sources do. In Part 3, you will encounter a huge swath of scenarios—some emotional (what to eat when you're hangry), some medical (what to eat when you want to prevent heart disease), and some situational (what to eat when you cannot sleep). All have different answers, because your body needs different nutritional solutions as it manages the various stresses, insults, and dynamics of life.

On the other hand, *when* also refers to the time of day during a normal 24-hour cycle. This is all about how your body reacts to food and how food affects your body throughout the rhythms of a day—and this is what the root of this book is all about, nudging you to switch your eating habits to optimize how food works to improve your body.

Let's take a closer look at this clock—and how food works as you chug, churn, and chew throughout the day.

CIRCADIAN RHYTHM 101

Many diet and eating plans focus on the best kinds of food to eat—for good reason, because that notion is really at the heart of smart eating. Some plans also address the element of timing, perhaps advocating several small meals throughout the day, while others might assert that the *when* doesn't matter at all: It's all about calorie counting and portion control.

This is one of the many reasons why eating well can be more confusing than a 225-box Sudoku. Although you won't get much argument about some health-related things (few would disagree that processed sponge cakes aren't as healthy as snap peas), the area of when to eat is hotly debated and not well understood.

But we can end that confusion here, by looking deep into a part of your biology that you are rarely thinking about when it comes to eating: your biological clock, also known as your circadian rhythm. Sure, we talk about it when it comes to sleeping, and we throw around the phrase when talking about fertility. But we rarely discuss the biological clock in the context of jalapeño omelets.

This, however, is the key to shifting your body to optimal function: Align your eating with these natural rhythms, and you'll have food working better with your body, rather than against it.

Here's how it works. All energy sources originate with the sun. But because the sun isn't always present, plants and animals had to develop mechanisms for storing energy and reducing energy consumption when light was scarce. So life on Earth developed automated or instinctual processes to conserve energy, which improved the chance for survival. No sun, no energy. No energy, no life.

Now, you may consider instincts as things you just *do* without conscious thought, like nurturing a baby or hightailing it in the opposite direction of a saber-toothed cat. But you also have instincts that lurk much deeper in your biology: organ-level or cellular-level reflexes that you don't necessarily notice, but that are just as important. The biological clock—your body's automated system for conserving energy—is one of them, as it influences behavior from sunset to sunset.

It achieves this by sending messages throughout your body via hormones. The signals—a biological Batman signal, if you will—tell us when to sleep and when to eat. Over and over and over. This cycle is your circadian rhythm. These natural cues—whether for animals or plants—are relatively consistent from day to day, so that your biological clock dictates a rhythm that you follow effectively and efficiently.

Your body wants to work as efficiently as possible, and these instincts help ensure it doesn't waste time or valuable resources. The internal clock conserves your body's reserves, allowing you to live in this rhythm every day. (Modern-day humans seem to have developed an internal clock requiring 7 a.m. Starbucks stops.)

In mammals, the master biological clock that sets the circadian rhythm is located in the brain. It's a tiny area of just 20,000 brain cells in the hypothalamus called the suprachiasmatic nucleus (you have around 86 billion neurons in the brain total).[1,2] This clock keeps time in a near 24-hour cycle, requiring light input that travels to it from the eyes and allows it to keep its rhythm set at exactly 24 hours.[3] The clock sends chemical signals out to the rest of the body that prime it to engage in certain activities, based on the time of day.

You probably understand this phenomenon mostly by the way it works in regard to sleep. Although you may interpret getting tired at certain times of day as a signal to tuck in and snooze, you may not realize that other things are also happening as a response to your biological clock. For example, your body temperature changes throughout the day based on your circadian rhythm. At night, it decreases, and melatonin rises, which encourages you to sleep. In the morning, it rises along with corticosteroid hormones, encouraging you to wake up and take on the day.[4] Your big brain gives you the ability to override these biological cues and stay up all night if you want. But we all know the price we pay when we don't live in tune with our natural body clock.

Now, some people choose to live their lives in opposition to their body's natural instincts—and this is an important example of how food plays a role in the rhythm of life. About 15 million Americans have jobs as shift workers, where they work during the night and sleep during the day.[5] Studies examining the health of these populations find that they have increased rates of both sleep issues and obesity.[6] People who work the night shift tend to gain more weight than people with a normal nine-to-five schedule.[7] One study of nurses found that when they switched to a night shift, they actually burned fewer calories than they did when working the day shift, even though they were engaging in the same activities.[8] Other studies determined that shift workers have a 40 percent increased risk of cardiovascular disease as well as heart attacks, strokes, and abnormal heartbeats than those working daytime hours.[9]

Although we don't completely understand the cause, the main suspect behind the disturbances in the health and metabolism of shift workers is that they are fighting their natural circadian rhythms—and their body's instinctual notions of when to eat.

CIRCADIAN RHYTHM AND YOUR FOOD CLOCK

You may not know it, but you feel the effects of your clock every day. You may pretty consistently feel hungry or sleepy or energetic at the same times from day to day. Maybe you nap for 10 minutes when you hit the couch at 7:30 p.m., or maybe you reach for something to nosh on at three or four in the afternoon. If you're a pet owner, you've probably observed this in dogs; those that are fed at the same time each day change their patterns in anticipating food. Scientists examining these displays found that animals indeed have individual food clocks,[10] an instinct that ensures we get the right amount of food throughout the day so that we have plenty of energy for survival.

Humans seem to have a food clock, too—and this is the area that few of us have really tapped in our daily habits. This is what serves as the scientific backbone of *What to Eat When:* Sync your body clock with your food clock.

What makes this tricky is that our bodies have a natural tension point: We crave food at night, but we function better when we eat earlier. Let's see how this works.

In an amazing 2013 study, researchers at Brigham and Women's Hospital in Boston put volunteers into a lab to measure how changes in light govern our circadian rhythm. Normal periodic light cues were removed and replaced with constant artificial light, so that researchers could see what the natural cycle of the body's clock was. Researchers fed the brave participants, who lived in the lab for 13 days, at different times of day throughout the study and asked them to rate their hunger. (No word on whether TV networks wanted to turn this into a reality show.)

They found that in the absence of normal light and time cues, people are naturally most hungry around the time that would correspond to 8 p.m., and least hungry at the time that would correspond to 8 a.m.[11] That basic instinct was an advantage in the early days of man—but in modern times, it may actually be hurting us (more on this in a moment).

Another interesting note: Your organs—including the liver, heart, muscle, pancreas, fat, lungs, and kidneys—seem to have their own food clocks, too.[12] That is, they all can develop "preferences" about when you eat, depending on their functions.

What sets the clock? The suprachiasmatic nucleus, as it happens. But these organs have an intrinsic rhythm, meaning they're trying to run based on what's best for your body.

One of the body's most important hormones for dealing with food is called insulin. You've probably heard of it, because its levels are abnormal in people who suffer from diabetes. In fact, diabetes starts when muscle and fat cells become resistant to insulin—meaning that even though insulin might be there, it doesn't have the effect it is supposed to (we'll talk about insulin a lot more in the following chapter). Studies of animals have demonstrated that the body's secretion of and response to insulin follows a circadian rhythm.

Scientists have examined the time of day mammals are the most sensitive or resistant to the effects of insulin; they found that sensitivity is the highest during active phases (when they are awake). When a mouse is active, its muscles are moving and it needs energy (in the form of glucose) to perform optimally. Insulin helps glucose into the muscle cells.

On the other hand, animals are normally the most insulin resistant during their typical sleeping hours (this is also the time they have the highest levels of fasting blood sugar).[13] During the rest phase, the mouse is typically inactive and food is not coming in. But whereas muscles don't need as much energy, the rest of the body does not shut down during sleep. In fact, this is prime time for crucial processes like DNA repair. One theory as to why we have higher insulin resistance at night: Your brain needs energy while you sleep because it is actually doing work during this down period (like storing memories and getting rid of waste). But because your muscles do not, their insulin resistance may allow more glucose to go to the brain during this period (the brain is not insulin resistant, so it can receive the extra circulating glucose).

What It Means for You: Studies of humans suggest that these same phenomena occur in you. Your body is most sensitive to insulin in the morning and becomes more resistant as the day goes on.[14,15] Now you've probably heard that eating a carbohydrate-rich meal causes a rise in blood sugar, and the more carbohydrates you eat, the higher this rise will be. At least that's what nutritional scientists thought. It turns out that the time of day you eat that meal has a big effect on what happens to your blood sugar levels. If you eat the same meal in the morning and at night, your blood sugar will actually increase more in the evening than in the morning.[16,17] Fat cells also appear to be the most insulin sensitive early in the day, with a peak at noon; they are about 50 percent more sensitive midday than they are at midnight.[18]

This means that your body is primed to eat at certain times and that the "what to eat when" principle really does matter. In fact, it matters so much that eating at the wrong time can throw off everything. Scientists at the University of Alabama at Birmingham have studied what happens to mice when they eat at the "wrong" time. Researchers gave mice access to food either during the night only, when they typically eat, or during the day only, when they are typically sleeping. The rest of the time, they had no food available.

Compared with those on a more normal schedule, mice that only had food available at the wrong time ate more when food first became available—10 percent more total calories a day—and gained more weight. In addition, mice fed during the inactive phase tended to use carbohydrates more for energy rather than burning fat, compared with mice fed during the active phase.[19]

Tinkering With Timing: These same researchers then conducted another series of experiments. They gave the mice either a high-fat or low-fat diet early or late. This time, they found that mice given a high-fat meal at the end of the day, rather than at the beginning of the day, had more insulin resistance, ate more calories, and gained more weight.

When mice ate more closely to when they were going to sleep, their bodies were not able to compensate for the extra calories by increasing energy expenditure. But the researchers weren't satisfied. They wanted to know what would happen if the two groups ate the same number of calories in this scenario. So they decided to give one group a high-fat meal at the beginning of the day and one at the end; both groups received the same number of calories. This time, they found that those in the group that ate at the end of the day weighed more—and had more body fat and increased insulin resistance.[20] So it looks like *when* the mice eat is just as important as *what* they eat. Their bodies are primed for food during the active phase— and the earlier they eat, the better.

Research is starting to show these same effects in humans. One study on weight loss that compared the times of eating among participants over a 20-week period revealed that those who ate lunch earlier lost more weight than those who ate it later.[21] And a related study found that those who ate later burned less energy than those who ate earlier.[22]

The take-home in all of this: It's better for your body to eat earlier. We need to shift our habits to front-load, rather than back-load, our daily eating rituals.

THE MICROBIOME'S CIRCADIAN RHYTHM

Your gut has more to do with your eating habits than just the hungry roar that comes from it. In fact, it's manipulated by an ecosystem of bacteria that influences many, many parts and systems of your body.

The bacteria that make up your gut are called your microbiome. The bacterial species that inhabit your microbiome can change—and that's a good thing, because people with more diversity of bacteria in their gut seem to be healthier than people with less. You can influence that diversity not only by what you put in your mouth, but also *when* you eat.

In studies of mice, it has been found that many types of gut bacteria populations fluctuate throughout the day. This means that the relative abundance of particular bacteria change on a rhythmic cycle. One group of scientists from Israel tested mouse feces to try to find out what might be going on. They collected the mouse poop (dirty job, but someone's gotta do it) and analyzed it for bacterial genes.

What did they find? (No, not digested cheese.) When mice were active, they found more signs of cellular activity that promoted metabolism, cell growth, and repair. When the mice were resting, the researchers found more genes related to activities like detoxification.[23] In mice that have had their circadian clock systems knocked out, the normal microbiome schedule disappears. This is because these mice lose normal feeding behaviors. Controlling when these mice eat can restore a more normal pattern to the fluctuations of the gut microbiome that happen throughout the day—once again showing the importance of when you eat.[24]

The Israeli group went on to study how eating at the wrong time could affect health. They shifted the light-dark cycle that the mice saw in the lab eight hours at a time to simulate international jet lag. As you would expect, the microbiomes in the jet-lagged mice were different than in the normal mice. When the scientists fed a high-fat diet to the jet-lagged and the normal groups, only the jet-lagged mice gained weight and became glucose intolerant.

To determine whether the composition of the microbiome caused this circumstance, they killed the gut bacteria with antibiotics. The antibiotic-treated jet-lagged mice did not gain weight or have glucose intolerance, suggesting that the microbiome was playing a significant role. Next, the researchers performed a fecal transplant from the jet-lagged mice to mice with no gut bacteria; after the transplant, the mice had an increase in body fat.[25]

So what's the takeaway here? Eating early is generally better for your microbiome, which is better for you. And the best time to eat whole grain carbohydrates, protein, and dietary fat is early as well.

EAT EARLY

Here's why the *when* part of the eating equation is so tough: Research has shown that our body's natural rhythm is to want food later, even though it has a negative effect on our overall health.

That's the major conflict: Our bodies were designed to want more calories at the end of the day and fewer in the morning. But the optimal way of eating—from a circadian rhythm point of view—is to consume more energy earlier in the day and less energy later in the day.

Why are our bodies' food cravings out of sync with our circadian rhythm? During times when we didn't know when our next meals would be coming, the human body may have evolved the need for a food-storage mechanism. In that era, humans didn't live long enough to experience the harms of late-night eating—and in any case, that impulse didn't make much of a difference: The body only cared about surviving the next day, not the next decade. Today, we no longer need that extensive storage ability; our modern world has outpaced the human body's ability to adapt to its new environment where food is plentiful.

We have to override our reptilian instincts using the executive function of the brain to make smart choices about, well, what to eat when.

If we can take one lesson from the existence of our biological clock, it's that our bodies will work best when we stay in sync. So remember this mantra: *More in the morning and less later on.*

Now, it's important for you to understand some food fundamentals. In the next chapter, we will explore the *what* of food and how it works, so you can combine it with the *when.*

CHAPTER 2

A NUTRITIOUS BREAKDOWN

Understand the Building Blocks of Your Diet

To understand the power of food, you have to learn about what it does once you chomp, chew, and churn it through your body.

In other parts of life, you probably don't give a hoot about the inner workings of your stuff as long as it functions properly. Who cares what hoses, tubes, and wires go where as long as your car gets you from point A to point B? Do you really need to understand the Instagram algorithm as long as you can post your favorite sunset pic? Unless you have a special or professional interest in looking under the hood of your day-to-day machinery, you, like us, probably take a lot of things for granted.

Food, however, is different. You should know about how it's built and how it works because its effect, function, and composition aren't the same from bite to bite. And its behavior is certainly not the same once it's torpedoed from your mouth to your digestive system. Taking your food for granted is a recipe for bigger jeans, more doctor visits, and an earlier expiration date.

The reality is that when you understand the fundamentals of food and how your body reacts to it, it becomes that much easier to manage the When Way of eating. Here, we'll take you through three major macronutrients and how they're broken down and used in your body. Then, we'll explain why they're so important to your health.

THE MACRONUTRIENTS: POWER AND EFFECTS

Food is more than just photographic fodder for your Facebook feed; it contains the building blocks you need to develop and maintain your body, supplying energy and raw materials so that organs, tissues, and cells are powered to work and renew 24/7. No fuel, no you.

This task of fueling is achieved through a cocktail of components that mostly come in the form of the big three macronutrients: carbohydrates and fat (used for energy) and proteins (the building blocks of the body). These are called macronutrients because we need them in large amounts.

Food also includes other necessary elements, known as micronutrients, which include vitamins, minerals, phytochemicals, and antioxidants. Together, these macro- and micronutrients help dictate your overall well-being, including your weight, your waist size, and your overall health risks.

Now, keep in mind that although it may seem simple to classify particular foods as proteins, carbs, or fats, the reality is that most foods include a combination of macronutrients (that is, fish has protein and fat; beans have protein and carbohydrates).

What does that mean for you? Well, you don't have to think about fractions or do complex calculations every time you eat. But you should understand why certain foods are good sources of macronutrients, so you can learn how to use their benefits to your health advantage.

Carbohydrates: Carbs are like 1980s hair bands—like them or not, they usually elicit an immediate reaction. Some of us associate the word "carb" with breads, pasta, and cake; for others, just looking at them means gaining four pounds. Athletes employ them skillfully, often "carbo-loading" before a big race or game. Today, the diet industry seems to contain two camps: carb haters and carb embracers. So let's break down what exactly this hot-button macro is all about.

Put simply, carbohydrates are sugars. Hang on, hang on—that doesn't mean that all carbohydrates look like a bowl of pudding. Sugar is a chemistry term for certain types of molecules. Because there are many forms of sugar molecules, there are many forms of carbohydrates. The main ones? Simple sugar, starch, and fiber. The most basic building block of these is a sugar molecule, which the body can break down and turn into glucose, the main energy currency of the body.

Glucose is like the body's form of Red Bull; it provides quick fuel as soon as it's available in the bloodstream. Insulin, which is secreted by the pancreas, delivers that glucose into your cells to be used for energy. Glucose isn't stored, so if it's not immediately used, it is converted into a substance called glycogen. (Think of glycogen as six extra cans of Red Bull sitting on your shelf, ready to provide energy if yours runs out.) Glycogen is a form of medium-term energy stored in your liver and muscles; your body can call on it as needed and can reserve about two days' worth. Glycogen is always stored in a hydrated form—again, like Red Bull—meaning it has about three times its weight in water. So when you go on a low-carb diet, most of the weight that you lose rapidly is water that disappears when you deplete glycogen stores. As soon as you go back to carbs, you build up the stores and associated water, and the weight comes back.

Although your body relies on carbohydrates for energy, it's better to obtain it from complex carbohydrates, rather than simple ones. Simple sugars—for example, those found in table sugar, white flour, and cornstarch—immediately start acting out in your body, supplying instant energy, but wreaking biological havoc on many of your inner systems (including damaging the lining of your blood vessels, which can lead to high blood pressure, high inflammation, and greater risk of heart, brain, and kidney trouble).

Complex carbohydrates—for example, whole grains and fiber—are broken down by the body more slowly, so the sugars are released gradually into the blood. This way of supplying energy provides for a more calm, efficient functioning of your bodily systems.

As you'll see later on, simple sugars are the ones that are more associated with weight gain and diabetes, not to mention wrinkles and impotence. That's why processed foods, baked goods, and other "white carbs" are the ones you should generally try to avoid, while fruits, vegetables, beans, and whole grains are the carbs to cultivate.

Think about it as the difference between frantic and calm. Simple carbs are like crazy partiers who are bouncing off walls, breaking lamps, and creating all kinds of messes. Sure, they can be fun for a moment, but the long-term damage probably isn't worth it. Complex carbs govern your body with stoicism and confidence, exuding a quiet leadership that makes your body work efficiently and cleanly.

Fat: For a long time, people considered fat to be a four-letter word (and we're not talking about "phat"). Experts believed that a high-fat diet was associated with a big-belly body; fat in food equaled fat on the body. Thank goodness that dogma has changed. Today, many, many people realize that fat isn't necessarily what makes people larger (more on that in a moment). Instead, fat (the macronutrient kind) should be thought of as a component of food, one that has a variety of chemical interactions.

Used for long-term storage of energy, fat contains more than double the energy of carbohydrates (2.25 times, to be exact). It comes in two forms: saturated and unsaturated.

Saturated fats are solid at room temperature and are typically derived from animal products (coconut and palm oils are exceptions as plant-based saturated fats). These are the least healthy kinds of fat, as they're associated with increased inflammation and increased blood LDL cholesterol.[1] Worse, they come with proteins that change the bacteria in the gut to make them produce inflammation throughout the body.[2] Recent studies suggest that saturated fat may also increase the risk of insulin resistance.[3]

Unsaturated fats are those derived from plants. There is consistent evidence that replacing saturated fats with unsaturated fats decreases inflammation, risk of cancer, mental decline, "bad" LDL cholesterol, and risk for heart disease.[4,5,6,7,8] Unsaturated fats can be broken down further into polyunsaturated fats (corn oil, sunflower oil, safflower oil, and omega-3 fatty acids found in fish) and monounsaturated fats (olive oil, peanut oil, canola oil, avocados, and most nuts). Studies have suggested that a diet rich in monounsaturated fats is associated with less visceral fat[9]—the worst kind, which can accumulate around the organs.

Polyunsaturated fats make up the outer coating of cells, but cannot be made in the body; therefore, we rely on outside sources for these (wild salmon is by far the best). Numerous studies show that people with higher levels of omega-3 fats in their blood have reduced risk of heart disease and better

What's the Deal With Trans Fats?

Trans fats—hydrogenated oils—are the worst kinds of fats. They've been linked with heart attack and stroke, and possibly with cancer and brain dysfunction. Trans fats were originally used to help improve the taste and texture of processed foods, but the health risks have made them a major villain in the nutrition world. The U.S. Food and Drug Administration (FDA) has banned them from food manufacturing—and they'll be off the shelves by 2020 if regulations stay in place. But trans fats are naturally present in some foods like beef, pork, butter, and milk, which are also high in inflammatory ingredients. This is one of the reasons we don't recommend these foods. (See Chapter 4 for more on this.)

cognitive function.[10,11] (Salmon, by the way, don't make the precious fish oil—DHA—themselves; the fish get it by eating algae.)

Protein: Proteins can be used for energy by being turned into glucose, but that's not their main purpose. Proteins are truly the building blocks of life. They are made up of amino acids that, like metal, can be combined into wide varieties of machines that the cells of your body need to run. Although most people think of meat as protein, all cells contain a lot of it—even the ones in celery. The big difference between the proteins in plant cells and animal cells is the amino acids; animal proteins contain a wider variety of amino acids than plants. The body cannot internally make many amino acids, which is why vegetarians should eat a wide variety of foods to receive the full mix.

These days, our culture is as obsessed with eating protein as it is with viral cat videos. In fact, many Americans eat almost twice as much protein as they actually need.[12] Proteins are worth four calories per gram, just like carbs, so eating too much of them can lead to weight gain. Although high-protein diets are all the rage, we don't recommend eating more than the average American already eats—about 82 grams a day, the amount in about 10 ounces of a grilled chicken breast—because very high-protein diets can stress the kidneys.

WHY FOOD MATTERS

It's one thing to know your macros and how they function. But the real value is understanding their interactions in the body. What happens as your body breaks them down?

The Digestive Process

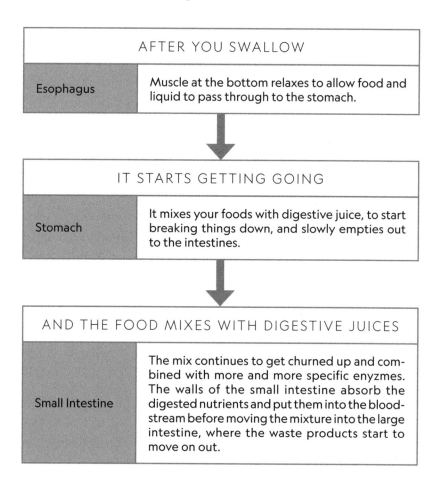

AFTER YOU SWALLOW	
Esophagus	Muscle at the bottom relaxes to allow food and liquid to pass through to the stomach.

IT STARTS GETTING GOING	
Stomach	It mixes your foods with digestive juice, to start breaking things down, and slowly empties out to the intestines.

AND THE FOOD MIXES WITH DIGESTIVE JUICES	
Small Intestine	The mix continues to get churned up and combined with more and more specific enyzmes. The walls of the small intestine absorb the digested nutrients and put them into the bloodstream before moving the mixture into the large intestine, where the waste products start to move on out.

Now, the reason that the *kind* of macros you ingest is so important is because of their impact at any given time. Take carbs, for instance. Your body needs to tightly control the amount of glucose in your blood; when it loses that ability, we call that diabetes. Elevated levels of blood sugar are associated with a whole host of health problems, including blood vessel damage.

Why is that important to avoid? These vessels are key to supplying your essential organs with nutrients and to removing waste. Disease in these vessels leads to damage throughout the body. Most notably, people with diabetes can develop kidney failure, eye disease, heart disease, stroke, mental dysfunction, and poor wound healing.

The Blood Sugar Problem

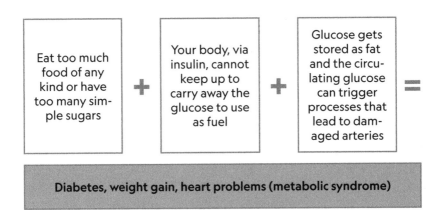

| Eat too much food of any kind or have too many simple sugars | + | Your body, via insulin, cannot keep up to carry away the glucose to use as fuel | + | Glucose gets stored as fat and the circulating glucose can trigger processes that lead to damaged arteries | = |

Diabetes, weight gain, heart problems (metabolic syndrome)

There's a simple action-and-reaction equation that everyone should know: When you eat carbohydrates, your blood sugar goes up. The simpler the carbohydrate and the more of it you eat, the more your blood sugar increases.

With that rise, insulin is released from your pancreas into your blood to help deliver the glucose that will be used for energy—and to bring your blood sugar back to a level that won't cause damage. Insulin stimulates muscle and fat cells to take glucose out of the blood, delivering it like a Fed-Ex package from the outside to the inside of those cells. In addition, insulin stops the breakdown of fat stored in fat cells (no need to break down fat if there is a lot of glucose around) and stimulates the liver and muscles to store glucose as glycogen (the stored form of carbohydrates used for energy).

Here's the catch: Your liver has a limited capacity for glycogen. Any extra glucose that is delivered to the liver is converted to fatty acids called triglycerides, which are the main type of body fat. They are stored in the liver or are packaged in the form of LDL (the bad cholesterol) to be shipped out into your bloodstream. Triglycerides are designed to help repair nicks in your blood vessels, but in excess they accumulate to become fat and then atherosclerotic plaque in the walls of your blood vessels.

That's why eating extra glucose increases your risk of developing fatty liver diseases (yes, this has nothing to do with alcohol, and 30 percent of the U.S. adult population is estimated to have a fatty liver condition).[13] Fatty liver is associated with insulin resistance, the inability of insulin to be an effective driver for delivering glucose out of your blood and into your cells. More sugar in your blood means more damage to your body and more stored fat.

Insulin resistance is as if the cells are a little hard of hearing. To get the attention of the cells, the pancreas (the organ that makes insulin) has to yell by making even more insulin to get a response. If you develop insulin resistance, three things happen: One, when you eat a typical amount of glucose, your blood sugar is going to be higher than normal because the insulin cannot get the glucose into the cells; the cells don't hear the insulin ring the bell. Two, because your blood sugar remains elevated, your pancreas is going to pump out more insulin than is actually needed. Three, that extra sugar attaches to your proteins, causing them to be less functional.

This scenario is a problem: One in three Americans knows they have prediabetes[14] (and countless more are not aware), which makes them even more vulnerable to full-blown type 2 diabetes.

And remember from the last chapter: *When* you eat also plays an important role in your blood sugar levels. Our bodies tend to be more resistant to insulin later in the day (it's almost like we have prediabetes at night), so the later we eat, the more likely we are to raise our blood sugar higher.

Being overweight can make you insulin resistant, but scientists are still debating whether or not such resistance sends you into a spiral of accumulating more fat (and thus becoming more insulin resistant). That's because eating a meal that increases your blood sugar substantially can cause a roller coaster ride of blood sugar levels. In other words, eating a high-glycemic food (see glossary) is associated with a rapid rise in blood sugar, which in turn is accompanied by a rapid increase in insulin. The insulin causes your cells to take up the glucose and drop your blood sugar below normal fasting levels. When this happens, you crave carbohydrates and start the cycle again. So eating carbs that have what are called a high-glycemic index can cause a vicious cycle of rising and falling insulin levels, which cause you to overeat.

This begs the question: How *do* you get fat? Any of the macronutrients—fat, carbs, and even protein—can cause you to gain weight if you eat too much. Because fat is the most energy-dense of the three macronutrients, eating a lot of it can quickly lead to too many calories in and not enough out.

What the body cannot use for energy or fit into those limited glycogen stores will be stockpiled as fat that your body wants to keep in case you run out of energy. (In terms of evolution, this process came in handy during times of famine.)

You store some fat under your skin (that's called subcutaneous fat). But the fat that surrounds our organs, called visceral fat, is more dangerous. It's been linked to metabolic disturbances like insulin resistance and type 2 diabetes, as well as increased risk for cardiovascular disease.[15] It may also be associated with certain types of breast cancer in women, and with prostate cancer in men.[16,17]

To find out how much visceral fat you have, you could do a body scan. But an easy way to determine your risk is to measure your waist-to-height ratio. A recent study has shown this is the

How to Lose Weight

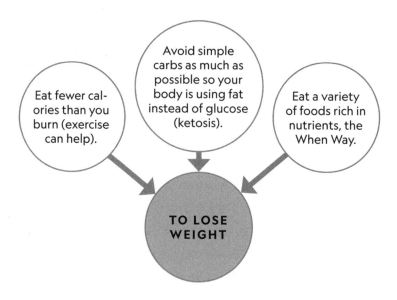

Eat fewer calories than you burn (exercise can help).

Avoid simple carbs as much as possible so your body is using fat instead of glucose (ketosis).

Eat a variety of foods rich in nutrients, the When Way.

TO LOSE WEIGHT

best approximation of body fat—even better than the BMI measure.[18] The ideal ratio is a waist size that is half your height or less. To measure your waist, measure around the belly button, and feel free to suck in your gut because we are more concerned about the fat inside than on the outside.

The million-dollar question, of course, is how do you get rid of the fat? Your body wants to use glucose as fuel first, because fat is better for long-term storage. You're always using a combination of both, but to burn more fat than glucose, you need to burn through your sugar stores and get to the fat.

Eating the When Way can help. As you go through the next few chapters—offering major eating guidelines and the optimal eating plan for eating every day—keep the what and when in the front of your mind. We'll front-load your days to be circadian-friendly, and we'll pack them with the nutrients that are best for your body. This combination has big payoffs: You'll be healthier, you'll lose weight (if that's one of your goals), and you'll have more energy.

| PART 2 |

The When Way

CHAPTER 3

TIME TO EAT!

Four Guidelines
for Setting Your
Food Clock

Before you read this chapter, do us one favor: Take every assumption you have about eating, toss it in the garbage disposal, and grind it up with your apple cores and onion skins. Why? An assumption, in many cases, can be what's holding you back from changing your diet, changing your health—and in effect, changing your life.

Think about how many assumptions you already make about the timing of meals. That if you eat very little during the day, you can feast at dinner. That the supreme dictator of your health is the number of calories you eat, no matter when you eat them. That having chicken breast for breakfast sounds as wacky as a bare-bellied fan at a December football game in Green Bay.

All those assumptions have come about for a variety of reasons—some through folklore, some through tradition, some through science. But that doesn't mean they're always accurate, healthy, or the best for you in the long run. So while you read this chapter, try to suspend your preconceived notions about the timing of eating as we take you through our major guidelines for how to best structure your daily diet.

From Chapter 1, you know the importance of your circadian rhythm and food (something we also call chrononutrition—the idea that food patterns should align with your body's internal clock for optimum health). Here, we'll take those big-picture science concepts and put them into action, so you can see the way they work in your daily life. Of course, the tricky part here is that everybody (and every *body*) is different. Every day is different. Every stressor is different. Every food interaction with your biology can be different.

The key to eating smartly is knowing how to adjust to certain circumstances. After all, that's the focus of much of this book: learning how to eat in a variety of situations (see Part 3). But here, we want to provide you with a science-based food foundation, so that you can use the When Way style of eating for the majority of your life.

Now, we also know that some of these principles will fly in the face of the way you may eat now. And although change isn't always easy, what we ask is that you simply give this approach a try for two to three weeks. That will go a long way in helping you form new habits. More importantly, we believe that you will feel better—and *that* will be the inspiration you need to make these four guidelines the basis of a new way of eating.

GUIDELINE 1: *EAT WHEN THE SUN SHINES.*

There are a lot of culprits behind the number of health problems Americans face: lack of exercise, lots of fries, food portions the size of beach bungalows. We know that health problems are a complex soup of causes and biological reactions, and part of this book will help you navigate that complexity.

As we tinker with strategic adjustments you can make to nudge your biological systems toward good health, one of the best places to start is to limit the window of time in which you eat. This counteracts the one-two punch of eating at night and eating for a long window during a 24-hour period—that is, feeding from the time you wake until the time you go to sleep.

- To best maximize chrononutrition, eat only during daytime, or during an approximate 12-hour window (or shorter) every day.
- To the best of your ability, try to align when you eat with when your body is ready to eat. In other words, eat in chorus with your circadian rhythm. Remember, this biology is determined by the light and designed to most efficiently utilize your most scarce resource: energy.

Why do humans have a circadian rhythm? Because your biology evolved to favor the conditions your primitive ancestors lived under. Your ancestors didn't have electricity (how they managed without Instagram, we'll never know) so they couldn't see well at night. That meant their active period was confined to the daylight hours; they rested when the sun set.

Considering that it's pretty much impossible to eat when you are sleeping (with a few exceptions), your body evolved to be primed for food during the day. Although electricity allows us to extend our day (and it may be more romantic to eat by candlelight), it's not ideal for our biology. The changing light cycle that trains your circadian rhythm helps set the cycle of your hormones. As evening comes, cortisol starts to drop and melatonin starts to rise as the body prepares for sleep. In addition, your insulin resistance increases throughout the day and is at maximum capacity during the overnight fast. All of which is to say, your body wants you to eat when the sun shines and fast when the sun sets.

Not only does this make sense based on what we know about circadian rhythm, but studies of animals and even a few of people have shown significant benefits to time-restricted feeding, that is, eating only during a limited window. (For any of our South Pole readers—howdy!—this does not apply to those in extreme climates with long days or nights.)

We get some of these insights from work in fruit flies, those pesky little bugs that swarm in your kitchen around ripe fruits and vegetables. Turns out these flies (known by scientists as *Drosophila*) are often studied to better understand the genetics of cardiac dysfunction; humans actually have more in common with these little guys when it comes to the development of the heart than you might think.

When aging fruit flies are allowed constant access to their favorite laboratory chow, they sleep less, don't fly as well, and have more variability in their weight; their hearts don't work as well. But when scientists allow them access to food for only 12 hours a day instead of 24, there's a dramatic difference. Older flies sleep more like babies, their weight remains constant, their flight improves, and their heart function remains stable.[1]

We see similar patterns in mice. When they're fed around the clock with a high-fat diet, they gain a significant amount of weight and develop markers for metabolic syndrome (like high blood pressure, high blood sugar, and low healthy HDL cholesterol). But when scientists restrict the time they have access to the high-fat diet to an eight-hour window during their active period, something dramatic happens: The mice eat the same number of calories but do not become obese or develop insulin resistance, fatty liver, or as much inflammation.[2]

The studies of humans don't have enough data to make definitive statements, but they do yield interesting findings. One study from a group at the Salk Institute in La Jolla, California, found that when people reduced their total feeding time from 14 hours a day to 11 hours, they were able to lose weight, have more energy, and sleep better after just 16 weeks.[3]

What to Do Now: Try to eat your daily calories while the sun shines within a 12-hour window for three days. That means no night eating (if you find yourself in a nutritional emergency, reach for some crunchy raw vegetables). If you can make it three days, try for a week. Ideally, we'd like to see you work up to three weeks in a row. But if you need to adjust, try eating this way five days a week, allowing yourself more flexibility.

GUIDELINE 2: *EAT MORE IN THE MORNING AND LESS LATER ON.*

If your day starts like ours, it's probably a tornado of to-dos: shower, brush teeth and hair, shave face and/or legs, get the household going, check your phone 437 times before you get in the car, and get rocking. If you're lucky, you'll cram some kind of breakfast bar down your gullet and get on with your day. Or maybe you'll just skip that part, instead ingesting a gallon of coffee and grabbing some grub for lunch.

About 25 percent of people almost never eat breakfast.[4]

Guess what: The two of us used to fall into that category, too. Indeed, the "breakfast is the most important meal" doctrine had been shoved down our throats for years. But we just didn't eat it all that often because we weren't hungry in the morning (maybe because we ate so much at night). As with many of you, the demands of the day distracted us.

After reviewing all of the research, we've changed our minds—and our habits.

The When Way of eating tells us that we should front-load our day with food. But that doesn't mean you have to do it at breakfast. The key: Breakfast and lunch seem to be the most important meals—not necessarily one or the other.

Breakfast didn't always have the nutritionally regal status it's ascribed today. In fact, according to culinary historians, eating it was tantamount to committing a sin during the early Middle Ages.[5] (According to us, it's still a sin if breakfast involves the words "Froot" and "Loops.") But as the centuries passed and tastier culinary options like coffee and chocolate were discovered, the meal gained more universal acceptance. Some say Seventh-Day Adventist preacher James Caleb Jackson and doctor John Harvey Kellogg, who in the late 19th century invented what would become our modern-day cereal, cemented breakfast's role as a necessity for health into the cultural consciousness.[6]

Today, numerous studies support the importance of eating breakfast for health and find that people who skip it have worse nutrition,[7] increased risk of type 2 diabetes,[8] more hypertension,[9] more coronary heart disease,[10] greater obesity,[11] and higher risk of metabolic syndrome[12] than people who do eat breakfast.

And that's where the directive comes from: For optimum

health, you must eat breakfast. So case closed, right? Not so fast. The studies cited are observational, which means they cannot prove cause and effect in the way the gold-standard randomized clinical control trial can. So although there is an association between eating breakfast and decreasing all those health risks, that doesn't mean that breakfast is the reason why. In other words, no one has proved that breakfast or lack thereof is the cause. (To complicate matters further, there is a lot of bias among people who do research on how great breakfast is for health—and often, researchers are more likely to draw stronger conclusions than their research findings actually support.)

So what's an oatmeal lover to do?

Studies of circadian rhythms show that our peak hunger occurs at night (around 8 p.m.), but that our body is actually primed to interact with food in the healthiest way in the morning. That's the central conflict at the core of what makes eating healthy so difficult. Our stomach wants one thing, but our biology wants another.

In the morning, our bodies are the least insulin resistant and our microbiome is ready for a meal. But as the day goes on, our cells become more resistant to insulin, which isn't good for our health. So, yes, it's better to eat early. But it's not just about one meal; it's about how you eat throughout the entire day.

- **The case for eating breakfast:** It turns out that there are actually a few gold-standard randomized trials that examine how eating versus skipping breakfast affects weight. The best trial, conducted at Vanderbilt University in 1992, gathered people who normally ate breakfast, as well as people who normally skipped breakfast, and randomly assigned them to keep up their normal habits or switch teams. The study found breakfast had no effect on weight loss, except that people who ate it were less likely to snack and ate less fat throughout the day.[13] Other trials also found no difference in weight but determined other health benefits of eating breakfast. In one study, the people assigned to skip the meal ended up with higher LDL (bad) cholesterol;[14] another found that people with type 2 diabetes who skipped breakfast had higher blood sugar after lunch and dinner, compared with when they didn't skip the meal.[15] Many other studies have shown that blood sugar rises or is inconsistent (which is bad for your health as well) throughout the day in people who skip breakfast.[16,17,18]

- **The case for less late eating:** Not eating breakfast also means that you may eat more later in the day—and that has disadvantages. One study found that eating after 8 p.m. was associated with an increased risk of obesity.[19] Another study followed more than 1,200 people for six years and found that those who ate a larger percentage of their total daily calories at night had a much greater risk of developing obesity, metabolic syndrome, and a fatty liver compared with those who ate a smaller percentage of their total daily calories at that time.[20]
- **Eating early versus eating late:** An important study examined the effect of meal timing on a low-calorie diet plan for women who were overweight. Women were assigned to either eat the largest proportion of their calories early in the day (at breakfast) or late in the day (at dinner). The women who had consumed more of

their calories for breakfast lost more weight and inches off their belly by the end of the 12-week study. Fasting glucose, insulin, and a hunger hormone called ghrelin were reduced most in the group that ate early compared with the group that ate late. Triglyceride levels decreased in the early-eating group but increased in the late-eating group. That's all *good* for early eaters.[21]

More support for eating most of your calories earlier was found in a study conducted in Spain, where lunch is typically the largest meal of the day. Researchers compared people on a 20-week diet plan who ate their lunch before or after 2 p.m. Even though both groups ate about the same amount of calories, those eating a late lunch were more likely to have a smaller or no breakfast than those eating an early lunch; they also lost less weight and lost it more slowly than those who ate the early lunch.[22]

What to Do Now: Whether it's the most important meal or not, the evidence is clear that breakfast should either be your largest meal of the day or your second largest. But we get it. Sometimes, you don't have a lot of time in the morning. If that's the case, make lunch your largest meal. Together, aim to get three-quarters of your daily calories before 2 p.m., between breakfast and lunch. Snacks and dinner should make up about a quarter of the day's calories. In terms of your macros, breakfast should be made up of complex carbohydrates (not sugar), protein, and fat (unsaturated, please). Adding protein to breakfast reduces appetite and food intake later in the day. In fact, a small study even suggests that the satiating effect of protein occurs only at breakfast and not during other meals.[23]

GUIDELINE 3: *EAT CONSISTENTLY—AND AUTOMATICALLY—FROM DAY TO DAY.*

The world is full of contradictions (and not just George Carlin jokes—"why do we drive on a parkway and park on a driveway?"). Our bodies have them, too—like how our stomachs are hungriest at night, but our bodies adapt better when we eat early.

Here's another: Our brains crave novelty.[24] That's one of the reasons why some of us get excited about new and exotic foods. In general, what's different makes us excited. What makes us excited floods our brain with feel-good hormones. When we get that flood, we want more—so we keep seeking novelty.

But here's the catch: Our bodies don't want that randomized style of eating—this today, that tomorrow—ooh, look, a croissant! Our bodies want consistency. They want to be fed efficiently and with foods that love them to health.

That provides quite a tug-of-war between your reptilian brain and your biology. You will be better off if you can get into a consistent rhythm with your food by following the first two guidelines.

Remember, the purpose of the circadian rhythm is to optimize energy balance. It works by priming the body to be ready at the right time for certain activities to occur. Keeping the size of meals consistent from day to day will help align your eating with your circadian rhythm. An interesting study even showed that people who vary their energy intake from day to day are more likely to have metabolic syndrome (a condition that yields unhealthy numbers in a variety of markers, such as blood pressure and blood sugar), as well as an increased waist circumference.[25] Another study examined what happened to blood glucose and lipids in women who ate either their normal diets with regular frequency or meals and snacks with an irregular frequency for 14 days. Irregular eating led to increased insulin resistance and higher levels of LDL (bad) cholesterol.[26] A different study by the same group found that people who ate regularly burned more calories after meals and had lower total and LDL cholesterol as well as less insulin resistance.[27]

What to Do Now: Try to keep all of your meals and snacks the same size every day. One way you can do this is to automate your food choices. Eat the same few options for at least two meals and two snacks a day, so you don't have to think about what's healthy. Once you find foods and recipes that you love, have them a lot. Try to incorporate different ingredients into your same recipes once in a while to encourage a diverse microbiome. The more you can automate your actions (the same delicious and healthy meals for breakfast and lunch, with small variations, five days a week), the easier it is to get into the rhythm of smart eating. This will save you from making bad decisions. Plan ahead, keep it simple, choose what you love and what loves you back, and pick some meals that you can keep consistent.

GUIDELINE 4: *STOP STEREOTYPING FOOD.*

One of the things we hope you take away from this book is that pancakes and omelets aren't the only things that you can flip. You can also flip stereotypes on their heads. What do we mean? Well, who says you can't have eggs for dinner or a salad for breakfast? Just because our culture has reinforced certain foods to be eaten at certain times of day doesn't mean that's the way it should work. Many international cultures do a very good job of not stereotyping food. Recently a friend of Dr. C's sent him a picture of his breakfast while in Shanghai; it looked like a typical dinner plate—noodles, rice, fish, lots of vegetables, and larger portions.

In fact, throughout this book you will learn to eat different things at different times of day. Black bean burgers make for sensational day-starting meals, and a bowl of filling oatmeal with some walnuts? That may be your new norm for dinner. When you get past the cultural assumptions we make about food, you will open up your world to a new set of "rules"—and new opportunities for tastes.

If you want to maximize your health by eating in tune with your circadian rhythm, you have to forget societal norms around what foods belong with what time of day. Especially if you follow our guidelines and begin to front-load your day, you're going to have to rethink what constitutes "breakfast" and "lunch." Instead of adding extra calories early in the day with the traditional simple carb bombs associated with these meals, we want you to eat your dinner for breakfast or lunch.

Ideally, your breakfast and/or lunch should contain protein, fat, and whole grains. Dinner should be light. The ideal dinner is a salad or other green leafy vegetables. (Make sure to eat small bits of salad—that is, cut it up and chew it well. That way, you'll get more nitrates and better function from your blood vessels, as well as take advantage of all the benefits of fiber.)

Remember, your body is most insulin resistant at night, so you want to avoid simple carbs at dinner. Instead, have fiber-rich vegetables and proteins. The fiber can help you feel full longer, so you're not tempted to eat after dark. Plus, if you've followed the rules and ate most of your calories early, you should be much less hungry in the evening than you were before following our plan.

Now, the easiest (and healthiest) way to eat your dinner for breakfast or lunch is to actually still make dinner at night just like you always do—but to put most of it away for the next day. For example, Dr. R loves salmon burgers, quinoa, and broccoli for dinner. Instead of eating four burgers (they're small!) at night, he makes the four in the evening along with quinoa and broccoli but eats only one with a salad for dinner and has the rest of the meal for breakfast.

Dr. C is one of those people who just couldn't eat a big breakfast even though he knows he should. So he started slow by eating a plain full-fat Greek or Icelandic yogurt (these are strained so they are richer in protein than regular yogurt and have great texture), made from grass-fed milk with some berries. Now, he is cooking quick meals like whole grain pasta or seared salmon with wilted kale and a side of avocado toast (on whole grain bread, of course). If he doesn't have time in the morning, he sticks with yogurt and has a meal centered on plants and whole grains (what he used to eat for dinner) for lunch.

What to Do Now: Plan out your meals so that your biggest are the first two of the day, and eat a lighter dinner—a salad with a small portion of protein, for example. The following plan encompasses all four of our guidelines to help you take the thinking out of it.

Now, it's time to put the principles into action. And you don't have to go from 0 to 60 in one day. We'll give you plenty of ramp-up time to nudge your eating habits into the When Way style.

What's the Deal With Intermittent Fasting?

Diet trends come and go—cabbage soup, paleo, keto, you name it. Some are rooted in science, some in marketing. One of the most popular topics in conversation today is rooted in some very interesting science. Intermittent fasting—a catchall to describe various methods of restricted eating—does appear to have benefit for weight loss, health, and longevity.

Most of the data come from studies in simple organisms and animals, where fasting has been shown to increase the life span of bacteria, yeast, worms, and mice. Studies in animals have also suggested that fasting may slow the development of some cancers and the degeneration of brain cells. Fasting can also reduce inflammation and blood pressure, as well as increase insulin sensitivity.[28]

Of course, fasting is very difficult, so scientists have been studying how to mimic its potential benefits with less extreme diets. That's when *(ta-da!)* the concept of intermittent fasting was born.

This kind of eating plan can mean not eating at all every other day, severely restricting energy consumption on two or more nonconsecutive days a week, or even time-restricted feeding (shortening the window in which you eat). The advantage of intermittent fasting over many other diets is that you get to eat as you like on the nonfasting days (within reason, of course; you cannot mainline whole pizzas).

A fascinating study by Valter Longo and colleagues from the Department of Gerontology and Longevity Institute at University of Southern California examined the effects of an intermittent fasting diet on markers of health and disease. The plan they used consisted of five days of energy restriction a month (about a third of normal calorie consumption—1,000 calories the first day and then 750 calories a day for the next four days, with all calories sourced from plant-based foods). During the rest of the month, subjects in the fasting group ate normally. After three months, those in the fasting group lost more weight than those in the control group (who just ate normally), with most of the loss a result of losing fat. And most of the fasters saw a drop in markers of inflammation, as well as a possible increase in stem cell life span.[29] That implies a longer life span with less disability. Although more research in humans is needed, the practice is worth further experimentation.

If you're following the When Way guidelines, you should already be fasting around 12 hours each night—from sunset (dinner) to sunrise (breakfast). If you're willing to give it a try, the science suggests that you may get some additional benefits from stretching this window out a little further to 14 hours, and then 18. Not eating for most of the day causes your body to burn up all its circulating glucose, as well as stored glycogen; as a result, insulin levels begin to fall. Instead of burning sugar for fuel, your body starts to rely on stored fat, which can be more easily mobilized as a result of low insulin levels.[30] In fact, a study in young adult men showed that the mobilization of fat from storage increases rapidly between 18 and 24 hours.[31] Scientists theorize that the periodic switching of fuel sources may be a key factor in the advantages that intermittent fasting diets have demonstrated in the lab.[32]

CHAPTER 4

THE WHEN WAY: A 31-DAY PLAN

One Month to Shift Your Eating Habits and Improve Your Health

P atience has become the dinosaur of human qualities. Today, we want—and get—everything instantly. Our coffee. Our news. Our mail. That efficiency has changed the world, yes, but it has also helped create an environment where we cannot even tolerate waiting 30 seconds for a red light to turn green. This systematic impatience has extended to all areas of our lives.

And from where we sit, that message is loud and clear when it comes to your health. Maybe you've spent a year, a decade, or your whole life in a sort of a health malaise—not giving your body, your diet, or your habits a lot of thought or attention. But when something snaps (seeing a number on a scale, getting a cholesterol scare, or living life with general malaise), you're ready. Like right now.

All you want is to flip a switch or swallow a pill—and get your desired health outcome instantly. The body, however, cannot microwave your new desires in a matter of seconds. It needs a little time to let new habits take effect. It needs you to coax it in the right direction.

But here's the good news: Eating better, eating smarter, and eating the When Way doesn't have to take an entire ice age to take effect. In fact, in just one month, you can adjust your habits and eating approach so that your new normal becomes your new healthy. And you'll reap all the benefits we have outlined— with a healthier weight, healthier organs, lower stress, lower risk of disease, and better energy.

With this 31-day plan, you're going to gradually shift your eating habits to achieve two things: consume better foods, and maximize your chrononutrition by syncing your food intake with how your body wants to operate.

THE GOAL: EAT BETTER FOODS AT BETTER TIMES

Ultimately, you're going to learn how to pair *what* to eat with *what time* to eat it. One doesn't work without the other. Why? It doesn't matter what time you eat if everything you rocket down your piehole is a relative of cherry Popsicles and tortilla chips.

As we've discussed, you should strive to avoid processed foods and all simple sugars (including table sugar, brown sugar, and syrups, as well as white flours). Processed foods are designed with salt, fat, and sugar to make them palatable and delicious—but as the term "processed" implies, you can think of these as partially digested and addictive. Processed foods are typically low or completely lacking in fiber and/or the binding of sugar to the fiber. Your body quickly accepts all the calories in these so-called "foods," which can cause your blood sugar to spike and mess with your appetite hormones. Every once in a while won't hurt you. Even our friend Dr. Oz enjoys a dessert from time to time. But long-term chronic eating of processed foods is a health hazard.

During these 31 days, you're going to gradually shift to the When Way lifestyle, eating whole foods like fruits and vegetables, whole grains, healthy fats, and plant- and sea-based proteins. Specifically, your diet will morph to emphasize the following:

- **Non-starchy vegetables** like broccoli, onions, and asparagus in unlimited quantities. Starchy vegetables like hot white potatoes are essentially a long chain of sugar molecules that can spike your blood sugar. But a resistant starch like cooled sweet potatoes (cooled potatoes have less problematic effects on blood sugar) acts more like fiber, helping you feel full and improving the health of bacteria in your gut.[1] (See page 156.)
- **Whole grains,** which are also made up of carbohydrates, but because they usually have a low glycemic index and contain resistant starch, they take a long time for the body to break down. Look for quinoa or whole farro, as well as 100 percent whole grains, as the only grain ingredients in pasta or bread.
- **Healthy fats** are derived from plant sources such as olives (omega-9 is the healthiest fat here), avocados, and nuts, especially walnuts, and constitute the unsaturated fats we discussed in Chapter 2. There are also healthy fats in fish like wild salmon, which is a great source of DHA omega-3 and omega-7 fat. (Walnuts and

avocados also have healthy ALA omega-3 fats; notice they are all odd numbers—3, 5, 7, or 9. Dr. R calls them the Odd Omegas.)

- **Proteins** derived from plant foods and fish. You can eat lean animal proteins like chicken and turkey as well.

- **Fruit,** especially berries, which come with a great reservoir of phytonutrients, as well as elements that are euphemistically called antioxidants (they don't function as antioxidants in your cells, but that's another chapter). Fruit contains sugar, but also a lot of fiber, which the sugar is often bound to. It's best to eat fruit whole, rather than in juice form, so that you always receive the benefits of the fiber (which we often refer to as pulp) along with the sugar. This slows your body's ability to get the sugar into your blood, which (no magic here) helps keep your blood sugar in line.

YES FOODS: NON-STARCHY VEGETABLES

At the right time of day, you can eat unlimited quantities of non-starchy vegetables, including the following:

- Artichoke
- Asparagus
- Beans (green, wax, Italian)
- Beets
- Brussels sprouts
- Broccoli
- Cabbage
- Carrots
- Cauliflower
- Celery
- Cucumber
- Eggplant
- Greens (like collard, kale, mustard, turnip)
- Hearts of palm
- Jicama
- Kohlrabi
- Leeks

- Mushrooms
- Okra
- Onions
- Peppers
- Radishes
- Rutabaga
- Salad greens

(like arugula, chicory, endive, escarole, lettuces, radicchio, spinach, watercress)
- Sprouts
- Squash

(crookneck, spaghetti, summer, zucchini)
- Sugar snap peas
- Swiss chard
- Tomato
- Turnips

YES FOODS: RESISTANT STARCH VEGETABLES

- Cooked—but not fried!—and cooled (so they are cold) sweet or white potatoes
- Green (not fully ripened) bananas

YES FOODS: HEALTHY FATS

- Extra-virgin olive oil (not for frying); you can use avocado oil or a combination of avocado and olive oil for higher temperature cooking. But this doesn't mean you should drink it—a good rule of thumb is around 4 tablespoons a day.
- 1 ounce of raw or dry-roasted nuts (make sure no oil or salt is added) and seeds a day
- Avocado (don't go nuts; half an avocado a day is fine)

YES FOODS: WHOLE GRAINS

You should plan to eat four servings of 100 percent whole grains a day—about four ounces if you're into weighing things, or four slices of bread, or two cups of cooked grains.

- Buckwheat
- Buckwheat flour
- Bulgur
- Millet
- Popcorn
- Quinoa
- Triticale
- Wild rice
- Whole farro
- Whole grain barley
- 100 percent whole grain bread
- Whole grain corn/cornmeal
- Whole grain pasta
- Whole oats/oatmeal
- 100 percent whole wheat flour

YES FOODS: PLANT- AND SEA-BASED PROTEIN AND POULTRY

Plan on eating up to seven ounces of the following proteins a day:

- Legumes (beans and peas)
- Tofu
- Tempeh
- Fish, shellfish, seafood—salmon and ocean trout are best
- Nuts
- Skinless chicken and turkey (white meat is best, but you can also have dark meat)

LIMIT FOODS:

- Animal protein: red meat (less than four ounces a week) and pork (less than six ounces a week). Be sure to avoid egg yolks, cheese, or other red or processed meats in the same week.

- Egg yolks (at most once a week and without cheese or red meat that week). Egg whites are OK.
- Dairy (limit most, but OK to go for plain, no-sugar-added, strained yogurt like Greek or Turkish yogurts, which have probiotic benefits). Alternative nut milks like almond or walnut are OK, but check labels and avoid added sugars or other food ingredients that will age you.
- Cheese (less than four ounces a week)
- Starchy vegetables (including parsnip, plantains, hot or warm potatoes, pumpkin, acorn squash, butternut squash, green peas)
- White and brown rice
- Alcohol (limit to one drink for women and two for men a day; men and women tend to metabolize alcohol differently because they have different levels of alcohol dehydrogenase in their stomach's lining).

AVOID FOODS:

Except on special occasions (see page 189), never consume the following:

- Sugar (especially in drinks and desserts)
- Added syrups (including maple, honey, agave, and so on)
- White flour
- Processed foods
- Fried foods
- Coconut and palm oil

THE PREP: WHAT KIND OF EATER ARE YOU?

Fill in the following information for a baseline portrait of when you typically eat and how hungry you usually are at those times. This will help inform how you approach the 31-day plan and adjust it to your specific eating habits and personality.

At the start of your 31 days:
Sunrise Time _____a.m. **Sunset Time** _____p.m.

Typical Wake Time _____

Breakfast Start Time _____
Hunger Rating (Not Hungry) 1 2 3 4 5 (Starving)
Breakfast Size S M L
Time for Breakfast Rating (None) 1 2 3 4 5 (Lots)

Snack Time _____
Hunger Rating (Not Hungry) 1 2 3 4 5 (Starving)
Snack Size S M L

Lunch Time _____
Hunger Rating (Not Hungry) 1 2 3 4 5 (Starving)
Lunch Size S M L
Time for Lunch Rating (None) 1 2 3 4 5 (Lots)

Snack Time _____
Hunger Rating (Not Hungry) 1 2 3 4 5 (Starving)
Snack Size S M L

Dinner Time End Time _____

Hunger Rating (Not Hungry) 1 2 3 4 5 (Starving)
Dinner Size S M L
Time for Dinner Rating (None) 1 2 3 4 5 (Lots)

Snack Time ⸻
Hunger Rating (Not Hungry) 1 2 3 4 5 (Starving)
Snack Size S M L

Bed Time ⸻

Think about the day you just logged. Fill in the graph on the left based on the percentage of calories you think you ate at each meal, as well as the start and end times. Each box in the chart represents 10 percent of the calories you eat in a day. So in the example on the right, dinner represents 50 percent of the day's calorie intake.

10%	10% **Breakfast Start 7 a.m.**
20%	20% **Lunch**
30%	30% **Lunch**
40%	40% **Lunch**
50%	50% **Midday Snack**
60%	60% **Dinner**
70%	70% **Dinner**
80%	80% **Dinner**
90%	90% **Dinner**
100%	100% **Dinner Finish 10 p.m.**

A 31-DAY PLAN

Now that you've figured out your baseline and know the best foods to eat, you can begin the 31-day When Way plan. We've designed this to make it easy for you to gradually adopt healthy practices, so you can slowly skew your eating routine to maximize your body's fuel intake and stay lean, healthy, and strong.

DAYS 1 TO 3

Record what you eat and when you eat. Take note of all foods, portion sizes, and the time of day; this will count for meals, snacks, and "nobody's looking" swipes in the cookie jar. Then, make charts like the one on page 77, where you estimate the portion of your calories in relationship to the time of day you're eating them. On day 4, we will use this information to figure out the perfect plan for you.

DAYS 4 TO 8

Your goal for the next few days is to eat more of your daily calories earlier in the day and fewer calories later, without worrying too much about *what* you're eating. Take a look at the charts you filled out over the last three days. Do they look like any of the following three we listed, in terms of what time of day you eat most of your food?

Like most people, you're probably eating a lot more of your calories at night for dinner or even after. Starting today, we want you to shift to eating your calories earlier. We recommend you do this over the next three or four days to give your body

10% **Breakfast 7 a.m.**	10% **Breakfast 8 a.m.**	10% **Breakfast 7:30 a.m.**
20% **Breakfast**	20% **Breakfast**	20% **Breakfast**
30% **Breakfast**	30% **Lunch**	30% **Breakfast**
40% **Lunch**	40% **Lunch**	40% **Breakfast**
50% **Lunch**	50% **Lunch**	50% **Lunch**
60% **Lunch**	60% **Lunch**	60% **Lunch**
70% **Snack**	70% **Lunch**	70% **Lunch**
80% **Snack**	80% **Snack**	80% **Lunch**
90% **Dinner**	90% **Dinner**	90% **Dinner**
100% **Dinner Finish 7 p.m.**	100% **Dinner Finish 7 p.m.**	100% **Dinner Finish 6:30 p.m.**

time to adjust to the change. But if you are like Dr. R and that doesn't fit with your personality, go ahead and make the change all at once; your body will catch up with you.

You also have to decide if you want to shift your calories to breakfast, lunch, or somewhere in between. So, let's take a look at your log again. If you find that you're not at all hungry and don't have any time in the morning, then it might be better to switch your calories to late morning or an early afternoon lunch. But if you do have time for breakfast, earlier is always better. You could also split the calories between the two meals. Your log can help you decide what would work best for you. Whatever time you choose, try the following few techniques over the next four days:

- Look at your regular dinner. Let's say it represents about 50 percent of your typical daily calories, based on the estimate you made in your log. Your goal is to bring it closer to 20 percent. Therefore, you essentially need to cut your typical dinner in half. If you're like Dr. C whose dinner used to represent almost all of his calories, you may need to cut dinner by 75 percent.
- Divide your dinner into quarters in your head. Starting today, we want you to take the food in one of those quarters and save it for breakfast or lunch tomorrow—whichever meal you've decided to increase in size. If your goal is to cut your dinner in half, then the next day, plan to do the same. On the third day, take two of those quarters (half the plate) and save it for breakfast or lunch the next day. By the third night, you should be eating a When Way–size dinner. On day four, do the same thing again.

Now, to pull this off, you're going to have to think the When Way and *stop stereotyping foods*. It's OK to eat the same foods for breakfast, lunch, and dinner.

You may be worried that you're going to be really hungry eating a much smaller dinner—but in all likelihood, you probably won't be. You're still eating the same total amount in a day; you've just shifted the timing of the main calorie consumption. The meals you ate earlier should help make you less hungry at dinner. Both Drs. R and C have successfully shifted most of their eating to breakfast and lunch, and both saw their hunger patterns change very quickly to fit the new schedule.

That said, if you do find yourself hungry anyway, we have a few tricks to try:

1. Add a salad or two. Actually, add as much salad as you want. Salad contains fiber and other micronutrients, but not that many calories (as long as you don't load it up with meat and cheese and tons of creamy or sugary dressing). We are talking about lettuce and other fiber-rich vegetables, extra-virgin olive oil, and *maybe* balsamic vinegar.
2. Expand your plate with as many vegetables as you want. Again, vegetables are fiber rich, filling, and low in calories—provided they aren't smothered in cheese or dressing.
3. Eat a pear for dessert; it's a fiber-rich fruit with a good amount of sweetness. A pear or berries at the end of dinner can help satisfy cravings for sugar and make you feel full.
4. Save one of your snacks for 20 minutes before dinner. It can take about this long for your body to feel full after you eat, so having a snack before dinner may dull your appetite and help you feel satisfied with a smaller meal.

Want to see how this works in practice? Here's how Dr. C pulled off this switch to make his bigger meal earlier. On most days, Dr. C was an intermittent faster. He may have had a very small breakfast in the morning (a half cup of yogurt), then ate nothing all day until the evening (usually 7 or 8 p.m.), and was typically finished eating around 9. He had the fasting (or time restriction) right, but his biggest meal was at the completely wrong time.

His day looked like this when he put it on the chart:

10% **Breakfast 8 a.m.**
20% **Dinner**
30% **Dinner**
40% **Dinner**
50% **Dinner**
60% **Dinner**
70% **Dinner**
80% **Dinner**
90% **Dinner**
100% **Dinner Finish 9 p.m.**

Dr. C realized he needed to make a big change. He needed to shift his calories from dinner to earlier in the day. On most

Night Snackers

If you're a late-night snacker, we want you to count that snack as part of your dinner. Based on all the biology we described in Chapter 3, it should be pretty clear that snacking late at night is just about the worst thing for you, as this is when insulin resistance is at its max. As a result, regular late-night snacks have no place in the When Way of eating.

days it would be hard for him to make breakfast his largest meal, so he decided he would start by shifting the bulk of his calories to lunch. He wanted his chart to look more like this:

| 10% Breakfast start 8 a.m. |
| 20% Breakfast |
| 30% Lunch |
| 40% Lunch |
| 50% Lunch |
| 60% Lunch |
| 70% Lunch |
| 80% Lunch |
| 90% Dinner |
| 100% Dinner Finish 7 p.m. |

To do it, he used the strategy mentioned previously, quartering his dinner. When Dr. C made dinner, he ate just a small amount and saved the rest for his lunch the following day. Now he typically doesn't eat dinner at all and saves the meal he makes at night for the next day.

DAYS 9 TO 14

After shifting your eating schedule, you may feel different. When Dr. C began eating most of his calories earlier, he started to sleep better and wasn't hungry in the evening. The downside: Even though he's now eating the same amount of food as before, he's had to buy new, smaller pants.

You can take these few days to work on making a further adjustment: trying to eat all your meals between sunrise and sunset. If you're eating after dark (it's especially hard not to in the winter), it's time to move your breakfast later or your dinner earlier. Now that you're eating a smaller dinner, you should be able to nudge it a little earlier if you need to (take a few days to get there; you can do it in increments, starting 30 minutes earlier a day).

If you're already eating only when the sun shines, you can skip ahead to an advanced technique like time-restricted feeding. Ideally you should be eating within a window of 12 hours or less. Remember the studies we mentioned earlier: Humans and animals with shorter eating windows tend to be healthier. So, use this time to shorten the window during which you eat even more.

DAY 15

Take today to log how you eat. See how much you've changed since you started. If you haven't quite made the full shift—eating more of your calories earlier and shifting your eating window to between sunrise and sunset—that's OK. Just keep working toward that goal as you start focusing more on the kinds of foods you eat.

DAYS 16 TO 19

Now is the time you're going to start focusing on *what* you're eating. On Day 16, take this quiz to note how you're doing with the When Way foods.

AVOID FOODS

How often do you eat processed foods?

Never	1/Month	1/Week	2-6/Week	Daily	Multiple Times a Day

How often do you eat simple carbs (sugar, white flour foods)?

Never	1/Month	1/Week	2-6/Week	Daily	Multiple Times a Day

How often do you eat fried foods?

Never	1/Month	1/Week	2-6/Week	Daily	Multiple Times a Day

How often do you eat processed meat, red meat, or pork?

Never	1/Month	1/Week	2-6/Week	Daily	Multiple Times a Day

WHEN WAY FOODS

How many servings of vegetables do you eat a day?

5 or more	4	3	2	1	0

How many servings of whole grains do you eat a day?

4 or more	3	2	1	0

How often do you eat nuts or seeds?

Daily	2-6/Week	1/Week	1/Month	Never

How often do you eat plant protein, fish, or skinless chicken or turkey as your protein source?

Multiple Times a Day	Daily	2-6/Week	1/Week	1/Month	Never

Take a look at how you answered these questions. Ideally all your responses would be on the lighter end of the spectrum. If your answers are toward the darker end of the spectrum, your goal over the next two weeks is to shift what you eat toward the lighter end of the spectrum.

Of course, just stopping isn't easy, so we have devised a series of substitutions (called the Sub Shop) that will make it simpler for you to eat under this new schedule.

For the next three days, we want you to focus on processed foods. On your first day, substitute healthier options for processed snacks. Collect all the processed food snacks you would have eaten and put them in a plastic bag. This will help you see what you've been eating—and you'll feel good at the end of the day when you haven't touched any of it! (Just make sure you throw the bag away at the end of the day. Temptation is real!)

Crunch Time

One of our favorite foods—which you can use as a go-to snack and to help you feel satisfied—is the almighty nut. We especially like walnuts, because eating them is associated with eating more fruits and vegetables, as well as with weight loss.[2] Also, nuts (especially walnuts) are known to lower the risk of heart attacks and strokes,[3] as well as the risk of death.[4] Walnuts in particular are a powerhouse snack that appear to help boost four types of good gut bacteria (*Faecalibacterium, Clostridium, Dialister,* and *Roseburia*).[5] In practice, that means that nuts, especially walnuts, on breakfast cereal or avocado toast make for excellent choices to help you start the day.

THE SUB SHOP

Crackers, chips, and pretzels. If you tend to indulge in these crunchy, salty, fatty snacks, we have some great new alternatives. Eating these kinds of processed foods is often done mindlessly; you meant to have just a small handful, but ended up eating a whole bowl or bag. The way to beat this habit is to pay attention to what you eat and be prepared:

1. Every time you think about having a processed snack, drink a glass of water. This will help slow you down so you are eating more deliberately. Also, water may help satisfy your hunger (and it keeps you hydrated).

2. Pack a small plastic bag with walnuts and two or three 22-calorie dark chocolate discs. This snack should help satisfy cravings for fatty foods—and has the benefits that come with healthy fats and phytonutrients. Other alternatives are carrot sticks, pepper strips, and radishes. These will help satisfy the need for a crunch and add more vegetables to your day. Skip the dressing.

3. Eat a slice of 100 percent whole grain or sprouted wheat bread such as Ezekiel brand. These breads are packed with good carbohydrates, so they will help satisfy those carb cravings. Add half of an avocado and lemon juice if you like, or a no-sugar-added nut butter.

4. Make some air-popped popcorn. If you want a flavor boost, sprinkle a homemade spice mix on top, like chili and lime or olive oil and everything-bagel seasoning.

Cookies, candy, pastries. Although delicious and momentarily satisfying, these foods will spike your blood sugar and can actually make you hungrier once it rebounds. Fortunately, alternatives can help you feel fuller longer. The trick is to substitute fiber-rich foods that satisfy your need for a sweet treat or dessert:

1. Go for in-season organic berries. These little bursts of flavor are sweet, yet packed with phytonutrients and fiber. They are also on the expensive side, so that should keep you from overeating them. If you prefer out-of-season berries, go for defrosted frozen organic versions.

2. Try a green banana. These are easy to transport and come in their own wrapper. But bananas can ripen quickly so eat them soon after you purchase them. They are not too sweet, but do have resistant starch that feeds the good gut bacteria.

3. One ounce of dark chocolate goes a long way. It doesn't have fiber, but it's a legitimate low-sugar dessert—and it contains antioxidants.

4. If you think of sweets as a reward, this sub isn't another food; it's an activity. Give yourself a different kind of gift with some time by yourself (listen and/or dance to your favorite song, do 20 jumping jacks, write down three things you are grateful for, take a bath, read a book, watch a new TV show) or with friends (give them a call or go see a movie together—just skip the buttered, oil-popped popcorn).

Preparation V

You've heard the word a thousand times: vegetables. Maybe it conjures nightmares of Meemaw trying to force sprouts down your throat. Maybe you just yawn at the very mention of what you consider no-taste plants. Or maybe you hear the word "vegetables" the way you hear the word "colonoscopy": good for you, yes, but once every 10 years is plenty.

Now, we all know the restaurant version of veggies: They smother them in butter, cheese, or some other calorie-dense sauce that for all intents and purposes robs them of their nutritional powers. Zucchini isn't zucchini when it's fried. Broccoli isn't broccoli when it's blanketed in melted cheddar. Potatoes aren't potatoes when they come in a bag and can be ordered in small, medium, and backpack.

And that's the real problem: The average American doesn't eat a very wide variety of vegetables. Even worse, the ones we do eat aren't exactly model citizens. Three individual vegetables compose about half the total average Americans eat: (1) potatoes, frequently consumed as fries and chips; (2) tomatoes, often in the form of processed ketchup and sauce; and (3) onions, often on top of burgers.[6]

The real power of vegetables—of which you can have unlimited quantities, with a few notable exceptions (see page 75)—is that the way you prepare them can make a huge difference in the way they taste. And isn't that really the end goal here? If you like the way good-for-you foods taste, won't you be likely to eat more of them? If you hate broccoli, it may be because it is typically oversteamed or boiled, rather than prepared in a way that maximizes flavor, texture, and even color.

To master the When Way, you have to learn to cook the When Way. Only when you prepare your own food can you truly control exactly *what* and exactly *when* you eat. Now, if the last sentence has you thinking about ripping this chapter out of the book and burning it, because you [fill in the blank with *can't, hate to, don't want to,* or *don't have the time to*] cook, hang with us. It's actually easier, cheaper, more delicious, and more efficient to cook the When Way than to pick up takeout or dine out.

So take a gander at the following easy cooking techniques. As you'll see, they'll add a ton of flavor and satisfaction without pumping your food full of fat, sugar, salt, cheese, or meat.

Technique	How to Do It
Blanch (cook quickly in water)	Chop vegetables in evenly sized pieces and drop them in boiling water. Cook them for 30 seconds to 2 minutes; they are usually done when the color brightens. Remove from water and drain, put in freezer for 5 to 10 minutes to cool quickly.
Sauté (cook over high heat quickly)	Cook small pieces of vegetables with a mist of extra-virgin olive oil in a sauté pan for 3 to 5 minutes, until tender but with some bite left. Add chili flakes, rosemary, garlic, and/or lemon to the oil for extra flavor.

Oven roasting	Coat veggies with olive oil, salt, or other spices and spread in an even layer on a baking sheet. Roast in oven at 350 degrees for about 15 to 30 minutes.
Braising (slow cooking in liquid)	Start like a sauté, but on much lower heat. Add liquid like water, wine, and/or tomato sauce to the pan, then cover and cook at a gentle simmer until tender. If you want less liquid, uncover and let some evaporate when the vegetables are almost cooked to your liking. The best vegetables to cook this way are Swiss chard, broccoli, green beans, and fennel. (Tomato-braised broccoli and greens are Dr. R's favorite—a double healthy choice with lycopene from tomatoes.)
Steaming	Put vegetables in a steamer above a pot of boiling water; the food will never touch the water. Let steam until the vegetables soften and the colors brighten, typically 3 to 5 minutes.

If you don't want to cook veggies every night, try freezing them: It allows you to buy, prep, and store in bulk so you have healthy meals on really short notice. But it's a mistake to think you can just toss them in the freezer. A few tricks will help you get the best out of your veggies:

- Freeze food as soon as possible after it's cooked and cooled.
- Remove air from any packaging. You can do this by plunging the bag into a bowl or pot of cold water (keeping the open end out of the water). The water pressure forces air out of the bag. Seal the bag before removing it from the water.
- Label your packaging with the date that you stored it. Eat it in a timely manner to ensure you retain taste, texture, and nutrients.
- Cook blanched veggies right from the freezer; they don't need to be thawed first.

DAYS 20 TO 23

We hope you are well on your way to eliminating processed foods from your diet. (Don't worry if you need more time; just keep working on it.) For the next three days, focus on this When Way principle: Stop stereotyping your foods.

Probably no meal is more stereotyped than breakfast. People often think of breakfast as either bacon and eggs; an egg, ham, and cheese sandwich; sugary cereal with milk; pancakes; waffles; or muffins and pastries. Hmm, none of those really fit into the When Way of eating, so if you are a breakfast person, this could mean some big changes are in store. But if you realize that "traditional breakfast foods" don't actually have to be eaten for breakfast—or ever—and that lunch and dinner foods are just fine in the morning, you'll be well on your way.

THE SUB SHOP

Breakfast skippers should try a plain, strained no-sugar-added Greek or Icelandic yogurt with some added fruit and/or walnuts to start. Even the most time-pressed person can fit in this deliciously simple, protein-rich food.

Cereal: Most cereals are loaded with sugar and simple carbs, but they don't all have to be. If you have to eat cereal, opt for one with very low sugar, 100 percent whole grains, and at least six grams of fiber (the more the better). Instead of milk, we recommend eating it with strained yogurt (Greek or Icelandic are our favorites). This will give your breakfast a boost of protein and probiotics. For a dairy-free option, you can try alternative nondairy milks like walnut or almond. Even better, swap out dry cereal for something that still falls into the traditional breakfast category: oatmeal. We like steel-cut oats the best, but even instant oatmeal is a great and superfast choice. Just don't buy the one with any added sugar; stick with plain oatmeal made with boiled water and add your own cinnamon and fruit if you like to sweeten the deal. The beta-glucans in oatmeal help feed your healthy gut bacteria. Bonus points if you eat it cold—that's when it becomes a resistant starch.

Bacon and eggs: If it's not morning for you without two eggs and two slices of bacon, then try giving an egg-white frittata a try (and once a week, you can add a yolk to it; or even a tofu scramble). A frittata is basically an omelet you flip instead of fold. We like them best loaded with green vegetables like kale. Vary the veggies for added pleasure. You can even add sweet potatoes and eat it cold if you're in a rush. This is a great way to sneak more vegetables into your day, which you probably don't think about doing with breakfast. Looking for the smoky flavor of bacon? Try putting some smoked salmon on top of your frittata when it's done (don't cook it with the eggs).

If you're really ready to take the plunge into eating the When Way and not stereotyping your food, try a salmon burger over

What's the Deal With Red Meat and Egg Yolks?

It's best to avoid these in the When Way. Yes, red meat contains protein, which is our body's main building block. But it often contains a large amount of saturated fat, which isn't good for heart health. That's one of the reasons red meat isn't always the healthiest choice. The saturated fat in red meat, as well as cheese and egg yolks, also comes with amino acid derivatives like carnitine, lecithin, and choline that gut microbiomes turn into a substance that increases platelet stickiness and is associated with heart disease, stroke, kidney failure, and maybe even inability to appropriately weed out cancer cells and dementia (not to mention impotence).[7,8,9,10,11] In the future, we may find a probiotic or other substance that reduces bacterial production of this substance. Although red meat and eggs in moderate amounts are OK, please eat no more than four ounces of red meat, six ounces of pork, or one egg yolk in a week, as more is enough to change the bacteria in your gut. It's best to stick with the other forms of protein— chicken and fish are the best, and you can also get protein in beans and nuts.

sautéed spinach or with broccoli for breakfast. This is what Dr. R often does. You'll get your healthy fats and protein in this totally nontraditional breakfast.

DAYS 24 TO 26

For these three days, we want you to focus on getting more whole grains into your diet. Carbs have been much maligned in recent years, but a study published not long ago found that we as a nation are not eating enough whole grains.[12] Eating them actually helps you live younger and longer, and they are delicious to boot! Remember, you want to eat about four servings of whole grains a day.

THE SUB SHOP

Bread and butter or bagels and cream cheese. Substitute white bread and bagels with 100 percent whole grain versions. Instead of butter or cream cheese, top with half an avocado and some chopped tomatoes or onions. Dr. R loves this for a weekend dinner after his Ping-Pong or squash game.

White pasta. Try substituting a whole grain pasta. Dr. C's absolute favorite is whole grain farro. (Using farro flour to make pasta is very traditional in parts of southern Italy like Puglia.) Other ancient whole grain pastas, like spelt and einkorn, are good too.

Always cook your pasta al dente; not only does it taste better, but it will also be richer in resistant starch (and even more so if you eat it cold). You could also try bean pasta, which

Better Than Butter

Who doesn't love butter on bread or cream in a salad dressing? These ingredients add luxurious mouthfeel and flavor. The problem is that those additions are loaded with saturated fat— the worst kind. But never fear: We've got a really cheap gourmet hack that cuts the fat and adds a ton of flavor.

The secret is something we like to call vegetable crema or cream—basically, pureed vegetables. Dr. C got the idea recently when he was perusing the olive oil section of his local grocery store. There, among the golden and green liquids, was a very small but very expensive jar labeled *crema di carciofi* (artichoke cream). Dr. C loves artichokes, which are not only delicious but also loaded with inulin, a prebiotic fiber that feeds good gut bacteria. A quick look at the ingredient list revealed there wasn't much to this interesting treat: just artichokes, lemon juice, garlic, and a little olive oil.

So, Dr. C decided to make it himself. He picked up a few cans of artichoke hearts, packed in acidulated water. When he got home, he threw them in a high-speed blender with some garlic and extra-virgin olive oil and let it whirl. He gradually added olive oil until the mixture was creamy and totally smooth. Then he tasted it: It was absolutely amazing. And he had a huge jar of it for just a few bucks!

Artichokes aren't the only foundation for vegetable cream; you can use the same method to create other variations with steamed carrots, roasted onions, and more. Want something really fast? Just blend some avocado with lemon or lime (no oil needed). The cremas are great on a piece of 100 percent whole grain bread or paired with some smoked salmon (just as good as cream cheese!). You can also add to hot soups, in place of crème fraîche or sour cream, to add extra body, or as salad dressing with its creamy texture.

doesn't really count as a whole grain, but is rich in fiber, resistant starch, and is a complex carb. We aren't huge fans of the taste and texture, but we find the lentil and chickpea versions to be the best of the bunch.

Rice. Rice can be a low or high glycemic carb, but it's also relatively high in arsenic, which can increase your chance of chronic disease. Lots of other whole grains—like quinoa, buckwheat, barley, and millet—are good substitutes. Despite its name, wild rice is not actually rice at all; it's derived from a totally different type of plant—so feel free to sub wild rice for white or brown rice as well.

DAYS 27 TO 28

Use these two days to focus on some of the previous steps you are still trying to achieve. If you haven't quite made the switch from your old lunch to the When Way option, now's your chance to catch up.

For most of you, lunch will probably be your easiest biggest meal. But it's also hard to prepare on the run. A good solution is to plan on eating your leftover dinner for lunch. One of Dr. C's favorites is a vegetable and bean stir-fry.

Soup for You

Making flavorful and healthy soups is easy, as well as a big time-saver when eating the When Way. Plus, soup is a filling meal that actually makes for a great breakfast or lunch because it's so easy to transport.

The trick to soup is developing a flavorful broth. The way to do it: Brown vegetables well in a pan. If you're going to add spices, toast them with your veggies at the bottom of the pan. For tomato-based soups, add tomato paste before the liquid so that it can caramelize a bit. All that dark brown stuff that sticks to the bottom (called the fond in technical terms) will be dissolved by water and add both color and flavor to your soup. Next, add water or low-sodium vegetable broth, bring to a boil, lower the heat to a simmer, and cover; cook for 20 to 40 minutes. When it's time to eat, adding a dash of fresh extra-virgin olive oil, lemon or lime juice, or chili flakes will soup up the flavor without adding too much salt.

This is yet another way to add more vegetables into your day, and it tastes great cold. You can eat it with some whole grains mixed in or on the side.

Another great trick, especially in the winter, is hot home-made soup. Believe it or not, an old-fashioned thermos can actually keep soup hot for 12 hours. Dr. C just started taking soup to work, and was skeptical that his old-looking thermos would do the trick. On the first day, he tried the soup after it had been in the thermos for six hours and he burned his tongue!

DAYS 29 TO 30

For this two-day period, focus on making your now smallest meal (dinner) something that's filling and satisfying. We like to make dinner a mini-feast of fiber-rich vegetables, soups, and salad. Both of us love broccoli and both believe we cook it the best.

Another great choice for dinner is a small bowl of vegetable soup with a little whole grain like quinoa or whole grain farro added in. As we mentioned before, you can have as much salad as you want.

DAY 31

Look back on all you've accomplished toward eating the When Way. Even if you skipped some steps or want to change your eating regimen and aren't all the way there yet, you've still come a long way. Remember that you don't have to fully make the switch in 30 days; after all, you've probably been eating the same way for a lifetime. You can revisit any of the days in this plan anytime to keep adjusting.

Now is the time to work on consistency with what you eat and when you eat. Even if you take a day off during the weekend, you're still doing great and well on the path to better health.

CHAPTER 5

FOOD FOR THOUGHT

Mindful Eating for More Majestic Meals

I f you look at the six basic questions of adopting the When Way—the who, what, when, where, why, and how—then it's clear this book covers most of them. The who is you, obvi. The what and the when are, well, the title of the darn book. The why—although individual for everyone—probably involves becoming healthier, fitter, or happier. That leaves us with two questions: where and how.

Now, you may initially think that those questions don't need addressing. After all, the "where" can be boiled down to a laundry list of typical places that include kitchen tables, driver's seats, and movie theaters. The "how"? Sort of elementary, right? Food to plate. Plate to utensil. Utensil to mouth. Mouth to belly.

That, however, is exactly the problem.

We don't think about the where.

We don't think about the how.

We don't *think* when we eat.

Truth is, eating has become such a vacuumlike process that the wonderful sensory experience that comes with it is generally lost to 99 percent of us during 99 percent of our meals.

Why does that even matter? A couple of reasons, actually. But perhaps the main one is this: Mindless eating—that is, the unconscious act of bulldozing in bite after bite without being aware of how you feel—is one of the reasons we overeat, and is the root of many health problems. Mindful eating, on the other hand, is about slowing down, focusing on food, not being distracted, and appreciating what you eat not only through the fullness of your belly, but also through the physical satisfaction relayed via your senses and emotions.

A recent analysis of 19 studies showed that mindful eating was effective in improving eating behaviors and producing better weight-loss results.[1] In a study presented at the 24th European Congress on Obesity, people who practiced mindful eating lost about three and a half more pounds than those who didn't.[2,3]

In addition, a 2017 study presented at the American Heart Association's Scientific Sessions followed 1,000 adults for five years. At the beginning, nobody had metabolic syndrome (the condition signified by such problems as high blood pressure, high LDL cholesterol, and high blood sugar). But five years later, those who ate fast (fast pretty much equals mindless) were about two to five times more likely to develop the chronic disease condition.[4]

So, although our main goal in this book is to get you to shift what and when you eat to maximize the way your body processes food, we also believe you should know a bit about the "how" and the "where" so that you're (1) allowing your body to really feel your food and (2) giving yourself a chance to enjoy the unique flavors and spices and tongue-tingling joy that can come when you stop and smell the flours (whole grain flour that is). The following are seven easy ways to get started.

MAKE PLACE A PRIORITY

There's no doubt that your life is in Autobahn mode: go, go, go. And that often means you have to eat on the run, grab what you can, and wolf down the quickest thing you can find just to keep you going throughout the day. Although we certainly cannot implore you to tell your boss or kids that you'd like to have a leisurely meal right now, we can give you a general eating goal: Focus on the food and the people you're with. Not traffic. Not your work. Not why the heck Aunt Edna posted that weird Facebook video involving a cat petting a baby duck.

To achieve this, your first step is getting away from a desk or the car when you can (and the second step is unfollowing Aunt Edna). If you already do this, great. If not, take one meal a week to consciously pry yourself from distractions and just focus on the food. You can increase the number of meals each week; they can be alone, they can be with family, or they can be with friends. The point isn't to sit by yourself or stay silent; it's to eliminate distraction so that you're not ignoring your food so much that you eat too much.

FOCUS ON SATISFIED, NOT FULL

When you're eating without thinking, your eyes want more than your belly can handle. That's because it can take up to

20 minutes for food to be digested enough to trigger the hormone responses that alert your brain that you've had enough.[5] When you slow down, however, you're more in tune with the amount of food you need. Your goal is to top off your tank, not make it overflow. When you're not buried pupil-deep in your phone, you can notice how you feel—and you're more likely to stop eating when your hunger has subsided. That's a totally different feeling than eating until you're full. And that one minor adjustment—over time—can be the game changer when it comes to keeping your weight down (and avoiding the problems associated with weight gain).

YOU CAN PRACTICE IT

One of the points of mindful eating is to teach you that healthy food has its own set of delicious tastes and satisfying qualities. (This fact has been masked over the last few decades with lots of overly sugared processed foods that have collectively taught us that you have to eat a silo worth of sweets to be happy.) Frankly, this is one of the hardest things to learn; people rarely say they'd rather have a radish than an oatmeal raisin cookie.

But here's the thing: You *can* practice mindful eating. Researchers suggest doing it with a raisin and following these instructions: Place a raisin in your mouth; don't chew. Close your eyes. Let the raisin sit on your tongue. Taste its flavor. Feel the texture, shape, and firmness. Begin to slowly chew. Notice how your tongue, teeth, and jaw move as the raisin changes in your mouth. Try it today. Practice it tomorrow. Integrate new foods. It only takes a few seconds, but the effects—if you keep it up—can last a lifetime.

REALIZE THE RELATIONSHIP BETWEEN TASTE AND SMELL

Taste and smell go together like almond butter and blueberries. In fact, smell is so much a part of taste that it's evolutionarily vital; it once acted as an early warning system. When people detected something was poisonous with their nose before they put it in their mouth, a life was saved (necessary in an era before labels included skull and crossbones on packaging).

Because of this, some of what we taste is actually influenced by smell. When food is placed in the mouth, some of the molecules actually move up into the back of the throat and into the nasal cavity. Your individual taste buds—and how they interact with food—certainly play a role in how you perceive food. The bottom line is that food should be experienced slowly, with all of your senses interacting with each other to fully appreciate what you're eating.

EXERCISE YOUR SMELL MUSCLES

OK, so maybe you're not going to go to the gym and do three sets of 10 nose sniffs. But you can exercise and improve your smelling ability in a similar way. Research suggests that you can do this by sniffing a variety of different aromas for 30 seconds, two or more times a day, using essential oils. Don't have essential oils lying around? Then pick distinct items you like, such as spices, coffee, berries, citrus, and herbs. For even better results, vary the items after a couple of months.[6]

Other studies suggest that you also take the time to smell different things around you and try to describe them as a way of becoming more attuned with a sense you may not pay much attention to except in extreme scenarios, from fresh flowers to foul feet. (By the way, some research shows that a leading cause of loss of smell is trauma, like car accidents.[7] That's because the part of your brain that receives smells can be easily damaged. So, yeah, we never thought that "wear your seat belt" would be a good eating strategy, but it is.)

Other ways to improve your sense of smell:

- Drink lots of water. Dry mouth can inhibit smell.
- Eat zinc-rich foods, like spinach, kidney beans, and seeds. Zinc deficiencies are associated with loss of smell.
- Go for a brisk 10-minute walk before a meal. Many people report an improved sense of smell after exercise. Bonus regular exercise can help prevent loss of smell.[8]

EAT PURPOSEFULLY

Eating shouldn't be a reflex; it should be characterized by thought and purpose. When you control the pace and duration of what you eat, you will allow your body to taste the flavors—and feel satisfied. Patience isn't easy if you're a speed eater, but you can tap the brakes with these tactics:

- Put your fork or spoon down after every bite. This forces you to slow down, rather than shovel in. We're not going to mandate a grandma-endorsed 45-chew rule—but yeah, you should make an effort to chew each bite a little longer than you normally would.
- Take one bite of one food and then a bite of another food (rather than eating all of the chicken at once and

then all of the quinoa). This allows you to move between flavors and prevent your sensory nerves from getting bored.

EMBRACE THE SPICE

Our number one way to be more mindful about flavors is to, well, be more mindful of new flavors. Don't rely on sugar, salt, and fat to provide your meal satisfaction; instead, go to the spice aisle (or the produce aisle for fresh herbs) and try new ones. You can use them on roasted veggies, grilled fish and chicken, and more. Our favorite spices are chili flakes, lemon zest, rosemary, fresh garlic, and basil. Some off-the-radar spices that you can also try include merkén, Aleppo pepper, harissa, za'atar, and shichimi togarashi.

PART 3

What to Eat When

WHAT'S THE
SITUATION?

Now you know how to follow the When Way, especially focused on these two actions: (1) Eat when the sun is up, and (2) eat the majority of your day's calories before 2 p.m. These two actions—along with eating a healthy mix of macronutrients—will take your body to a good place, with better health, less disease, more energy, and lower weight.

Our goal is for you to make this style of eating your new normal. This allows you to take full advantage of chrono-nutrition: syncing your body's clock with your eating schedule.

We also know that life is *never* normal. Stuff happens. Habits are threatened. And there are a zillion and one things that can derail even the best of intentions.

This is what Part 3 of this book is all about—the second definition of *when*. What do you eat when life happens?

Using the When Way as a baseline, these 30-plus life scenarios will show how to navigate whatever circumstances come your way. Consider it the ultimate nutritional playbook—

one that will allow you to adjust the kinds of foods you eat to the situations that you find yourself in, from a day at a baseball game to a genetic disposition to a chronic disease. This information is based on scientific evidence that proves you can influence the health of your body through the macronutrients and micronutrients that you ingest.

We've also provided the tools you'll need to survive some of life's toughest moments. First, we give you the complete lineup: foods we're calling the MVPs and Key Players that will help get you through any situation, along with those that should be cut from the team. You'll find more in the Sub Shop for a number of these scenarios as well—for example, healthy alternatives that will keep you from falling back on old habits.

Feel free to read this section straight through; you'll find tons of useful little tricks and tips for a variety of everyday circumstances. Or flip straight to the scenarios that most apply to your life. The bottom line: When life hits you, you'll always know that the When Way can help you hit back.

| CHAPTER 6 |

WHAT TO EAT . . .

When You're Stressed and Hangry

W hen you eat the When Way, you'll spend a fair amount of time boiling water—blanching those vegetables, whipping up a soup, hardening eggs. Anyone who's watched a pot knows exactly how it works: stovetop on, tiny bubbles appear, then bigger ones, until—finally!—the water rumbles and is ready for action.

But what happens when your blood boils? When you get so mad or frustrated or hopped up on the injustices of the world that you feel like your head's going to explode? Well, it's kind of the same thing: Like the water in a pot, your blood rumbles and rages until you're ready for some action.

Most of us have the ability to manage our emotions well enough that "some action" doesn't involve fists (or worse). Unfortunately, though, "some action" can mean you're ready to go 10 rounds with Mr. Häagen-Dazs. Once you tangle with a pint of Pralines & Cream, you may feel like you've lowered the temperature on your blood boil. But you wind up losing the big battle in the end. That's the effect of acting out of "hanger." You may temporarily numb, mask, or forget what set you off—but when you reach for an instant soother that hurts more than it heals, you're ultimately doing much more damage to your body in the long run.

Think of it this way: Even if a truckload of chips stops your blood from boiling, all you're really doing is turning the temp down to a stealthy simmer—a simmer that comes in the form of high blood pressure, high LDL cholesterol, high blood sugar, and more.

Now, we know what you're thinking. It's one thing to *say* skip the chips, but when you're in the heat of the moment—and your brain is setting off the hangry fire alarm—you need to *do* and *chew* something immediately. There ain't no time to whip up a bowl of minestrone when junior decorated your new walls with crayons, markers, or the goodies he found in his diaper.

Rule number one: Don't go near a fast food establishment when you're hangry. These restaurants use smells, images, and sounds to reel you in[1,2,3]—and these cues can trick you into eating more than you want or need. When you're hangry, you're especially vulnerable to food cues like scents and aromas. The key is to keep your blood sugar balanced with foods that will bring your emotions to a low simmer, and keep you healthy to boot.

It's no surprise that emotional eating is a real biological phenomenon. We see it play out in all kinds of ways, and theories abound as to why hunger and emotions go together like sweat and stink. For one, several parts of the brain, including the hypothalamus, thalamus, and insula, among others, deal with hunger. These areas can influence the way your body is aroused. (Arousal, for the record, can come in many forms;

whether it's positive, as with sexual arousal, or negative, as with anger, both your heart rate and body temperature will rise in these states.)

In addition, the physical state of hunger works as a sort of trigger that leads to an emotional response. For example, low blood sugar (caused when you're hungry) has been linked to aggression and impulsivity, both of which can certainly play a role in a spur-of-the-moment rendezvous with a vending machine.[4] Ultimately, though, hunger can seem to impair self-regulation, our own ability to make decisions with the executive function part of our brains.[5] So, combining the two—hunger and anger—leads to the perfect storm of coaxing you to ditch the When Way and grab a Milky Way.

That begs the question: What to do? It's not as if you can simply ignore everything that triggers intense feelings of anger, nerves, or frustration. But you can do two things to help take the edge off.

First, if you are able to stay satisfied during the day, it's less likely that hunger will inhibit your impulses. This actually works incredibly well with our front-loaded way of eating. That is, if you're satisfied with a generous breakfast and/or lunch, you're less likely to feel the impulse to eat emotionally if something gets to you later in the day. Second, it's always wise to create your own emergency response system. Having healthy foods on hand—whether a bag of crunchy vegetables, a healthy, protein-rich bar (no added sugar or syrup or non–100 percent whole grains), or even a stash of turkey on 100 percent whole wheat that you can grab on the go—can get you through a wave of emotion. An extra step: Mute your TV during advertisements or pick an alternate route from work so you don't pass by your local fast food franchise. The "out of sight, out of mind" principle will help you stay healthy.

You can't always control what life throws at you, but you can control what you throw down your gullet. Ultimately, emergency foods should have a little fiber, a little protein, and healthy fat to help alleviate hunger and to satisfy you in a very balanced way. And although avocado toast is a nice choice, it's not always realistic in the heat of the moment. Here are some other foods you can try:

MVPs: Roasted chickpeas are our favorite anti-hangry snack. They not only contain those good-for-you macronutrients, but they're also an incredibly satisfying way to help you power through problems without the blood sugar spikes that can follow consuming processed snacks and refined sugars. In fact, studies have found that eating legumes, like chickpeas, helps control blood sugar and hunger even better than animal protein.[6,7,8] No, we don't expect you to jump to the oven and roast up a tray of them when emotion hits—but they're a great snack to prep ahead and keep on hand (plus, they are tasty cold as well).

To make roasted chickpeas: Dry the chickpeas by rolling them in paper towels, then spread them evenly on a baking sheet and sprinkle with a little extra-virgin olive oil and your favorite spices (if you like Indian food, they're delicious with some curry powder, or try adding garlic, rosemary, and cayenne, the way Dr. R prefers them; you can also place the beans in a small bag with some extra-virgin olive oil with seasoning and shake till evenly coated, then spread on a baking sheet). Roast in the oven at 425 degrees for 30 to 40 minutes, shaking the sheet pan every 10 minutes.

Key Players: In a pinch? Pop in a microwavable pack of no-butter-added popcorn. Filled with fiber, popcorn keeps you full, and will satisfy that oh-I-need-to-crunch feeling. If you like, you can sprinkle in a bit of sea salt, cinnamon, Old Bay Seasoning, or even a dusting of Parmesan cheese and pepper for a savory, salty, and crunchy snack, all at the same time. Have a little more time? Skip the premade bags and try your hand at an air popper. Or place dried kernels on the stovetop with a tablespoon of extra-virgin olive oil, cover, and cook over medium heat, shaking the pot every 30 seconds until the popping stops.

Cut From the Team: It's OK to engage in strategic dabbles with dessert, but your go-to food when you're feeling mad shouldn't be boxes of sugary treats. It doesn't matter if it's candy, cookies, ice cream, or doughnuts. Bottom line: The refined sugar will momentarily make you feel good (the sugar high), but you'll crash hard afterward—and your body won't have the much-needed energy sources to get you over the next slump.

The Sub Shop: Mad Meals

SUB OUT...	SUB IN...
Doughnuts	Plain instant oatmeal mixed with some no-added-sugar nut butter will be incredibly satisfying and a little sweet. Plus, it's filled with fiber to help you avoid blood sugar spikes and to keep you full longer. Add cinnamon if you like.

SUB OUT...	SUB IN...
Chips	Your crunchy vegetables of choice dipped in some hummus give you the healthy fat and fiber that will quell your rage.
Water	Water is awesome. You should drink a lot of it, but in the moment, you may want to reach for your coffee or tea. Why? That flavor you like can temporarily divert you from unhealthy cravings—like sodas or milk shakes.
Whatever's left in the fridge	It may be easy to reach for leftovers, but there's danger in overeating when you just grab and go. Make sure to keep some salad with your favorite vegetables on hand. You can bag it and crunch away without worrying about shoveling in three days' worth of calories in a single, teary-eyed sitting.

CHAPTER 7

WHAT TO EAT . . .

When You're Fighting Fatigue

he world spends billions fighting fat. It spends billions more when you add "-igue" onto the phrase. We're a tired bunch, for sure.

Trying to pinpoint the cause of fatigue is like trying to explain why your Uncle Lew still can't figure out Facebook—darn near impossible. That's because there are dozens and dozens of causes; some constitute the root of the problem, while others combine to produce mental and physical exhaustion. The reasons are myriad: not enough sleep, not the right foods, side effects of medication, hormonal issues, undetected conditions, not enough activity, too much stress, and on and on.

That's why the root problem—not getting enough quality sleep and feeling like a big blob of gelatin in the morning as a result—has to be addressed at a deeper level by identifying potential causes or triggers of fatigue. But here's a hint: Food is a major answer (after all, quite technically, food *is* energy).

Unfortunately, many of us turn to artificial or unhealthy stimulants to give us the spark we think we need. But in the end, they hurt us: Instead of raising and sustaining energy levels, these stimulants cause them to fluctuate like the stock market in a volatile economy. That's a problem because it makes us eat even more unhealthy foods.

This is where much of our collective energy problem lies. When we feel tired, we look for anything we can find to help restore our energy levels. Our gut reaction is to crave sugar, which is our body's most immediately available form of energy. And it works! We get peppy and zippy and think all is well. But that simple-carb high is very soon followed by a simple-carb crash, which leaves us feeling even more fatigued than when we started. And the vicious cycle starts again.

Ultimately, we want you to use quality sleep, regular exercise, and stress management to help restore energy levels (all subjects for a different time). But we can also show you how to add food to your power-boosting arsenal.

For starters, the When Way of eating will be a huge advantage. Eating earlier helps keep your energy systems primed and revved throughout the day. When you do find yourself looking for boosts, focus your attention on two forms: the kind of energy that can give you a non-crash-worthy quick jolt, and the kind of energy that can sustain you for a long time. Here's how to approach these.

YOUR FUEL TANK: KEEP IT FILLED

Water: Lack of water is one of the leading causes of fatigue. If you're not well hydrated, your body uses resources to maintain water balance instead of giving you energy. We keep water by us all day and constantly sip it. We also recommend having a glass or two first thing when you wake up in the morning. And of course, you need more when you exercise. Drinking eight glasses is a good ballpark, but it's also worth investing in a half-gallon thermos so you don't have to worry about keeping count. Just finish the jug every day and you've got it.

Healthy fats: Fat is the most energy-dense macro, and most typical snacks mix it with simple carbs. These calorie bombs give you the up-and-down energy we talked about, plus help you gain weight. On the other end of the spectrum, healthy fats mixed with protein and fiber let you take advantage of the slow energy release fat provides without all the risks. That's one of the reasons why unsaturated fats—like ones found in salmon, nuts, and avocado—are such a crucial part of the When Way. It's probably also why avocado toast has become so popular as a breakfast food: It ensures you get some healthy fat and fiber at the start of every day.

Protein: Protein in lean meats (chicken, turkey, and fish) is excellent for energy; you can also get protein in beans and nuts. Having protein early in the day is also key.

YOUR PORTABLE CHARGER: QUICKER HITS

Coffee and tea: You already know these are staples of an energy-boosting diet. Both are great (and generally don't give you the energy swings that sugar will), so it's OK to have these caffeinated beverages provided you don't load them with sugar or other heavy add-ons, like cream and flavored syrups. First thing in the morning is fine. But our friend Dr. Oz likes to have some tea in the late morning, instead, before a natural slump may occur.

Complex carbs: These are slower burning than simple carbs (ones with white flour and sugar). Complex carbs like fruits and whole grains can satisfy those carb cravings you're having *and* give you that faster bump in energy without the risk of a great crash.

CHAPTER 8

WHAT TO EAT . . .

When You're Bummed

When you're in the kind of funk that has nothing to do with James Brown songs, it's hard to describe how you feel. Blah, gray, numb, blue. In fact, all kinds of artists—from painters to songwriters—have made careers depicting what emotional lows are all about. Feeling down is indeed one of our universal emotions. Even the happiest and most positive people you know can dip into pools of sadness.

This universal emotion has an equally universal response—chowing down in hopes of getting up. We've all been there: Things don't quite feel right, so we self-medicate with something salty or something sweet, something crunchy or some kind of treat (this is not a new wedding mantra, by the way).

We react this way not because we're rebelling, but because our biology wants nutrients to pick us back up (that's why we reach for fast-acting sugar).

We need to make clear that depression and feeling down—although very common—operate on a spectrum of severity. Those with serious depression (the kind that interferes with day-to-day life or is so debilitating that it can cause potential harm) need medical and professional assistance to help. What we're talking about here are the typical ebbs and flows of mood that we all experience: the kind of blues that can happen as a reaction to specific situations, lack of sunlight (common during winter months), or hormonal changes that alter your mood.

The brain, of course, is the most complex part of our anatomy. It works as a universe all its own; the medical and scientific world have not fully mastered the interaction between its physical structures and chemical parts. We do know, though, that mood is controlled by many things—such as the amygdala (the part of the brain that deals with emotion), as well as levels of various neurotransmitters (like feel-good dopamine and serotonin). This is part of the reason we reach for sugary treats: The immediate rush of juju makes us believe we're satisfying those parts of the brain.

The tricky part is overriding that instinctual urge to feed our brain with foods that can do the same thing—without the side effects that come with eating a whole jar of icing.

Although many things can help kick your mood up a few levels (exercise is a favorite, as is connecting with old friends), this guide to brain-boosting foods can also help turn your funk into spunk.

BLUES BUSTERS

In the Moment: Feeling down right now? Take a lesson from the almighty carbohydrate. Its very job is to provide you with energy, but research suggests it can also help boost your mood and handle stress.[9,10] But don't take it in its simple form. Instead, try a piece of 100 percent whole grain toast with all-natural peanut butter (no sugar added). Add a few berries of choice.

Best of all, peanuts are rich in an amino acid called tryptophan, which is a building block of serotonin.

For the Long Haul: To improve your mood and reduce chances of depression, a diet of fish, vegetables, and healthy oils is the way to go. In a recent study of people who were monitored for six years, those who ate more vegetables, fruits, and grains were less likely to have depressive symptoms than those who ate more of a Western meat-and-potatoes (with butter on them) type of diet.[11,12]

Best Anti-Blues Food: Fish like salmon and ocean trout are full of omega-3 fatty acids, which have been suggested in some studies (though the jury is still out) to help improve mood and reduce symptoms of depression.[13] This may be because the fat in the fish helps improve the function of neurotransmitters.

An All-Day Crutch: Keep green tea by your side. It has many health benefits, but one of them is that it includes an amino acid shown to have a calming effect.[14]

CHAPTER 9

WHAT TO EAT . . .

When You're Experiencing Grief

When you've lost a loved one, the last thing you want to think about is what to eat, how you should prepare it, and what time is best for your chrononutrition. And for good reason. Losing someone close to you is one of life's major stressors—one that makes your heart ache and your body break.

We're not here to tap you on the wrist and mandate that you stick to any certain plan during these dark days. After all, everyone goes through the stages of grief (denial, anger, bargaining, depression, and acceptance) differently. And frankly, it's inappropriate for us to talk about cauliflower and salmon in the context of mourning.

That said, we do believe there is a way to manage your health while your emotions are—rightly so—in a different place. That's because during these times, there is a real risk of developing what's called decision fatigue. You're doing so many other things (whether it's planning, meeting with people, or adjusting to a new life) that you simply don't have the energy to do *anything* for yourself. And that means you take the path of least resistance. This could mean anything from opting for fast food to something equally as bad: no food, which robs your body of necessary nutrients you need during this tough time.

So keep the following notes in mind when you experience grief. This way, you'll give yourself a fighting chance to fortify your body with healthy ingredients that can strengthen you during a period of loss.

Accept help. Your friends and family will offer to help. Your instinct may be to say, "no, thank you, I can handle it." Fight that impulse. Accept their willingness to bring meals, and don't be shy about asking for foods you have come to love—fish with vegetables, whole grains, healthy soups. To make things easier, ask a close friend to take the lead on organizing a meal system (this allows you to communicate your wishes without feeling like you're imposing).

Stick to the familiar. Studies show that in times of mourning, familiar rituals, such as eating regular foods and meals, help stabilize people emotionally by helping soothe feelings of grief.[15] So if you can muster the strength to prepare food, consider making large quantities that you can freeze, which will only require minimal prep time.

Use the express lane. Even just stocking your fridge and pantry with produce will help. If you're not up for a full grocery store trip, just run in for an express-lane visit, or ask a friend or family member to make a run for you. Making it easy to grab an apple or pear is half the battle. You'll get the vitamins and nutrients you need, rather than the bad stuff from emotionally eating bags of processed junk.

Create a pattern. Take the thinking out of what you have to eat. That way, it's automatic and you can focus your energy in other ways. Maybe you fall into a pattern with an egg white scramble for breakfast and a salad for lunch, plus some easy option for dinner. In normal times, that may feel a bit like a rut. But right now, it will be a comfort—and that's ultimately what you need at this difficult time.

| CHAPTER 10 |

WHAT TO EAT . . .

When You Cannot Sleep

W e live a life of verbs. We eat and drink. We work. We play. We scroll. We run, read, and riff about the latest news coming out of D.C. We love, listen, and learn. Every moment of every day is about "doing." These verbs— no matter which you engage in—form and define our lives.

Yet we treat one of the most vital verbs of every 24-hour cycle—sleep—as a footnote, rather than the main text (and that's not because some people would rather use the bed for other verbs). Sleep has become a cultural sacrificial lamb. We'd rather work late than get enough zzz's. We'd rather binge on Bravo. We'd rather stalk social media. Or maybe our bodies just cannot shut down, or health problems make it hard to fall or stay asleep.

In any case, the reality is a harsh one. Our lack of sleep isn't just a boon for the coffee shop industry. It's slowly killing us.

And the two of us don't say that lightly. People don't put lack of sleep in the same category as cigarettes or obesity because fatigue is more of a behind-the-scenes health threat—one that has a steady, creeping effect on our bodies. (See fatigue fighters on page 120.) But the risks associated with lack of sleep are big.[1]

Here's how it works: While you're sleeping, your body and brain cycle through various stages—ranging from light sleep to deep sleep. You go through that cycle several times a night. It sure feels like nothing is going on—after all, you're not aware of anything, except maybe that wacky dream about a tornado, a marching band, and your seventh-grade math teacher. That's maybe one of the reasons why people don't give sleep as much attention as they should: They don't feel anything the way they "feel" exercise or a change in eating habits. So it's easy to think that sleep is, well, just a whole lot of nothing.

But that's not the case. When you're closed for business, your body's cells start their work. Think of the inside of your body as a big factory of shift workers. Cells clock in when you shut down. All day long, your body—at work, during exercise, while you're going about your day—has been put through a series of cellular stresses. Through the course of living, the body gets broken down and beaten up. Even if you don't feel it, that's what's happening at the cellular level. For example, when you use your muscles, they can experience little microscopic tears. That same kind of stress happens all over your body in all kinds of organs, tissues, and systems throughout the day.

To maintain itself and recover from these cellular insults, your body needs a repair crew. Enter your shift workers. While you're sleeping, they're repairing your muscles, growing and strengthening neurons in your brain, fortifying your body's damaged cells. These cells cannot do their jobs optimally unless your body is shut down and in deep sleep.

So you can imagine what happens if you don't give these cellular fixers enough time to work. Your body never fully gets repaired, making you weaker, more susceptible to further insults, and a lot less healthy. In practical terms, that means lack of sleep can contribute to immune problems, memory issues, higher stress levels, and even obesity. Because your brain never fully rids itself of its waste products (the "poop" from your brain cells is removed at night, and is done more efficiently the longer you sleep), you can develop inflammation in your memory centers as well.[2]

Yes, perhaps one of the greatest effects of lack of sleep is a high inflammatory response, which is your body's way of fighting problems. When this response is at high levels all the time because it never shuts down, that leads to a sort of friendly fire within the body: Your attacking immune cells begin to damage healthy ones (and not just in your brain), putting you at an increased risk of heart disease, diabetes, and arthritis.[3] (Heck, research has even shown that lack of sleep increases hostility in relationships; the fallout can trigger higher stress, which has damaging effects on overall health.)[4]

These bodily damages work in various ways. But if you think about your body's function as a massive game of dominoes, you can see how it plays out. When you don't get enough sleep, you feel fatigued. When you feel fatigued, your body wants to raise energy levels, so it reaches for the fastest solution: sugar. When you reach for sugar, you gobble up stacks of cookies. And when you do that day after day after day, you gain weight.

Yeah, yeah, yeah, you say. You've heard it all before. Get more sleep. Sleep eight hours. Easier said than done, especially if you have a complex cocktail of problems that make it difficult to sleep (pain, hormonal issues, obesity, urge to urinate, and so many other things that can disrupt sleep cycles). Like many other health issues, sleep is one in which you may need to consider lifestyle and medical tactics to determine what will work best for you. But you can also use food and nutrients to ease into some possible solutions to help change your verbs from "tossing and turning" to "sweet dreaming." (As long as that sweet dreaming doesn't actually include sweets!)

MVPs: No magic sleep-inducing piece of fruit or secret ingredient will induce drowsiness (though, as you'll see in the following, some are better than others). But setting yourself up with a good last meal of the day can help prepare your body for sleep. Research shows that having meals high in fiber and low in foods with saturated fat and simple carbs (sugar) should help.[5] So that's why a dish like beans, grilled fish or chicken, and a large side of vegetables is the best meal choice to help your body prepare to shut down (and as we've learned, the earlier you eat it, the better). One recent study in *The Journal of Clinical Sleep Medicine* found that this kind of meal was associated with people falling asleep faster—in less than 20 minutes, in fact. When subjects consumed more saturated fat and sugar, the process took closer to 30 minutes.[6] If you have the choice (and you do!), make your protein fish, which, when eaten regularly, has been linked to helping prevent poor sleep.[7]

Key Players: The two nutrients most associated with better sleep are magnesium and tryptophan.[8,9] You've heard of tryptophan; it's all over headlines in late November as the reason why you want to zonk out after eating a big plate of Thanksgiving turkey. Although tryptophan may not actually make you tired after a big holiday meal, the foods that contain it, or magnesium, are certainly good options if you're trying to improve your sleep *quality.* Tryptophan is an amino acid that converts to the body clock–regulating hormone melatonin. Foods that contain it include egg whites, soybeans, chicken, and pumpkin seeds. And when you choose your vegetables for dinner, consider leafy greens like spinach that contain magnesium.

Cut From the Team: Feeling cravings at night? Don't be tempted by a midnight snack. Research on circadian rhythm and eating cycles reveals that midnight is actually the worst time to eat—even if you think you just need a little something to make yourself more comfortable. Instead, have a fiber-rich dessert before the sun sets—for example, a big bowl of berries or a pear. The fiber will slow things down so you feel full longer—and thus less likely to crave something later at night.

The Sub Shop: Snooze Foods

SUB OUT...	SUB IN...
Caffeine less than six hours before bed	Water with a squirt of lemon or lime juice
Large meals within four or five hours of bedtime	Larger meals as your first or second meal of the day
After-dinner sugar bombs	Kiwi fruit and tart cherry juice both have been shown to help improve sleep. Tart cherry juice may help improve levels of melatonin—a hormone that induces sleep.[10]

CHAPTER 11

WHAT TO EAT . . .

When You Get a Lot
of Headaches

The word "headache" feels like a catchall metaphor for calamity. You invoke it when you're stressed, when people annoy you, to describe tough projects, and when you're not in the mood. But for many people, the phrase is more than just a clichéd way to decline a romantic rendezvous.

Persistent headaches cannot always be fended off with a couple of ibuprofens and a good nap. They can be debilitating. And they can feel like someone's taking a j-j-j-j-j-j-j-j-jack-hammer to your forehead.

The trouble, as you likely know, is that there is no one-size-fits-all solution. That's because headaches are like dog breeds: There are many kinds. Some can be triggered by hormonal changes and fluctuations. Others can occur because of blood flow changes that cause constriction and dilation of the vessels feeding the brain. Some come about as side effects of medications or other conditions; others stem from changes in your sleep or diet patterns (not eating for a certain amount of time can certainly do it, as can lack of caffeine in regular users). Some headaches arise from environmental factors—whether exposure to toxins or stress or allergens or cranky mothers-in-law. And some people may simply have a genetic predisposition to getting a lot of those skull-knockers throughout their lives.

Because the neurons that make up your brain don't have pain sensors, it begs the question: Where do headaches come from anyway? Well, although the cells that make you think don't sense their own pain, other parts of the brain do—for example, the dural or larger cerebral vessels, along with the large veins and dural sinuses (the dura is the name of the tissue that covers the brain). When movement, constriction, dilatation, or inflammation stimulate these areas, they can activate pain fibers in the fifth cranial nerve (known as the trigeminal nerve). The stretch or pressure on a nerve fiber (or the pressure or instability of a blood vessel in the brain area) can cause pain. Some headaches, though, are also caused by

Caffeine: Yes or No?

Caffeine can help you get rid of a headache—but it can also backfire on you. When you don't have your regular amount in the course of a day, you can experience a withdrawal headache. This can happen if you drink two, three, or more cups of coffee a day (Dr. R averages 8-plus), then skip a day entirely. As with any food, you need to identify whether caffeine is a consistent trigger and reduce or eliminate it if it is. But keep in mind that caffeine can also work as a short-term cure to help reduce the headache as well.

muscles in and around the head; a strained muscle there (just like one you'd feel in other parts of your body) can cause your noggin to throb.

Because the causes (and treatments) are so varied, no one magic meal will help you fend off headaches. However, a lot of evidence suggests that food can be a common trigger, so being in tune with what and when you eat can be the first step to figuring out how food can help.[11]

Start by creating a food and headache journal in which you write down everything you eat (and the time you eat it), then make notes about when headaches come about. Over a period of a few weeks, you may be able to notice patterns (more often than you'd expect) and thus be able to perceive what foods might be triggers. Chocolate, red wine, and monosodium glutamate (MSG) are common culprits.[12] Note: The headache often happens within 12 hours of eating the food, so don't just look to what you ate immediately before the onset. You'll have to sleuth a bit to see if you can find patterns during that time frame, so share your journal with your doctor. Eliminate those triggers and you have a good chance of reducing the rate at which you get headaches.

The interesting factor here is that food can also play a role by bolstering nutrient levels that may have some influence in the onset of headaches. If you're a persistent sufferer, you should learn how to adjust your diet (through addition and subtraction) to lower the chances of your head feeling like it's constantly being bulldozed.

MVPs: Spinach and other leafy greens (kale and arugula included), already in your healthy food arsenal, are good staples because of the vitamins they contain. Spinach contains lots of folate and B$_6$, as well as some vitamin B$_2$ and omega-3 fatty acids; all have been found to reduce migraines.[13,14,15] Vitamin B$_2$, also known as riboflavin, has been shown to help reduce the length and frequency of migraine headaches.[16] Use leafy greens in salad, sauté them with garlic and extra-virgin olive oil, or blend them in a smoothie (a stealth way to get more of them into your diet). Egg whites are also a good choice; four of them contain about half of your daily requirement of riboflavin.[17,18] So say yes to that spinach egg-white omelet.

Key Players: It appears that many chronic headache sufferers may have lower-than-typical magnesium levels.[19] This means that your snack of choice should be a handful of nuts or seeds, which are high in this important nutrient. Good choices include almonds, sesame seeds, cashews, sunflower seeds, walnuts, and Brazil nuts. One study found that those who took magnesium supplements reduced their migraine frequency by 41 percent. Still, experts recommend increasing dietary magnesium, rather than taking supplements if at all possible.[20,21]

Cut From the Team: Red wine and other alcohol might make you feel buzzy and happy in the moment, but they're common triggers for headaches (and not just the ones associated with hangovers). Why? First, booze can cause dehydration, which triggers headaches. Many people think the sulfites in red wine are to blame for headaches, but experts say no. Instead, most now believe it's the tannins and the phenolic flavonoid components (the chemicals that affect the taste of wine), which vary greatly from vineyard to vineyard.[22] Chocolate, caffeine, MSG, and other foods are also linked to headaches. The best bet: Start that food and headache journal to see what *your* triggers are and then try to eliminate suspects.

The Sub Shop: Stop the Pounding

SUB OUT...	SUB IN...
Fasting	Regular complex carbs, like whole grains and veggies with fiber to make sure you don't experience hunger dips that can trigger headaches.
Red meat	Grilled salmon and ocean trout. Chronic headache sufferers can benefit from an increase in omega-3 fatty acids and B_{12}, which is found in salmon and ocean trout.[23,24] Plus, red and processed meat can often trigger headaches.
Artificial sweeteners	We don't advocate the use of *any* sugar, but a dash of it, or better yet, a little cinnamon, can sweeten your coffee, instead of the artificial packets that are associated with headaches. Or better yet, try decaffeinated black coffee to reduce the possibility of two common triggers: sweeteners and caffeine.
Chocolate	If chocolate is one of your triggers, try roasting walnuts and mixing them with berries to get your sweet fix.
Soy sauce	Soy sauce contains MSG and sodium, which is linked to dehydration. Instead, sprinkle food with other spices you love, acids like lemon, or your favorite type of vinegar.

CHAPTER 12

WHAT TO EAT . . .
When You're Sick

Weall get hit with it. A cold, the flu, or just a few days when we're feeling downright cruddy. Some of us get walloped harder than others, while others seem to avoid sickness the way tweens avoid their parents on social media. Our friend, Dr. Oz, for example, very rarely gets sick, even though he shakes hands with hundreds of people a day; he attributes this to his overall eating approach. (A well-constructed diet done the When Way will fortify your immune system.)

Although we cannot necessarily say that food choices can help make a cough disappear or ease a scratchy throat, we shouldn't diminish the fact that it can play a role in how you handle the random sicknesses that can get you from time to time.

That, of course, is no surprise. You've probably heard (and may even subscribe) to the well-known adage "Feed a cold and starve a fever." This mama medicine philosophy is pervasive, in part because many people have discovered anecdotally that food can in fact affect how your body prevents and recovers from illnesses like colds and viruses.

What About Vitamin C?

When Dr. C was young, his father insisted that he drink lots of orange juice and take vitamin C tablets if he was sick (or felt like he was about to be). Dr. C—the good boy that he was—obeyed. But as he grew up, he grew skeptical. And he treated vitamin C tablets with the same respect he treated three-hour-old gum—straight to the trash. To this day, Dr. C and his dad cannot agree.

Turns out, the same debate has been raging in scientific journals, newspapers, and households since the 1970s. A few years ago, a comprehensive review of top-level studies examined the issue and found that large doses of vitamin C had no effect on the prevention of colds. However, it had some effect on shortening the symptoms of colds in some people.[34] So an apple or orange a day may not keep the doctor away, but eating foods rich in vitamin C is still a good idea because of the long-term effect on your overall health (as well as perhaps playing a role when you do get sick).

As for zinc, a review of studies found that doses of less than 75 milligrams had no effect on cold duration, whereas taking doses of 75 milligrams or more resulted in a 20 to 42 percent reduction in cold duration. Although this may imply zinc looks promising, the safe recommended dose is only 40 milligrams. Taking higher doses of zinc supplements over a long time for an occasional cold carries a risk of significant side effects that range from a metal taste in your mouth to nausea, vomiting—even an increased risk of prostate cancer. The best source of zinc may be our recommended zinc-containing foods like pumpkin seeds, cashews, and beans.[35]

But is there actually science that links what you eat with these stay-in-bed-and-moan sicknesses?

It's worth noting that the meals-as-medicine mantra is somewhat flawed in that a cold is an actual illness and a fever is a symptom. It's sort of like comparing apples to oranges—both of which are fine illness fighters! When you get a cold, you could be suffering from any number of symptoms (cough, congestion, runny nose, loss of appetite, even a fever). A fever itself, though, can be a symptom of any kind of infection that's causing your immune system to fight whatever bacteria or viruses are invading.

As far as science goes, the data are minimal—and somewhat conflicting. In one study, for example, different immune-boosting benefits were found for both those who were given a nutrient-rich broth and those who refrained from eating.[25] A recent study showed that starvation protected mice infected with bacteria and feeding was detrimental—but that the opposite was true when the mice were infected with a virus.[26] Alas, the research in humans is as sparse as the supermarket water aisle before a hurricane.

So what's the bottom line? You should let your body—not a mantra—dictate some of your decision making. Your immune system does need nutrients, so if you're able to eat—and you feel like eating—you should get some calories in your body (see the following for what kind). But if your symptoms are making you nauseated or you don't have an appetite, you shouldn't force it down. No matter what, make sure you're getting plenty of fluids, because hydration is the key to bouncing back from an illness. You can easily get dehydrated from sweating and producing lots of mucus, and you need to make plenty of urine to clear the waste from your immune system.

MVP: Grandma was right about more than just her philosophy on hugs. She also knew a thing or two about sickness when she pumped you full of chicken soup. Although there aren't double-blind placebo-controlled studies looking at the effect of chicken soup on curing a cold, some creative studies have been done. In one of the most often cited, from decades ago, scientists found that drinking chicken soup helped with nasal mucus velocity (#bandname).[27] Other research has found that ingredients in chicken soup have an anti-inflammatory effect (perhaps because of the chicken, broth, and vegetables all working together).[28,29] Bottom line: Chicken soup will help you stay hydrated, which is important, and may have a soothing effect that can both help speed up your recovery and make you feel better, too.

Other Starters: The best part about some of the other foods to prevent sickness is that you can throw them into your soup. Garlic, for example, has been shown to help prevent colds by giving your immune system a kick in the pants.[30] And in one experiment, ginger was shown to block viruses.[31] Finally, mushrooms (an ancient medicinal remedy) have been shown to help prime immune cells to better fight an infection.[32]

Cut From the Team: Just because oysters have zinc doesn't mean they help you shorten a cold's duration. Zinc lozenges do—but extra zinc can cause big toxicity, so only take it while you have a cold and not year-round.[33]

The Sub Shop: Sick and Your Stomach

SUB OUT…	SUB IN…
Orange juice	An orange. Yes, you want the hydration and nutrients of an orange, but orange juice gives you a high sugar load that just makes bacteria and viruses (and even cancers) feel good about propagating within you.
Sushi	Broiled medium salmon or well-cooked ocean trout. When your immune system is busy fighting off an infection, you do not want to test its breadth of action with another potential opponent like something hiding in raw fish.
Chia seeds	Unless fully hydrated, chia seeds will suck needed hydration from you. Waterlogged oatmeal may be much better.

CHAPTER 13

WHAT TO EAT . . .
When You're
in Pain

Pain is usually associated with lots of four-letter words. But just because pain can make you squirm, yelp, curse, or plead for mama to bring you a blanket doesn't mean that all pain is made equal. As you know, there are all kinds of pain. There's emotional pain (it's why we call it heartbreak, after all), and there's a whole spectrum of physical pain. Some of that physical pain is both specific and acute: when you twist an ankle, bang your elbow, or stub your toe on the bedpost during a 3 a.m. bathroom trip (four-letter words indeed!).

Then there's chronic pain. This kind, which affects more than 25 million Americans every day and more than 100 million every year, is just always there. A bad back that aches, joints that throb, waking up every day with a headache, or even an overall feeling of malaise that just *hurts*.

The first kind of pain is simple enough to understand: You hurt something temporarily, eventually it stops (whether in a few seconds, as with a paper cut, or a few weeks, as with a sprained ankle), and you go on your way. The second kind of pain is much trickier, in that it's not always easy to diagnose or ease. For example, backs and spines can be more complicated than an advanced physics exam, and pain associated with hormonal or autoimmune issues doesn't just resolve itself with a couple ibuprofen. (Back x-rays, CT scans, and MRIs often reveal problems like disk protrusions, which have existed for years without causing pain but just as often mask other problems.)

The first thing to note is that in cases of complicated or chronic pain, it's essential to have physical therapy (PT) to help get rid of the problem, and professional medical care if PT doesn't get to the bottom of it. That *has* to be the foundation. That said, there are things you can eat to help with many chronic pain problems. Here's why: Good foods are some of the Earth's most effective natural pain fighters.

Important point here: Pain is NOT a bad thing, at least evolutionarily speaking. It's our anatomical watchdog, alerting us that our bodies—and potentially our lives—are in some kind of trouble. In fact, the body part that hurts is not actually controlling the pain. Instead, your brain—via various pathways in your nerves—is sending signals that you need to get out of the situation. Makes sense, right?

Put your hand on a dish that comes right out of the oven, and your fingers hurt; that's your brain telling you that, uh, maybe you ought to walk those little fingers of yours to the drawer and get some pot holders. Pain is your "stop" button: Stop doing what you're doing so you can stay alive. That doesn't mean pain is pleasant or we want it in our lives. But it does give you some perspective as to how it works and why it's essential to our survival. No pain, and we—as a species—don't make it very far.

Here's how the pain-messaging system works: Let's say you miss the last step on a set of stairs, trip, and fall. You slam your knees against the ground, and wow, that hurts like heck. If it doesn't hurt immediately from the damage you may have done, then the long-term pain is triggered by your body's immune system responding to a five-alarm fire call and rushing to the injured area. Your immune fighters come in to start healing the damaged cells and tissues. As those fighters arrive, it means more blood is flowing to the area, which becomes inflamed with immune cells trying to put out the fire. That inflammation is sending signals back to your brain via your nerves that something's wrong, basically a signal saying that the smartest course of action isn't to immediately get up and run (see Chapter 38 on inflammation).

When your knees heal in a few days or weeks, the inflammation will quiet down and you will sense less pain. So you can see that one way to help ease pain symptoms is to help quiet your body's systemic inflammation. That's not to say that eating pain-fighting foods will help your knees hurt less if you trip on the stairs. But if you suffer from chronic pain, systemic pain, or a low-grade pain that's difficult to diagnose, you can help ease it by quieting your body's inflammation.

That's where food comes in. Anti-inflammatory foods aren't going to work like medicinal pain relievers (have a headache, eat two pieces of dark chocolate!). But over the long term, they enable your body to more efficiently handle what hurts.

MVP: Research is showing that people who eat a traditional Mediterranean diet (low in saturated fat, rich in olive oil, fruits, vegetables, and nuts) seem to have fewer conditions related to pain and inflammation, such as joint problems.[36] That makes a case for a steady dose of extra-virgin olive oil and walnuts; in fact, studies show that extra-virgin olive oil might have compounds similar to ibuprofen.[37] Therefore, use olive oil for salad dressings and to cook with whenever you can. There's a good chance that one of the reasons it's so effective is because it's a healthy fat, which makes the case that avocados, walnuts, and salmon (a fish full of omega-3 fatty acids) should also be a steady part of your diet (don't get Dr. R started about how many salmon burgers he has in a week!).

Other Starters: Spicy food can also help with easing inflammation. For example, ginger has been found to have anti-inflammatory compounds that may help relieve pain.[38,39,40,41] And turmeric (or curcumin) does, too;[42] that's the spice commonly used in Indian cooking and other Asian foods. Best of all, these two spices taste great used together in one dish.

Cut From the Team: You want a surefire way to hurt *more?* Keep on rocking the simple sugars and carbs. These are the foods that will actually spike inflammation as your body tries to deal with them.[43,44,45] And here's the tricky part: When you're in pain, you reach for the quick fix—comfort foods that make you feel better in the moment. But though that simple sugar— whether from a cookie, chip, or cold piece of pizza—may feel good in the short term, it will hurt the rest of your body in the long run.

The Sub Shop: Hurting Helpings

SUB OUT...	SUB IN...
Diet soda	Coffee. Low doses of caffeine have been shown to help reduce the perception of pain.[46] Chocolate also has caffeine and may help as well. (That doesn't justify ordering the café mocha; instead, have your cup of coffee with a square or two of dark chocolate.)
Canned fruit with added sugar	Cherries or tart cherry juice are rich in phenolic compounds associated with decreased inflammation and pain.[47]

CHAPTER 14

WHAT TO EAT . . .

When You Have
Digestive Problems

W ith its tubes, pipes, and sludge, the digestive system is most often compared to plumbing. Clogs, stop-ups, leaks—all kinds of issues can arise in the home, and in the body. Altogether, the organs involved include some darn impressive tools that take your food and nutrients on a long journey through your body and out.

But when you look at the entire digestive system—from the consumption of foods and drinks to the way your body processes them, to how it delivers, stores, or expels them—you may think of these processes a little differently. It's part magic, part thrilling, part crazy.

In a lot of ways, your gut is really your anatomical amusement park. When things are going well, you've got a lazy river shuttling your food through the park so that your body can use calories as energy. Eat something that doesn't agree with you and your gut may feel like it's on a triple-loop roller coaster. Or when things are really bad, your food may be purchasing a ticket for an extreme gravitational ride—sometimes shooting straight up and sometimes dropping straight down. No seat belt is going to hold anything back.

This is the nature—and majesty—of our digestive system. It's responsible for so many parts of our health because of how it processes our food and energy.

From our discussion in Chapter 2, you already know the basics of how digestion works—but here's a quick refresher: Food moves down the esophagus to your stomach, which breaks it down with various acids and enzymes so it can move through the intestines in a more liquid form. In the small intestines, food is broken down even more as it prepares the nutrients to be absorbed into the bloodstream to be shuttled to other parts of the body. The colon's main job is to remove water, which is the part of the process that creates your stool. While these things are happening, your pancreas, liver, and gallbladder are all performing various functions to remove toxins and help your intestines do their job. The waste that's left over moves through the colon to ship out to its final destination.

That system doesn't always run smoothly, as you know. Sometimes you feel rumbles, sometimes you feel cramps, sometimes you feel blah after eating certain foods, and sometimes your body rebels in a full-scale assault that threatens the cleanliness of your porcelain bathroom fixtures.

Why? Seems like there are millions of different causes for digestive problems. Some of them have to do with your microbiome—that is, the population of bacteria in your gut. You remember from our earlier discussion that good and bad bacteria have to coexist to have a peaceful environment; when they don't, you can experience digestive and other issues. Your gut health can also be influenced by the foods you eat; some people have intolerance to certain foods or ingredients (gluten and lactose being some of the most prevalent). And viruses can invade your body to cause your digestive system to go haywire for any period of time.

In any case, it's important to pinpoint the root issue that's causing any turmoil in your gut. Oftentimes, you can settle it down by identifying foods and nutrients that might act as triggers to a certain discomfort or problem (and then eliminate those triggers from your diet). In many instances, though, you can use food to help heal your problems. Here's the menu for four of the most common digestive issues you may encounter:

Diarrhea/vomiting. If food is quickly shooting out either the North or South Pole, there's a good chance that you don't want to eat anything. And in most cases, that's the right thing to do: Take it easy on your stomach, because many foods can actually make symptoms worse. The following are two major exceptions:

The BRAT diet—bananas, rice, apples, or toast. These choices work because they're gentle on the stomach, so won't likely trigger any further rebellion. They also can help solidify the gunk in your gut to help ease symptoms of diarrhea. If you're vomiting, it's best to eat nothing and give your stomach a break for about six hours after your last bout. Sip as much water as you can tolerate to stay hydrated. Then, ease back in by sucking on some hard candy or a frozen fruit pop and drinking clear liquids. After about a day without vomiting, start eating again with the BRAT foods.

Homemade hydration drink. If you've experienced a lot of diarrhea, the biggest concern isn't that you're running low on TP; it's that you're running low on nutrients. You've likely lost a lot of fluid that you need to replenish. An oral rehydration solution (ORS) is a simple recipe that you can use to treat both children and adults with diarrhea and related illnesses. To make it, take 6 teaspoons sugar, ½ teaspoon salt, and then mix with a liter of water. Stir it until the salt and sugar dissolve. The combo will help replace what has been lost and prevent you from losing more fluid.

Note: This is the one time we recommend *adding* sugar to your diet. It works because sugar helps electrolytes into your system, and electrolytes are what drags water through it. ORS has saved many lives, and Dr. C learned in a few bouts with a stomach virus that it tastes pretty good too.

Constipation. This is the body's version of a traffic jam. Nothing's moving, and no horn honk is going to get anything to move any faster, no matter how frustrated you get. Thank goodness, some foods can clear the road and help traffic move a little more smoothly:

***The CRAP diet*—**cranberries, raisins, apricots, prunes. A diet rich in fruits, veggies, and whole grains will help get your system going, but these four foods are great choices to start. That's because the fiber in these foods helps keep you regular. Fiber has been shown to help reduce constipation and diarrhea, and to help lower bad cholesterol. It also plays a role in keeping many of us satiated, which helps prevent weight gain.[48] Most Americans simply don't get enough of fiber; men should have between 20 to 24 grams of fiber a day, while women should have 24 to 28 grams.

Water. One major source of constipation is dehydration; without enough water to help your waste move through your digestive system, things get slowed down or stuck. Water is the shuttle driver that helps move things along. So drink, drink, drink.

Reflux. Anybody who's ever experienced a little heartburn, acid reflux, or a burrito-tasting belch knows that the sensation isn't as pleasant on the way up as it was on the way down. But there's a reason, evolutionarily speaking, why our bodies need to take food *up* the anatomical escalator every now and then. Our stomachs are strong enough to digest just about anything. But we developed a mechanism to reject poisonous foods: the vomiting response. When it comes to reflux, what travels upward is the acid that's in the stomach to help break down foods.

The problem with reflux isn't just the burning you feel in your esophagus, but also the chronic effect it can have on your body—namely, increasing dangerous inflammation. You can do a lot to help prevent or ease reflux by what you do directly after eating (for example, not lying down right after you eat or eating too close to bedtime). But for changes in eating habits, your best bet is to avoid acid and go bland:

Bland foods. Certain foods can increase the amount of acid in your stomach and thus increase the chances your throat will feel like fire. The biggest ones to avoid are peppers and spicy foods, as well as caffeine and alcohol. For some people, reducing chocolate may help. Citrus fruits and tomatoes—both very acidic—also promote reflux. Stick to bland foods like quinoa, skinless poultry, and non-spicy vegetables.

Bloating. Bloating means different things to different people. Some associate it with gas, gurgles, and that distended feeling in your belly. Those symptoms can be associated with reflux— but in general, it sort of feels like your innards are gargling. That gassy feeling can be reduced by what and how you eat. For example, by eliminating carbonated beverages and beer, you'll reduce the gas (bubbles in the drink cause those bubbles in your belly). By eating more slowly, you can help reduce the chance that you'll suck down a lot of air, which also contributes to that distended, gassy feeling.

There's another kind of bloating feeling—the kind that makes you feel more puffy than gassy. This happens when you retain water, often after meals loaded with sodium. Sodium used to be rare in our diets (not the case anymore!), so our bodies learned to retain it; our kidneys were responsible for maintaining balanced sodium levels. Now that we consume so much more of it (averaging 3,400 milligrams a day when we only need 200 to 500 milligrams), our kidneys are working overtime to filter it out through our urine. Because that doesn't happen instantly, extra sodium can trap water—and your belly feels like a massive wave pool. The following are your best bets:

Slow-digesting carbs. Think fiber, so lots of veggies. Not just salty foods make you retain water; sugar and simple carbs also do. Simple carbs cause a spike in blood sugar and insulin—and insulin works to actually save sodium, which can lead to even more water retention. Instead, eat complex carbs like oatmeal and whole grains or any type of beans.

The Sub Shop: Digest and Conquer

SUB OUT...	SUB IN...
Spoiled or unwashed foods	Bacteria from outdated or uncooked foods can get into your system and cause a whole range of issues, such as food poisoning and cramps. Go for whole grains and washed vegetables, which amp up the fiber to improve your digestive health.
Spicy and hot foods	If you have digestive issues, spicy meals can trigger even more problems, especially heartburn. Ginger is a traditional remedy for all kinds of tummy troubles and may help your stomach properly empty. Studies haven't proven it works, but it's worth a try.[49] You can also season your food with cinnamon or caraway for a gentler effect on your stomach.
Dairy products	Get your vitamin D from salmon and leafy greens (or even mushrooms exposed to sun) instead of traditional dairy products, which can be tough on the stomach for those with an intolerance to sugar lactose. Try Greek yogurts (with no added sugar, syrup, or fat), which don't include lactose.
Acidic foods like oranges, grapefruit, tomatoes, and lemons	High-acid foods can irritate your stomach lining and cause discomfort. Try blander options like apples and bananas, or fiber-rich vegetables, like asparagus and artichokes.
Alcohol	Not only will alcohol give you a buzz, it can also relax the sphincter in your esophagus and increase heartburn. Water, on the other hand, will keep everything moving smoothly, as it's one of the most important things you can ingest for a healthy digestive system.

| CHAPTER 15 |

WHAT TO EAT . . .
When You're Being Tested

Testing: ugh. Just seeing the word might inspire flashbacks to calculus exams or spelling tests or the seventh time you took the SAT. Whether the outcome was a good one or a "don't show mama" scenario, there's a decent chance that most of those tests came with a side order of anxiety. After all, that's the nature of exercises like these: They're small blips to gauge whether you have mastered the material and can do so under a bit of pressure. Maybe when your formal schooling ended (assuming it has), you thought that your days of pencils and Scantrons were over. And most likely, they are.

But let's be real. We take tests throughout our lives, and they don't all come in the form of old Mrs. Hatchet watching over us as we sweat to remember the 118 elements of the periodic table (if you got them all correct, you got an *Au* star).

Yes, there are always going to be moments when you are asked to perform in a very short time window—and when they come, you'll need your brain firing to the best of its abilities. Maybe you need to recall certain information quickly at work. Maybe you're doing a big presentation for your boss. Maybe you're taking an online test for a certification. Or maybe you require some intense neuro surges here and there.

Your brain—like the rest of your organs—relies on glucose to give it the energy it needs. That's why we're now seeing research signaling that mental and memory tasks improve when subjects ingest some form of carbohydrate,[1] the nutrient the body uses for immediate energy. Yes, your brain can get a glucose high from that surge (it's why we crave sugary stuff when we need a pick-me-up). But the downside is that your body can experience a big old crash fairly soon afterward. So for any performance-related tasks, a sugar rush may give you a jolt if it's a relatively short assignment. But it could backfire on you if it isn't.

Of course, the best approach to increasing your short-term cognitive function is to eat a diet rich with brain foods all the time so that you're primed and ready to go at a moment's notice (see brain-friendly foods on page 267).

MVPs: Coffee or green tea. There's a reason why caffeine has become the ubiquitous morning crutch. It triggers a number of chemical responses that make you alert, give you energy, and make you sharper. One of the ways it achieves this is by influencing your brain chemistry so that more neurons are firing. That's a good thing come test time. Aim for one or two cups about 30 minutes[2] before you need to perform the mental task.

Coffee and green tea have wonderful health benefits too, including being linked to reduced heart issues and lower inflammation.[3,4] But overdoing consumption can diminish its in-the-moment effectiveness. If you're a habitual user, you may not get the big boost you're looking for when the time comes.

And if you experience side effects like jitters, you should avoid caffeine in these situations.

Key Players: If you're under the microscope for a few hours at a time, your best bet will be a meal that contains 100 percent whole grains, slow-digesting carbs that will give you a steady drip of energy. A choice like a whole wheat English muffin with natural, no-sugar-added peanut butter is perfect here, because it also contains some protein and fat to give you nutritional balance for hours.

Cut From the Team: Just about anything you find in a vending machine. It's tempting to grab a colorfully wrapped bar of sugar to give you a surge. That influx of glucose can feel like a good thing in the short term, but it won't last. You'll experience a drop in energy, likely after 40 minutes. That's a formula for tanking any mental task.

WHAT TO EAT . . .

When You Have
a Job Interview

There are all kinds of job interviews—the one-on-ones, the group get-to-know-you meetings, the all-day visit that entails bouncing from one office to the next. No matter the kind, there's a good chance that they all take on the same emotional aura: You've got some nerves, some excitement, some paranoia, some confidence, and a whole lot of hope that you will dress the right way, say the right thing—and not sneeze on your interrogator.

Although you've done all the prep to make sure you present yourself in the best light (research, wardrobe, practice answers), you can also use food to your advantage. That's because certain foods can help keep you sharp, your energy levels high, and give you the juice you need to fire on all cylinders for the duration of the interview. Use the following food plan to count down to the big moment:

The Morning Of: You already know to avoid the breath vandalizers like garlic and onions in a morning omelet, but also make sure to avoid simple carbs, too. A muffin may feel like something you can grab and scarf down, but the simple sugars will cause your energy to spike and dip, something you don't need when your interviewer asks you to name your three greatest achievements of the last year. Instead, go for whole grains in your breakfast, like whole grain toast or oatmeal with some fruit, which will yield long-lasting energy. Added bonus: Sprinkle some ground flax on the oatmeal. It's a wonderful source of alpha-linolenic, a healthy fat that improves performance of the cerebral cortex. Flax also contains B vitamins, which can increase your mental alertness, concentration, and focus. As for coffee, moderate amounts are OK, but don't overdo it. Nobody needs a job candidate jumping over a desk with rah-rah-rah enthusiasm.

Meal Before the Meeting: You want to make sure to eat about 90 minutes before your interview, if possible. That way, the food will be partially digested, so you won't be dealing with bloating or stomach issues. That's also enough time to give you sustained energy. Aim for a meal with a balance of your three macros—something like a chicken sandwich on whole grain with an avocado slice works well. If you don't want too much, try a handful of nuts with a piece of fruit and some coffee. It's important to get some protein in there for energy. One Massachusetts Institute of Technology (MIT) study compared people who ate a high-protein breakfast with those who ate a high-carb one. Those eating the high-carb diet had tryptophan levels (that's the substance that may make you feel sleepy) four times higher than those eating the high-protein diet. (Let's face it: You don't want to crash on your interview.)

About 45 Minutes Before: Have that cup of coffee (hold the cream or go for almond milk). Researchers have found that coffee helps short-term memory, attention, and problem solving. Stick to one or two cups, so you don't get the jitters upon jitters.

Bring With You: A bottle of water. And it's not just to make sure your mouth isn't as dry as laundry lint. Hydration helps with energy and focus. If you've got a long session with multiple meetings (and no meal built in), it's not a bad idea to bring a bag of nuts—not just for the energy that comes from the protein and fat, but also for the amino acids lysine and arginine. Research has found that they can help reduce anxiety.

CHAPTER 17

WHAT TO EAT . . .

When You Have to Make a Big Decision

In life, there's probably nothing you make more of than decisions (except maybe your bed). Decisions come in all shapes and sizes, and you probably make most of them without skipping a beat—you're driven by your experience, your values, your expertise, and your wisdom. Some of them are relatively simple (why yes, I will delete that email), and some of them are more complex (what project do I need to work on next?). Then, there's that whole category of decision making that is, well, life changing.

There's a good chance that many of these tough decisions are tied to work—things like changing jobs, changing career paths, finances, and more. (Of course, there are plenty of major life decisions that have nothing to do with work, but the same principles are still in play for any decision you make.)

We don't want to imply that decisions you make are hanging in the balance because you ate a stick of beef jerky instead of a banana. A lot of factors are at play. Still, it is worth noting that because food influences everything—mood, clarity of thought, brain function, and so on—it can play a supporting role in how you handle both everyday and major life choices.

It's not for us to say what you decide and what you're grappling with. But as you manage the many complexities of life, it's worth thinking about how you can use food in your favor to help steer your mind in the direction that will pay you whatever dividends you're after.

The Tough Choice

FACTORS THAT INFLUENCE DECISION MAKING	HOW TO USE FOOD TO HELP
SLEEP: Getting quality sleep will help you make decisions with a clear mind to sort out pros and cons.	Eating the When Way will naturally help as you shift meals to earlier in the day (meaning you'll likely have fewer sleep disruptions caused by a full belly). Dr. R's favorite sleep-inducing meal (a few hours before bed) is a salad with one half slice of whole grain toast; his favorite pre-decision meal is a small portion of salmon, walnuts, and some whole grain toast and a glass of water.
CLARITY OF THOUGHT: Impulses can be destructive if you make decisions based on emotions, rather than critically thinking through consequences.	Avoid alcohol while trying to come up with answers. Same goes for making a decision on an empty stomach. After all, an empty stomach is an empty brain.

BRAINPOWER: You want your mind at its sharpest.	Eat brain-friendly foods that are loaded with healthy fats, especially omega-3 fatty acids found in fish like salmon and ocean trout.
OPTIMAL TIMING: Studies show that the best time to make a big decision is early in the morning, a few hours after you wake.[5] That's when you're most alert.	Moderate coffee or tea is great to help with alertness because of the caffeine boost. Too much may make you jump to conclusions in a fidgety state—so stick to one or two cups, max.

WHAT TO EAT . . .

When You're
on the Go

When it comes to healthy eating, there's one word that dictates the whole battle. (And no, it's not cheesecake.) It's control. Maintaining control over your choices, your environment, and your temptations (see our 10 commandments on page 311) is the key. The more you control—through shopping, keeping your hunger in check, and the time of day that you eat—the better your chances of changing unhealthy eating habits to healthy ones.

As we know, control isn't the easiest thing to, well, control. Life happens, and sometimes your schedule looks like an air-traffic log—everything coming from all directions while you're just working to take off and land every item on your to-do list. Sometimes, that means your commitment to eating healthy gets sacrificed.

Here's a common scenario for those who are always on the go: You're out and about with one appointment after another, and the only choice you have when your stomach is growling like a mama tiger is to run into the gas station and grab something on the fly. We get it. Our lives are so busy that you cannot always have salmon burgers packed in your pockets. (Just ask Dr. R about the time he was stuck in the desert after giving a talk without having eaten for more than 20 hours; the only place to pull over was an old-time gas station. He ended up using its microwave to heat up some sweet potatoes to go along with his nuts and water. Now that's commitment!)

You know exactly what we're talking about: Walk into a convenience store and just about every choice looks like it's going to make a beeline from the shelves to your thighs. Packaged pastries, gnarly hot dogs, soda cups the size of gas tankers. Convenience foods are convenient not only because they're quick to buy, but also because they're an easy way to fast-track you to an appointment with the diabetes doc.

So what to do? Have a strategy. When you're in a pinch—and your only option is a pit-stop purchase—your fuel could look like this:

Bag of nuts. Nuts have protein and healthy fat. And thank goodness, it's becoming more and more common to see packages of unsalted nuts in gas stations. Avoid the sugar or honey-coated versions.

Bottle of water. Hydration is important, and a bottle of water is the best choice among all the other high-calorie and high-sugar options in the gas station fridge. Or you can grab a cup of joe or tea (skip the sugar and milk).

Fruit pack. No, not the gummy kind. Many gas stations will have apples or bananas to purchase, and sometimes prepacked apple slices or berries.

Cup of Greek yogurt. If you can find it in the store, there's a good amount of protein here. Go for no-sugar-added versions, if they're available.

Hummus. Often sold in small packages with pretzels for dipping, this snack is loaded with protein and healthy fat.

One final note: Be wary of items that "sound" healthy. Granola bars and trail mix can appear healthy, but they're often loaded with sugar. And that stick of beef jerky that looks so easy to eat with its high protein? Stay away, as processed meats are loaded with ingredients that, in our opinion, cancel out the positive power of protein. Finally, if that soda fountain looks tempting, fill up one of those jugs with ice, then buy a bottle or two of sparkling water. Fill 'er up and get on your way.

| CHAPTER 19 |

WHAT TO EAT . . .

When You Have an Event

Some things are impossible to separate: Peanut butter from bread, Dr. C from his phone, Dr. R from his Cavs jersey (and salmon!). Here's another: food and work.

No matter what line of business you're in, there's a good chance that your work will somehow overlap with eating. Let us count the ways: a lunch meeting, baked goods in the office kitchen, candy passed around the conference room, a happy hour, the vending machine, "Who wants to go in on a pizza?!"

This can be a pretty tricky way to live—especially for folks who are always on the go or who constantly attend social functions that involve a lot of gabbing and a lot of gobbling. After all, it's one thing to know what to eat, how to prepare it, and when to eat when you're the one doing the cooking. But it's quite another when you're surrounded by trays of mini-hot dogs, cheese dips, and plum-size bonbons that have a four-digit calorie count.

Let's be clear: Occasionally partaking in less-than-healthy food at social events isn't going to make you unhealthy. But if you always succumb to the barrage of buffets, that could mean trouble when it comes to your health—and frankly, you won't perform as well with the wrong kind of nutrients.

Our goal here is multifold: One, we want to give you healthy strategies that will help you manage the bombardment of temptations. Two, we want these strategies to help you manage energy levels (and professionalism) throughout these events.

Here's our memorandum for how to pay extra-special attention in these sneaky situations:

MEMO
To: You
From: Dr. R, Dr. C
Re: Eating in Business Settings

It has come to our attention that you have recently fallen prey to mid-meeting munchies and after-hours hors d'oeuvres. We offer the following tactics for making strategic decisions that will allow you to reach your daily and annual goals, and we are excited about the opportunities that await as you make the smartest investment in your life:

Prep your pregame. If you know you're attending a function where there will be lots of unhealthy options, have an apple (maybe two) before you go. Not only will you preempt some potentially indulgent behaviors, but you'll also load up on fiber and other nutrients that will help fill you up and reduce the urge to eat everything you see.

Hydrate and caffeinate. Water, water, water. It works well before the function, and it's smart to constantly sip it during the event as well. Water can help stop you from drinking too many alcoholic beverages (stay away from ones that are mixed with empty-calorie sodas or sugary mixes, by the way). In addition, having coffee at hand will take the edge off and give you something to sip on so you'll have less of a drive to fill your meeting plate with the doughnuts that are passed around.

Survey the landscape. Anytime you're in a buffet situation take time to see *everything* before you take *something*. That way, you can make strategic decisions about what you really want to eat. Multiple all-you-can-eat options tend to trigger your basic biological urge to eat all you can; if you're having trouble controlling your inner Neanderthal, remember that you can eat as many vegetables as you want.

Focus on the work at hand. In these party scenarios, food is often the backdrop to what you need to be doing work-wise, whether it's networking, presenting, or listening. Therefore, you have a greater risk of engaging in mindless eating. Really think about the purpose and joy you get from the work itself. When you're engaged in the subject, you're less likely to be distracted by bacon-wrapped shrimp.

Make a promise. We know that you're not going to avoid every single nutritional party challenge every single time. But if you know that an upcoming event has the potential to contribute to bad health, try this one little trick: Promise yourself you're going to have some vegetables (carrot sticks or sautéed greens, for example) and some kind of lean protein (grilled chicken skewers or shrimp cocktail). Make a commitment to those things first, and then you can dot the rest of your night with a few unsavory characters. In addition, pick one food that you will avoid at the event. This will allow you to eliminate one problem food while still sneaking in a few bites of another.

ADDENDUM: *If you're the organizer of business functions, try to serve more foods that follow the When Way of eating. You can find lots of suggestions at* healthymeeting.org.

I CHAPTER 20 I

WHAT TO EAT . . .

When You're on Vacation

We all have different definitions of what constitutes a vacation. And, frankly, when it comes to eating, it doesn't matter whether we're talking about a slump-in-a-hammock beach paradise or a walk-the-streets tour of a European city. When we're in holiday mode—a needed break to reset the brain, to see new things, to spend time with family—our regular routines go out the window.

Vacations can be monumental, yes. But they can also test the limits of your waistband, your arteries, and—over time—your longevity. A day or two of indulgent choices here and there aren't going to hurt. But what happens when your treat week doesn't just add a few pounds, but gets you out of rhythm of eating the When Way?

This is really why vacation eating is so important—not because we want to slap your hand for having wine and pizza when in Rome or umbrella drinks by the pool. We want you to enjoy your time away! But we also don't want you to bring home a souvenir full of risk factors that get worse because you've derailed your eating habits.

That's the challenge: How do you give yourself license to stray—and do it without ruining all that you've already accomplished?

Ultimately, it all comes down to some simple strategizing *before* you go. Just as you plan where to visit, when to update your passport, and making sure you have #alltheshoes, you should take some time to think about how you'll approach eating while on vacation. The simplest answer is that even when you're on the road, you can still eat the When Way by focusing on the nutrients and timing that we've already discussed. (In fact, you may even find it easier, as some international cultures naturally eat their biggest meals earlier in the day.)

You can practice this philosophy while eating out (yes, the salad loaded with veggies on the menu is always a great choice), and by making one of your first vacation activities a grocery store run to stock up on healthy snacks. (You can even commit to making a few meals in if your accommodations have a kitchen.) Even play a game to see who can find the best healthy salad bar. If you're vacationing in a place with a foreign cuisine, what better way to embrace the culture than to try shopping and cooking the local way?

So when you're making your packing list, leave the packing-on-the-pounds version at home by making these small commitments to integrating When Way tactics into your travel experience:

Make a split. Two-thirds of Americans say they always finish their restaurant entrées. That's especially a problem when portions are the size of a Prius. You can split entrées with people you're traveling with or ask for the meal to be split into two, with half boxed before it's even served to you (take the boxed half back to the hotel for breakfast or lunch the next day). Besides dividing up your calories, you'll also save money, of course. This works especially well when you're traveling with a group and can have your meals family-style by sharing a few items.

Redefine high-maintenance. You may feel like you're annoying your server and kitchen staff by asking for sauce on the side, or veggies instead of fries, or lettuce instead of a bun. But don't think of yourself as high maintenance. Think of yourself as "healthy maintenance"; you are teaching the waitstaff and kitchen how to prepare food that "a patron will love and love her back." A few adjustments from the way a restaurant typically serves its dishes can quickly turn them from artery cloggers to artery clearers, like extra-virgin olive oil instead of dressing. Keep in mind that you're not on vacation because you really want a cheeseburger. You're on vacation to be with people you love and to explore places you want to enjoy. That's what you'll ultimately remember.

Schedule strategically. When making your plans, incorporate a walking activity after meals. That will help offset some potential damage, burn off some of the immediate jolt of calories, and help with digestion. This works especially well if you eat a larger lunch and lighter dinner, so take your walk in the afternoon.

It will also help if you can find time to exercise in the morning before sightseeing. Even a 15- or 20-minute workout is game changing. Why? It's not just for the calorie burn. It also helps mentally: You're telling your body you're going to be healthy that day. You may be less inclined to splurge on sundaes if you've already put in some sweat time. Granted, it's not always easy, but if you can make a commitment to get in a few short workouts (most hotels have gyms) during your time away, you'll see a positive domino effect.

Count a little. Nobody wants responsibilities on vacation—that's what we're trying to leave at home! But just like you may get a kick out of seeing how many steps you walk while you're away, why not add something else to your daily counter? Challenge your group to see who can have the most servings of fruits and vegetables every day. Make it a little competition, and you'll inspire everyone to add a little more. Do that, and you'll be letting veggies do their job—not just shuttling high-quality nutrients through your body, but also filling you with fiber so that you're less likely to be tempted by a dirty water dog from a street vendor.

Check out the sides. Nowadays a lot of restaurants are pushing sides. If you're already having an appetizer and an entrée, sides are usually overkill. But often hidden in this section of the menu are great plates of seasonal vegetables. A vegetable side makes for a great app; a few different veggie sides (hold the butter) can easily substitute for an entrée. If you're at a creative restaurant, these will often be just as cleverly prepared as everything else on the menu.

Drink up. Water, water, water. It's what you need for hydration when you're on the move, and it'll also be your secret weapon against temptation. Stay full of water, and you're not going to crave high-sugar meals and treats throughout the day. It's worth getting a Nalgene or similar stainless steel bottle. Keep it filled, and take it with you when you're on the move so you're not reliant on finding plastic bottles on the go.

Keep the big picture in mind. And by "big picture," we're not talking about your health (though that really is the ultimate big picture). We're talking about remembering that the meals aren't why you're on vacation. Though no one can argue that you should try the paella in Spain or the lobster roll in Maine—we want you to taste the flavors of different regions—we're guessing that you're *really* there for different reasons. Remind yourself of what those are and soak in the joy of exploration, not the goop of melted butter.

Now, if you happen to be on vacation to try as many of the local dishes as possible (this is the case for Dr. C, who tends to only vacation in places he can take a cooking class), remember that just because you ordered something doesn't mean you have to finish it. You might have to turn in your membership card to the Clean Plate Club, but having just a bite or two of a wide variety of foods should be enough to satisfy your curiosity and keep you from getting stuffed, overeating, and feeling miserable.

One more thing: Remember to plan (time for shopping, etc.) for eating the When Way when you return. You've done so well during your vacay that you don't want to let a rushed return get in the way.

CHAPTER 21

WHAT TO EAT . . .

When It's the Holiday Season

Almost every holiday is associated with some kind of dietary decadence. Halloween has bags of candy, while Valentine's Day has boxes of it. Thanksgiving has pumpkin pie, gravy, three-story mounds of mashed potatoes, and sweet potato casserole smothered in marshmallows. Birthdays have cakes, New Year's Eve has champagne, and the Fourth of July has burgers and dogs. That's not even including the slew of smaller holiday parties, anniversary celebrations, or other special events that might as well be subtitled "just one more margarita."

Here's the trick with treats: We don't want to legislate a no-fun zone when it comes to eating otherwise off-limits foods during the holidays. We do not advocate perfection, because we know it's not always possible. Nor should you feel like you have to have a birthday cake made of hummus.

But there's something to be said for moderation. That is, even during times of celebration, you can manage your cravings, refrain from overeating, and avoid pummeling your insides with nougat-filled artery killers. When you attack your insides multiple times a week, you're asking for a whole host of problems, ranging from the destruction of arteries to changing the bacteria in your gut (which, as we know, can create waste products that cause inflammation). Save your indulgences for special occasions—birthdays, holidays, weddings, and so on. And no, binge-watching *Real Housewives* (of whatever city) is not a special occasion!

You can mitigate some of the damage from holiday eating with a smart and holistic approach using behavioral tactics (like going to the nut jar, instead of the chip and dip bowl), as well as limiting your exposure to sugary, processed, or high-calorie foods. Find our suggestions for healthy swaps in the following Sub Shop section. And perhaps the smartest choice you can make is never attending a celebration hungry. A fiber-rich snack like fruit or whole grains 20 to 30 minutes before a party will help you control your hunger and make you less likely to vacuum up marshmallow treats.

Although every holiday, family, and tradition is different, here are some basic strategies you can employ when faced with myriad pant-splitters around every corner:

MVP: Water. We know, we know. We mention the word "water" in the context of holiday eating, and you think we're about as much fun as a three-wheeled lawn mower. But hear us out: Water can be your main protector, distractor, and healer during the holidays. Why? Well, for one thing, it can help you manage your hunger so you're less likely to overeat (sneaking one Halloween candy can very quickly turn into a barrage of 234 Snickers Minis).

Additionally, sipping water in between alcoholic beverages can slow down your drinking pace. Because alcohol may inhibit your decision making, you're more likely to eat *a lot* of bad stuff when you're buzzed. Water can slow everything down and hold off that temptation. Plus, holding a water glass in your left hand while shaking hands or gesturing with your right leaves no hands for food. And that's not to mention all the other benefits of drinking water, such as keeping your digestive system moving, easing symptoms of hangovers, and avoiding headaches (they're often caused by dehydration). Drinking plenty of water—especially in the throes of temptation—will help you pump the brakes so that you can still enjoy some of your favorite foods without paying too steep a toll.

Key Players: The veggie tray. There's no better way to counteract the effects of chocolate treats than by mixing in plenty of veggies. That goes for your plate at a holiday dinner or as munchies when you're at a party. Besides being, uh, peppered with all sorts of polyphenols that build antioxidants and health-promoting compounds, veggies are also filled with fiber, which will help curb temptation. When you're having one too many appetizers/drinks/helpings, make a conscious effort to weave in carrot sticks, green beans, and a salad. And this fits with our strategy of eliminating simple carbs, especially after 6 p.m.

Cut From the Team: The holidays, as we said, represent the one time you get a free pass to indulge—as long as you truly do keep it to minor moments of gluttony. But foods we would urge you to take off the list are any baked goods made without 100 percent whole grains (sorry Christmas cookies and Thanksgiving pumpkin pie). Why? They contain stuff that raises your blood sugar and changes your bacteria, contributing double doses of inflammation. Most baked goods contain saturated fat (the worst kind) and until 2020 many are likely to be made with partially hydrogenated oils. These are the types of oils that contain trans fats, which the FDA has decided can no longer be "generally recognized as safe" because they increase the risk of heart disease. Until they are off the shelves, you can avoid trans fats by checking labels for any ingredients that feature the words "partially hydrogenated."

The Sub Shop: Celebrate Good Times

SUB OUT...	SUB IN...
Milk chocolate	Dark chocolate. It has less aging fat and more catechins and other flavonoids, which help protect against damaging free radicals.
Mashed potatoes	Roasted sweet potatoes with roasted garlic and a touch of orange juice. Delicious! And they have less fat than mashed spuds, which are usually heavy on butter and cream. Skip the marshmallows on top, too.
Butter and shortening	When recipes call for these, swap in unsweetened applesauce, which contains fiber and traps moisture in your baked goods.

Ways to Make Your Turkey Even Healthier

By nature, turkey is a healthy, lean source of protein. But the backdrop of Thanksgiving can turn this fine meat into a foul one. Some ways to make it as healthy as possible:

- Avoid self-basting turkeys, which are usually injected with butter or other high-fat or salt-containing additives.
- Baste with a broth you make yourself from turkey bones, onions, carrots, and herbs. This broth will also be the base of your gravy, which will help make it richer and more flavorful. If you don't want to make it yourself (it's really easy), use low-sodium broth that doesn't have trans or saturated fats.
- Cook the stuffing (yes, use 100 percent whole grains here) outside the bird so that it doesn't absorb fat.
- Try your gravy without a thickener like cornstarch or flour. If you want a lot of body, make stock from the turkey bones and cook it down thoroughly. It will become thick as it reduces. Still want it thicker? Add pureed vegetables, or if you are into modernist cuisine, try a few grams of xanthan gum.

CHAPTER 22

WHAT TO EAT . . .

When You're
at the Stadium

Whether you like baseball or hockey, basketball or tennis, football or *fútbol,* attending a sporting event can mean a lot of things. It can mean your emotions may roller-coaster with your team's performance. It can mean you're in a state of sensory overload with the bright lights, the loud jams, the PA announcer, and the dazzling entertainers on the sidelines. But it can also mean you're in a nutritional apocalypse. Nachos the size of a mountain (and that cost as much as a plane ticket). Fried this and that. And that's not even including the crazy concoctions that seem to come out every year (one ballpark serves a hot dog topped with Cracker Jacks and mac and cheese![1]).

Now, we don't want to spoil your fun (that's what the Cleveland Browns are for!). So if going to the ballpark is a once-in-a-while treat, you can still indulge a bit. That said, you can still eat smarter when you're at the stadium, so that you can enjoy game day without feeling like you could suit up as an offensive lineman when all is said and done. Dr. R attends a lot of games, and has made it a habit to bring along some celery sticks that

Watching the Game at Home

A Cornell University study showed that the more action a television program provided, the more people tended to mindlessly overeat.[2] Hosting a viewing party with family or friends? Make sure to have healthy options front and center. Veggies and hummus can be just as satisfying as chips and dips.

he can dip into guac or hummus. If you're permitted to bring in outside food, snacks with healthy fats help you feel indulged while cheering and jeering (Note: Dr. R doesn't really jeer, except at the refs).

The reality is that the best way to prepare for the calorie-bomb temptations that make up stadium staples is to go into the event without a hankering for the first fried creation you see. To do that, eat a healthy meal before you leave for the ballpark and drink plenty of water, which will help curb cravings. A small bag of nuts or celery sticks can serve as *your* crunch time during *their* crunch time. One more trick: Before you plop down your cash for the first cheesy delight that catches your eye, make a loop around the stadium. You may spy a few healthier options that still give you the ballpark feel without the artery-clogging ingredients (plus you get in extra steps of activity!).

Or consider skipping the stadium food altogether: When Dr. R first started attending a lot of games back in the 1970s, he made a habit of not eating a lot *inside* the stadium, but to have tailgates afterward (while he waited for the parking lots to clear out). The spread, made by his boss's wife, was wonderful and healthy—veggies with guacamole, salmon slices on whole wheat bread, dark chocolate drizzled over walnuts, and great wine (and water), too. That's when he learned that eating and celebrating (or drowning your sorrows) could be both fun *and* healthy.

It's OK for the play on the field to be heart-stopping—but we don't need your meals to be, too.

MVPs: Peanuts. These are usually by far the best option, unless you're at a forward-thinking ballpark that has filled its stands with healthier choices. Nuts (even legumes called nuts) contain protein and healthy fat. And although they are calorie dense, peanuts are good go-tos because they'll fill you up and keep you satisfied, keeping your eyes (and wallet) off big-ticket concessions. Best of all, if they need shelling, they slow down your eating, which in turn slows digestion so you're less likely to gorge.

Key Players: In some places, you may find a turkey sausage or grilled chicken sandwich. This is a better option than hot dogs, brats, and burgers—especially if you eat it without the bun. In other stadiums, you may find salads (easy on the dressing) or sushi—both of which could be excellent choices compared to usual fare as well.

Cut From the Team: Wings, cheesesteaks, nachos, soda, you name it. Although indulging every so often won't kill you, too many nights of ballpark treats are a recipe for once-is-enough nights in the hospital.

The Sub Shop: Buy Me Some Peanuts
(but not Cracker Jacks . . .)

SUB OUT...	SUB IN...
Chicken tenders	A grilled chicken sandwich. Grilled always trumps fried (make sure to skip all the gooey sauces).
Hot dog	With a turkey dog, you can get the feel and taste of a ballpark dog with fewer calories and unhealthy fat.
Cotton candy, Cracker Jacks	Peanuts. The protein and healthy fat are nutritionally superior compared with any fancy display of simple sugar.
Pizza	Turkey or chicken wrap, which will get you some lean protein.
Fries, nachos	In some stadiums, corn on the cob is the closest thing you'll find to a vegetable. If you can get it without butter and lightly salted, it's a nice crunchy alternative to the 1,500-plus-calorie portions that you find in a typical serving of ballpark nachos or fries. Popcorn can be another great option—as long as it's not loaded with butter.
Soft pretzel	Sushi. A soft pretzel looks innocent enough, but a large one can contain 700 calories (and loads of simple carbs). If your stadium serves sushi, that's often a great choice.
Beer, soda	Water, water, water. If you want to have a ballpark beer, go for it, but make it light and stick to one or two.

CHAPTER 23

WHAT TO EAT . . .

When You're on a First Date

In this day and age, there's a good chance that a first date is hardly your first interaction. Maybe you've tangoed on text or sassed on social media. Or maybe you're friends exploring the idea of taking it up a notch. You may very well "know" your partner before you dip your proverbial toe in the water. That may mean that you're less nervous than on first dates of yesteryear. But it doesn't mean these encounters don't come with some special circumstances of their own. You want to look good. You want to feel good. And that doesn't happen when gravy splatters on your shirt.

Now, you certainly don't need us to tell you about dating etiquette (no phones at the table, listen more than you talk, do not bring up previous partners). But there's a good chance that a first date may very well occur over a meal—and that's where we come in. Because there's no scientific data to confirm the ideal meal for finding an ideal mate, and because one meal won't make or break your health (unless you tally a lot of first dates!), our goal is for you to use food to your advantage. After all, you can put your best foot forward by putting your best food forward.

Let's test your first-date savvy!

1. **True or false: A good order would include a salad as an appetizer with light dressing and sprinkled with fresh pepper.**

Answer: False. The salad, yes. The dressing—unless it's oil and vinegar—no. And you want to pass on the pepper (or anything with fine ingredients), so you don't spend all of the date wondering if a piece has put a down payment on a space between your teeth.

2. **How should you ask for your marinara sauce?**
   a. As it comes on the dish
   b. None
   c. On the side

Answer: C. There's nothing wrong with fresh marinara, but you probably want to avoid having it served all over the dish. First, it helps diminish the splatter factor (who wants to stain a shirt on a first date?). On the side is also a good health tactic: You'll likely eat less of the marinara, which in restaurants can be made with unwanted added sugars.

3. **Which of the following ingredients would be most desirable to order?**
   a. Garlic
   b. Dark chocolate
   c. Pesto
   d. Red wine

Answer: B. They all have health benefits, but the best choice here is dark chocolate because of the feel-good constituents it has. It's also been shown to decrease anxiety.[3] Red wine can stain your teeth, pesto can get stuck, and garlic—although delicious and healthy—may not be the best thing to come between you and your suitor.

4. What food has been shown to increase libido?

a. Oysters

b. Asparagus

c. Chocolate

d. Avocados

Answer: None of the above. Sorry there is no good science behind any of these in terms of increasing libido, but feel free to give them a try anyway—they're all good-for-you options.

5. What is the best pre-date meal?

Answer: Any foods that increase energy levels slowly are good—so think of healthy protein and a little bit of fat and complex carbs, like walnuts, slices of turkey, and a bit of avocado on whole grain toast. You don't want to fill up, but you don't want to go into your date feeling famished. Having a bit of energy will help calm any nerves you may have. Tip: Add some celery, which can be a natural diuretic and may prevent bloating.

6. On a scale of 1 to 10, how important is what your partner orders?

Answer: 10! Well, maybe that's a little harsh for a first date. But if the first date turns into a second, a third, and a 40th, your partner's eating habits are important. Eating habits will show you whether the two of you have shared values when it comes to health, and experts say that's one of the best predictors of long-term relationship success.

CHAPTER 24

WHAT TO EAT . . .

When You Exercise

Sure, some people think that exercise is about as comfortable as a colonoscopy without sedation; others feel that sweat is about the ickiest thing your body can ooze. But the fact is that physical activity has so many beneficial effects you'd be hard-pressed to find a reason *not* to do it regularly.

List all the benefits of working out and it sounds like the magic bullet everyone wants but nobody believes exists. Exercise lowers the risk of heart disease, stroke, osteoporosis, cancer, and dementia. It helps you lose weight. It relieves stress. It improves your mood. It fends off depression. It enhances all your numbers, from blood sugar to cholesterol. And—cue the royal trumpet—it makes you *feel* good.

Geesh, the only downside of exercise is that it may double the size of your laundry basket—but we'll take that trade-off.

Along with the food you eat, the toxins you avoid, and the stress you manage, exercise is one of the basic pillars of attaining and maintaining good health and wellness. So we're going to assume you're doing *something*—preferably some resistance training and walking at a minimum. Many of you surely are doing even more, whether engaging in more intense exercises, diving deep into training for a big race, or getting so strong that you could shot-put a Ford Explorer a couple of blocks down the street.

And that's what makes this subject so tricky. With exercise, there are so many variables to consider that it's difficult to generalize what you should eat to meet your nutritional needs in relationship to your goals. Those variables include your age, weight, intensity of workouts, duration of workouts, types of exercises, number of times you exercise a week, your health history, and more. That said, the following are some of the major principles of eating and exercise:

Don't overcompensate. Unfortunately, some people fall into this cycle: Yay, I'm exercising! Wow, that makes me hungry! OK, I exercised so I guess I can eat! Looky-looky, four pieces of pie! It's very common for people who start exercising to think that working out gives them the license to eat more. And although it's true that you do burn calories and use energy to exercise, those calories represent just a fraction of your daily intake. Therefore, it's very easy to overeat if you're justifying dietary decisions by counting more calories burned than you actually knocked off. Be aware of food choices—and make sure they stay under the umbrella of high-quality foods with reasonably sized portions.

Eating after exercise generally trumps eating before. This mainly applies to those who are not doing intense training and those who are trying to lose weight. Here's the theory: As you know, your body uses sugar (glucose) as its primary fuel. When you eat, you store some of that fuel in your muscles and liver as glycogen for later use. But because you can only store so much of it, it's mostly meant for the short term.

The currency of long-term energy storage? Fat. Therefore, if you exercise after a fast (like overnight), your body will quickly burn through any remaining sugar fuel and move on to the fat.

One study examined what happened when eight healthy men ran on a treadmill after either fasting, eating a low-glycemic meal, or eating a high-glycemic meal. They found that although all the subjects burned fat, the subjects who exercised in the fasted state and ate their meal afterward burned more of it.[4] Another study explored what happens to the fat in muscle cells when you work out in a fasted state. It found that you break down more intracellular fat when fasting than if you exercise after a sugar-rich meal and continually consume a sugary beverage. These intracellular triglycerides (fats) may increase insulin resistance, so getting rid of them is a good thing.[5]

Although there isn't a lot of data that link fasting before a workout to losing more weight, we recommend eating after a workout rather than before. If you can exercise in the morning after an overnight fast, even better. And there's another reason why eating after a workout is better: You will help repair the muscle tissue that was damaged during exercise. By having something small with a mix of protein and carbohydrates (like Greek yogurt), that energy will be quickly taken up by muscles, where it can help aid recovery, rather than circulating as excess blood sugar.

Experiment! The fact of the matter is that all competitive athletes need to think of themselves as an experiment. Athletes tinker with their nutritional needs because of all the variables associated with exercise, as listed previously—and

Ready for Race Day

Handling nutrition when you're training hard and logging so many miles can be difficult, especially because many marathoners find that they gain weight when they train because their hunger levels shoot up fast. If this applies to you, try adding more protein to your diet and spacing out meals with a couple of healthy snacks (think almonds and fruit). As you get closer to race day, thinking about your nutrition is even more important. You have to prepare your body for the intensity of covering 26.2 miles. Consider this dietary schedule:

Two weeks out—Start hydrating by drinking more water and adding more complex carbohydrates, like whole grain foods and vegetables, to your diet.

Three days before the race—Complex carbohydrates should make up about 70 percent of your diet, fat 20 percent, and protein 10 percent.

The night before the race—No new foods! Stay as bland as possible to avoid any gastrointestinal (GI) distress. A little grilled chicken, whole grains, and veggies are great. Water, water, water.

Three hours before the race—A healthy breakfast of 800 to 1,200 calories will give you energy stores that last. Try oatmeal, a whole grain bagel, or nonfat yogurt. Drink plenty of water and skip the fatty foods, which can aggravate your stomach. Drink coffee if you're used to it, but don't go overboard—or else you may be spending more time in the Porta Potties than on the road.

During the race—Keep drinking water, but also add a sports drink that replenishes the electrolytes, sodium, and potassium you will burn after the first hour and a half. Energy gels are fine (provided you have trained with them and know they won't upset your stomach).

After the race—More sports drink to replace lost nutrients. Also make sure to have something light to replace blood sugar levels, like fruit or whole grain pretzels, and some of that lean protein.

also ones that can change, such as heat and the fluid loss associated with it. That means experimenting with macronutrient ratios (proteins, carbohydrates, and fat for performance purposes); the amount of fluid, salt, and electrolytes (when doing long-distance endurance events); and the timing of eating and drinking (before, during, and after races and competitions). Generally, you only need extra sugar or carbs during a workout if you participate for more than two hours continuously.

MVP: Grilled skinless chicken. Most likely, this healthy diet staple is already in your dining rotation. But it's a must for those who exercise regularly because it's a form of lean protein that will help you rebuild muscle after your workouts. (Runners, for example, need 50 to 75 percent more protein than non-runners.) In addition, chicken also contains selenium, a trace element that is important for muscle function and may help protect against the damage that can happen during exercise, as well as niacin, a B vitamin that helps suppress the production of triglycerides and lousy cholesterol.[6,7] Of course, salmon is also an excellent choice for protein and healthy omega-3 fatty acids.

Key Players: Side dishes of canned black beans (get low-sodium versions and add salt yourself) and a sweet potato. A cup of black beans contains almost 30 percent of your daily value in protein and 60 percent of the daily value for fiber. This will not only help control lousy LDL cholesterol, but also your hunger if exercise leaves you famished. A sweet potato is a great addition because it has a lower glycemic effect than white carbs. Moreover, it's full of vitamins and minerals that are crucial for muscle function.

Cut From the Team: The daily "I earned it" treat. Even if you do a lot of exercise, your body will not be able to keep up with a steady supply of sugars and refined carbs. There's an old saying—you can't out-train a bad diet—and it's true. Unless you're exercising at Olympian volumes, diet will always trump training when it comes to the overall effect on your body. Although steady and consistent training will incinerate the occasional "treat," making a sugary snack a daily habit will ultimately negate the positive effects of exercise.

The Sub Shop: Muscle Foods

SUB OUT...	SUB IN...
Pancakes	Egg whites. You don't need to carbo-load every morning, but stick to whole grains when you do. For a hearty breakfast, egg whites are a good choice because of their protein content.

Chips	Almonds. Although you may crave something salty after a good sweat, a better bet is almonds, which contain healthy fat, as well as vitamin E, an antioxidant that can protect our muscles from free radicals. It's best to get natural levels of antioxidants from foods; studies suggest that too many supplements may hinder the positive effects that exercise has on muscle cells.[8]
Cheese sticks	Oranges contain vitamin C, which may help with muscle soreness.[9]
Milk chocolate	Dark chocolate can help lower blood pressure, as well as inflammation.[10]

WHAT TO EAT . . .

When You're Trying to Get Pregnant (or Already Are)

For couples looking to start or expand their family, there's a simple biological equation involved:

Body part A + Body part B x 9 months =
"Welcome to the world, boo!"

Granted, with modern medical advances, it doesn't always happen that way. And it's well understood that fertility is so complicated that there's usually more than just one 10-minute attempt. The point is, people often think fertility solely depends on what happens in the bedroom. But what happens in the kitchen—and the way you prepare your body to carry a baby—is a vital part of the equation as well. And the same holds true once you're pregnant; the way you fuel your body is the way you fuel your child's body.

That's because the healthier you are, the better your odds of carrying a healthy baby to term. What does that mean in terms of food? It means you live at a healthy weight when you're trying to conceive (and healthy weight is largely dictated by what you eat), and as your pregnancy continues. It means that your body is peppered with nutrients that best enhance ovulation and other processes involved in fertility, and delivers proper nutrients to your developing child. And it means that you do what you can—via food and other lifestyle tactics—to manage stress.

When Trying to Get Pregnant: To be clear, bolstering your diet with baby carrots doesn't mean you'll be buying baby clothes in no time. Genetics and other conditions can influence fertility rates, so if you've been having trouble getting pregnant for more than a year and are under 35 (or have been trying six months for women over 35 and men over 45), then it's wise to talk with a specialist to identify any underlying issues.

A quick biology refresher about how it all works. Ovulation happens once in every menstrual cycle, when hormones tell a woman's ovaries to release an egg. At the same time, the hormone estrogen increases, which thickens the lining of the womb with nutrients a fertilized egg would need to develop. The egg can be fertilized for up to 24 hours after its release; if it doesn't happen, the lining is shed and a woman's period begins. (Even though the fertilization period is 24 hours, sperm can remain active for up to five days, so intercourse within that time frame before the egg releases can lead to conception.)

For women, many things can influence infertility. Sometimes they can be physical (as with fibroids, which can make the uterus less receptive to eggs). Infections or chemical reactions can also influence fertility, as well as how an egg matures, develops, and travels. Stress can play a major role too, and is one of the main reasons why food choices can impact conception. Remember, healthy choices can assuage the effects of stress.

In addition, food can prime your body to prepare for the process of carrying a child (also, see what men can do to increase their fertility odds on page 235).

Besides getting to a healthy weight, one of the most important things you can do when trying to conceive is to take prenatal vitamins, which include folic acid and other nutrients that increase your chances of conceiving a healthy baby. Folic acid (a synthetic form of the B vitamin, folate) has been shown to help prevent miscarriage and birth defects. One note: There are some instances when you don't want megadoses of vitamins and minerals that can be harmful to a developing baby, so be sure you choose a vitamin designed as a prenatal one. Take a supplement with 400 micrograms of folic acid for at least three months before you start trying to get pregnant, and increase to 600 micrograms when you are pregnant, or as your doctor recommends.

When You Are Pregnant: The main thing to remember is that you're not "eating for two." Although it can be tempting to add calories because you think you need to feed your developing baby with lots of nutrients, eating double the amount of food you usually do is a recipe for adding more weight than necessary and putting you and your baby at risk of developing gestational diabetes. When it comes to quantity, think 1.1 times the normal amount of food you have; that means just eating *a little* more than normal.

When it comes to quality, the same rules apply: Eat healthy ingredients, and minimize bad ones. You want to focus on healthy fats because they're important for the baby's developing brain. Avoid as many simple sugars as possible, as they'll raise your blood sugar. And avoid high-mercury fish like mackerel, sword-fish, tilefish, marlin, orange roughy, and tuna because mercury toxicity can affect your and your baby's brains.

During times when you feel nauseated, you still want to try to get some nutrients to give you and your baby fuel. This isn't easy, but you can try relatively bland foods like quinoa, whole grain bran, nuts, and plain chicken. Some studies have suggested that vitamin B_6 can help with morning sickness.[1] Our favorite sources, which may also be prepared on the bland side, include salmon, sweet potatoes, beans, and nuts.

Above all, you want a healthy diet whether you're trying to get pregnant (or already are). That means eating healthy doses of protein, complex carbohydrates, healthy fats, and essential nutrients. Do that, and you'll have done what you can to help your body prepare for perhaps the greatest job it will ever perform.

MVP: A grilled wild salmon salad should become your staple. Salmon is a fatty fish that has fertility-boosting benefits because of its high levels of omega-3 fatty acids (for both men and women). Higher levels of omega-3 are associated with better fertility, and may help improve egg quality and increase blood flow to reproductive organs.[2,3,4] Omega-3s may also enhance the work of your reproductive hormones[5] (and the omega-3s help sperm swim better[6,7]). Bonus: According to the FDA, eating low-mercury fish while pregnant may increase the baby's IQ—and salmon is one of the lowest, so it's good to get into the habit now.[8] Levels of mercury in fish can be fickle, though, so check with the EPA or other websites when the time is appropriate for you. You can sprinkle on a few walnuts, flaxseeds (ground), or pumpkin seeds for an even bigger hit of omega-3s.

Why the salad? Those B vitamins found in leafy greens will help prepare your body for the long journey of carrying a child by helping prevent pregnancy-associated problems (like pre-eclampsia) and aiding in fetal development.

Key Players: Now is the time to increase your intake of dairy. Not only will it help your own bones stay healthy, but there is early research signaling that women who have problems with ovulation may benefit from one serving a day of full-fat dairy.[9] Women who drank low-fat dairy products had an increased risk of infertility. Keep it in check with the full-fat versions, as overindulging can increase your weight and be detrimental to your goals. Remember our favorite source of dairy is Greek or Icelandic yogurt.

Cut From the Team: When you're pregnant or trying to conceive, you should avoid high-mercury fish. Research shows there's a connection between high levels of mercury and infertility.[10] Avoid the highest-mercury fish like swordfish, shark, king mackerel, Gulf tilefish, marlin, and orange roughy. According to *Consumer Reports,* pregnant women and women trying to get pregnant should also avoid all tuna—fresh and canned.[11]

The Sub Shop: Primed for Pregnancy

SUB OUT...	SUB IN...
White rice	Complex carbs like whole grains and legumes. Refined carbs can increase your blood sugar and insulin levels, which have been shown to disrupt reproductive hormones and the menstrual cycle.[12]

SUB OUT...	SUB IN...
Chips	Nuts, which contain some zinc. Zinc deficiency has been linked to lower-quality eggs.[13,14] Focus especially on walnuts, which also contain omega-3s that help with the fertility in sperm quality.
Baked potato	Yams, which may have fertility-boosting nutrients. Some researchers speculate that yams are part of the reason for higher rates of twins in certain populations.[15]
Processed meats	Fish and avocado on corn tortillas. Processed meats can disrupt fertility processes in both women and men.[16,17] Better to go for healthy protein and fats.

CHAPTER 26

WHAT TO EAT . . .

When You're Nursing

There's no question that a mother's job is not only the most important one in the world, but also the most diverse. She is a caregiver, a teacher, a hugger, a booboo kisser, a role model, a doctor, a provider, a police officer, a judge, a Yoda, a "keep-the-crayon-out-of-your-mouth" soothsayer. She is *everything*.

Most significant, you cannot overstate a mother's role in the development and growth of her children. One of the most fundamental influences comes from the simple biological process of nursing: the passing of nutrients from mother to child. And what you eat while you're nursing *is* what your baby consumes. That goes for whether you're having broccoli stalks or tequila shots. It doesn't get more important than this, because this is one of the rare times when your choices directly and biologically influence the health of others. (It is also important to note that we are not implying that the only option for mothers is to breast-feed; there are many medical and personal reasons why you may choose to use formula. Some 130 years ago before formula, if you couldn't breast-feed, your child had a hard time surviving. Now, many mothers choose to do both, which also can work well.)

Widely regarded as nature's most well-engineered nutritional cocktail, breast milk is full of nutrients, vitamins, and other compounds crucial to the cognitive development of a baby (whose brain doubles in size during the first year of life). Breast milk contains the three macronutrients:

- Fat, which is vital for brain development. Interestingly, the amount of fat increases during the feeding, so the milk that is secreted early has less fat.
- Protein, which has amino acids that agree with a baby's system. It contains less of a protein called casein than cow's milk, making it easier on a baby's digestive system.
- Carbohydrates, which primarily come in the form of lactose and help provide energy to the baby.

In addition, breast milk contains a variety of vitamins and substances that help build and support a child's immune system, helping the young fight viruses, bacteria, and other potential invaders. (Quick note: The milk that is secreted in the first few days after delivery, called colostrum, has a different makeup than milk that comes after. This special milk, in those vulnerable few days after birth, has more vitamins and immune-fighting properties than the milk that comes later.)

Breast-feeding moms should plan to eat a well-balanced diet with lots of fruits and veggies, balanced between lean protein, healthy carbs, and healthy fats. It's true that you burn calories while nursing (up to 500 a day), but that doesn't give you license to barrage your innards with buffet lines. You can add in some extra calories, but aim to get back to your pre-pregnancy weight and to keep your calorie choices healthy.

MVPs: Salmon and ocean trout, or DHA in pills (for vegetarians). DHA is instrumental in development of the brain; it's the structural fat that composes at least 20 percent of the portion of your child's brain that is made up of fat (yes, it is good if your child is called a "fathead").[18] Women who eat more DHA are found to have higher levels of it in their breast milk.[19] DHA serves as a key component in covering the connections between brain cells that allow for faster processing and memory storage—especially in the part of your brain that makes decisions. Plus, it's key for improving eyesight too.

Key Players: Zinc is important for immune function, wound healing, the breakdown of carbohydrates, and cell division (that's how cells grow.) Although the best sources of zinc in our diets are oysters and mussels, we would avoid those in uncooked varieties while breast-feeding due to potential contamination from bacteria and viruses. Instead, load up on legumes, like garbanzo beans.

Cut From the Team: Any foods that have potential safety issues, like undercooked meats and eggs. These can harbor infections that make it hard for mothers to have enough energy for their children, let alone produce milk. You may also want to be on the lookout for citrus fruits, which have been known to cause gastrointestinal problems in babies. And any fish high in mercury, like tuna, mackerel, tilefish, and especially swordfish, which may hinder brain development. Stick with salmon (wild is best and often available frozen), as well as ocean trout, for a big dose of DHA omega-3.

Breast-Feeding FAQs

Can I get pregnant while breast-feeding?

Although the hormone prolactin prevents the release of eggs, there is still a small chance you could get pregnant while nursing. We suggest using barrier methods (like condoms) or implants (IUD) for birth control. You should not take estrogen-containing birth control pills until after about six weeks of breast-feeding, as they can interfere with your ability to produce milk.

What's the deal with alcohol?

You shouldn't nurse while drinking or if you still feel the effects of booze. According to the American College of Obstetricians and Gynecologists (ACOG), you don't need to "pump and dump" if you have a drink. Just wait two hours; once the effects of alcohol have passed, it should be out of your milk and safe to nurse again.[20] Medications, by the way, typically are not transmitted via breast milk, so it's safe to take these while nursing. Of course, consult your doctor for specific recommendations.

What if I supplement with a formula?

That's fine. Just use one made with cow's milk instead of soy protein if you can. Cow's milk formula is more similar to breast milk. Remember that there is a difference between whole cow's milk and cow milk–based formula. The latter is specially designed to mimic breast milk, whereas the former is not. The American Academy of Pediatrics (AAP) recommends against giving children whole cow's milk before one year of age because their GI system might not be ready for it.

The Sub Shop: Feed Yourself, Feed Your Baby

SUB OUT…	SUB IN…
Salt that isn't iodized	Salt with iodine. Iodine helps with various thyroid hormones and functions and can also be found in seafood, seaweeds, and sea vegetables.
Coffee and energy drinks	Herbal tea and water. Keep your caffeine levels to 150 to 300 milligrams at most (that's about two to three cups of coffee, but three to six cups of tea) a day. Caffeine passes through your system while breast-feeding— and excess can lead to sleep disturbances and agitation in your baby.
Purified or distilled bottled water	Tap water (if from a major metropolitan system). You need at least three eight-ounce glasses to help you replace the trace minerals that you passed along to your child.
Junky stuff (like wings, croissants, doughnuts)	Olive oil or hummus with vegetables can help satiate cravings for fat and flavor. High-fat and high-sugar foods aren't optimum nutrients to pass along.

CHAPTER 27

WHAT TO EAT . . .

When You Have PMS or Period Pain

T he world is filled with all kinds of cycles. Circadian cycles. Laundry cycles. Motorcycles. But the one that needs no explanation is the menstrual cycle, which influences the pregnancy process and the many side effects that come with it.

If you're reading this chapter, you don't need us to mansplain the symptoms associated with your period—cramping, bloating, headaches, mood issues, and abdominal pain. They can certainly range in severity depending on a lot of factors, and some women don't experience much discomfort at all. But women who do suffer from these problems will know the way it works. Month after month, it's the same song and dance (though you have no desire to do either).

There's an explanation for all of it. For example, cramps can happen because of contractions in the uterus or surrounding muscles; those contractions can press against nerves or blood vessels. That cuts off oxygen that goes to the uterus—and that's what manifests itself as cramping. Muscle

What to Eat to Prevent or Treat Fibroids

These abnormal growths can inhabit your uterus and can come with symptoms (pain, heavy periods) or none at all. If they grow too large, they can change the makeup of the uterus and disrupt the receptivity of eggs, which makes getting pregnant more difficult. Fibroids can also die and lead to infection, and they can bleed. They are typically promoted by excess estrogen, which they feed on to grow. When starved of estrogen, fibroids shrink and die. That's why food can be so important here.

Above all, you should avoid foods that may make fibroids worse, such as processed and red meat, which can play a role in increasing inflammation and feeding their ability to grow.[30] Green leafy veggies, cruciferous vegetables (broccoli, cauliflower), and high-iron foods (beans, lentils) are all important if you have fibroids or want to prevent them.[31] Iron is key, because it helps replenish what can be lost in women who have heavy periods (often associated with fibroids). Although estrogen can make fibroids grow, phytoestrogens—estrogens from plants—are thought to help balance estrogen levels in the body and help shrink the growths (though studies in people have yet to prove this).[32,33] That being said, it certainly doesn't hurt to add more plant-based foods to your diet. Flaxseed is one of our favorite phytoestrogen-containing foods. Sprinkle it coarsely ground on oatmeal or include in a smoothie or on top of a salad.

contractions are also triggered by a hormone-like substance called prostaglandins. These inhibit blood flow to the uterus, which also deprives it of oxygen and causes pain and cramps.

(Excessive cramping and pain can also be associated with endometriosis; this is different from regular period cramping and a medical condition that diet probably won't solve.)

Hormonal fluctuations during various stages of a woman's menstrual cycle may also trigger other symptoms, from headaches to mood swings. To attempt to quell the pain, women may use all kinds of medical tactics and home remedies, ranging from over-the-counter medications and birth control pills (they help level out hormonal issues) to soaking in hot baths. If you suffer from severe symptoms, you need to talk to your doctor. But for moderate symptoms, don't rule out food choices to help take the sting out of your monthly visitor. You can use food to lower the volume of cramping and help ease other issues that make menstruation a period of frustration.

MVPs: Celery dipped in hummus should be your go-to snack (and maybe even meal). Celery is a water-filled veggie with almost zero calories that can help with bloating, and hummus has plenty of protein and healthy fat, which can help keep cramps at bay. Most of all, though, you should wash this combo down with plenty of water (and have lots of water throughout the day). Hydration is hugely important for beating back so many of the side effects associated with menstrual cycles, from acne to cramping to bloating.

Other Starters: Keep a stash of dark chocolate in your house as a little dark chocolate has been shown to elevate mood and may aid in lowering stress hormones in high-stress individuals.[21,22] Perhaps more than anything, though, dark chocolate can be your wonder food because it can help control cravings, which can be very intense around your period.[23] Just a little bit can take the edge off so you don't succumb to a whole bag of chips or pint of mocha swirl, both of which add to inflammation and pain sensation.

Cut From the Team: Alcohol and caffeine may seem like they help by diverting your attention to something you enjoy, but they can exacerbate period symptoms. Try cutting down on booze, coffee, and tea before and during your period to see if it makes a difference. If not, you can try eliminating some other common foods that can contribute to pain, such as salty snacks or those with added sugar.

The Sub Shop: The Periodic Table

SUB OUT...	SUB IN...
Croutons	Get your crunch from sesame seeds. They contain calcium, which has been shown to help reduce menstrual cramping and pain.[24,25] Pumpkin seeds can have a similar effect, likely because they contain magnesium, which fights water retention.[26,27]
Dessert	Tropical fruit—aka pineapples and bananas, both of which are rich in manganese. Low levels of manganese are associated with worse period symptoms.[28]
Coffee	Ginger tea. A systematic review found that ginger may reduce pain during menstruation.[29] To make it, just peel a small piece of gingerroot, slice it, and steep it in hot water with a wedge of lemon for five minutes.

CHAPTER 28

WHAT TO EAT . . .

When You Have
Hot Flashes

Hormones, like younger siblings, are often blamed for everything—sometimes, unfairly so. That said, hormones can be responsible for weight gain, weight loss, fatigue, pain, brain fog, fluctuating sex drives, and more. They're also responsible for the hot flashes and night sweats that women experience, especially before and during menopause.

You likely know the feeling—the heat wave and pool of sweat that cascades over your whole body out of the blue. These furious flashes can affect how you feel, how you sleep, and whether you're mad, happy, or some combination of the two (mappy?!).

Hot flashes happen because of changing estrogen levels. Estrogen, as you know, regulates many functions in your body, and plays a role in the development of secondary sexual characteristics (like breasts and hips). When interacting with other hormones, it also performs various functions, like giving women the ability to get pregnant and deliver children. As you age, those estrogen levels go up and down like a pogo stick.

This fluctuation interferes with your body's ability to maintain a steady blood flow, because changing levels of estrogen can cause your blood vessels to constrict or dilate. When the levels bounce around, it creates a not-so-rhythmic change of pace between the constricting and dilating of these vessels, meaning that it's very possible for you to experience surges of blood. That—and the fact that estrogen has a role to play in regulating body temperature—is what causes you to feel the heat.

Ultimately, eating the When Way—featuring plenty of fruits and vegetables—will help normalize blood flow, as fiber helps stabilize everything. And if you're experiencing a lot of hot flashes, you can use food to help calm them down. Of course, food cannot fix everything, so if your hot flashes are really bothering you, discuss them with your doctor.

MVPs: Soybeans. Soy contains compounds (called genistein and daidzen) that have been shown to help control hot flashes in some studies.[34] Foods like tofu and soybeans contain phytoestrogens, which help mimic biological estrogen and may help control hormonal levels. Great news: Almost all edible beans, like edamame, may have a positive effect, so make sure your diet is rich with them. Even better news: Large trials of moderate amounts of soy do not increase breast cancer risk.[35]

Key Players: The traditional Mediterranean diet seems to be the long-term solution for helping control hot flashes. In one study, women who followed this diet—with lots of vegetables, whole grain noodles, and red wine—were 20 percent less likely to experience hot flashes and night sweats.[36]

Cut From the Team: Coffee. A study from the Mayo Clinic found that caffeine intake is associated with more bothersome hot flashes.[37] The caffeine in coffee can also elevate your heart rate and cause dehydration, which may intensify those feelings. You can always have decaf if you are craving it, and green tea (in moderation) to help prevent caffeine withdrawal.

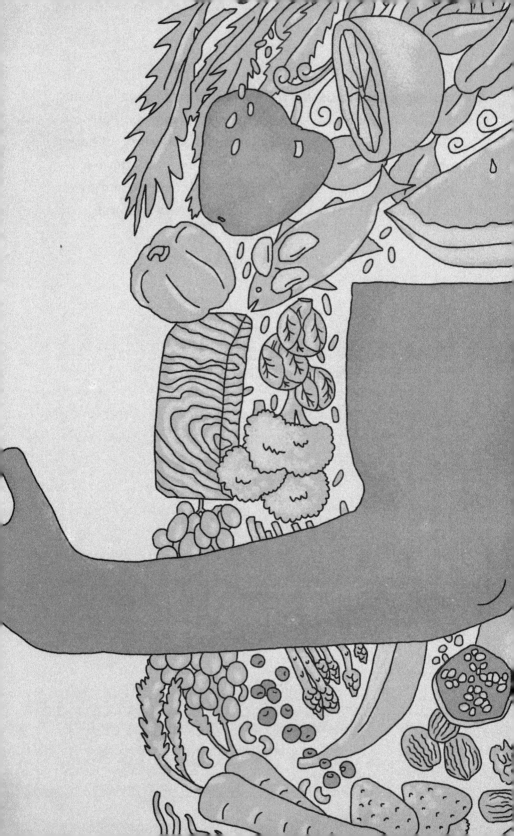

WHAT TO EAT . . .

When You Need
a Testosterone Boost

P lay a word association game with "testosterone" and chances are the first words that will come to mind are "muscles," "libido," and "erections." And that's for good reason: The male-trait hormone does play a role in everything from muscle mass to sexual sturdiness. We could certainly argue that when it comes to men's identity, satisfaction, and sexual health, testosterone is one of the chemical keys. But there's also some misinformation swirling around about testosterone.

For one, it's not just a male hormone; women's libido is also tied to adequate amounts of testosterone. Next, some believe a quick-fix dose of testosterone supplement or cream is all that's required to address low testosterone. But the fact is that many things—such as strength training and the food you eat—can boost T levels. And although supplementation can work for some, many variable factors (including the role of other hormones) could be causing symptoms like high fatigue, erectile dysfunction, and low sex drive.

Some automatically assume that experiencing certain symptoms at a certain age is the result of low testosterone.

The fact is, many factors can cause these symptoms, including side effects from meds, unrelated conditions, other hormonal fluctuations, a decrease in quality blood flow, and more. Which is to say: Just because you're a certain age (say, around 50) doesn't necessarily mean that you're going to suffer from the equivalent of "menopause" with low testosterone. Yes, we do gradually lose T as we age. But that doesn't mean that normally steel-solid body parts will suddenly turn to Jell-O.

If you do experience machine malfunctions in the bedroom or you notice you've lost a little zip, the first step isn't to knock on the door of the T-doc. It's to have a thorough examination that will get to the root of your troubles.

Nonetheless, naturally trying to bolster your testosterone can pay dividends in the way you feel, look, and function. The When Way, of course, focuses on food boosts that will up your testosterone levels. In fact, being overweight is associated with lower testosterone levels, while losing weight can boost them, so if you're eating the When Way, you should be on your way.[1]

The ultimate testosterone-boosting dinner looks like the following:

Bowl of fruit. This should include grapes, pomegranate, and chunks of watermelon. Researchers have found that resveratrol, a compound found in grape skins and red wine, could improve levels of testosterone, as well as improve the ability of sperm movement (known as motility).[2] Resveratrol supplements do not seem to lead to absorption of as much active ingredient in your body as getting it from food. A pilot study suggested that pomegranate juice may be worth trying for men with erectile issues.[3] And watermelon, although not specifically raising

T levels, is rich in L-citrulline, an amino acid that promotes the production of nitric oxide.[4] Nitric oxide can help open up blood vessels and is an important part of the erectile process.

Cabbage sprinkled with pumpkin seeds. Cabbage and other cruciferous vegetables contain a chemical that may help lower estrogen levels, which may be beneficial for preventing prostate cancer.[5] As for the seeds, they are filled with zinc. Zinc deficiency is associated with low testosterone.[6] If you prefer, use garlic instead of pumpkin seeds; a Japanese study found that garlic contains a compound that helps lower the stress hormone cortisol while increasing testosterone levels in rats.[7]

Salmon. Besides being one of the world's most perfect foods, it's high in vitamin D, which a small study found may be key for boosting testosterone.[8] Plus, it will help keep the blood vessels clear, making way for the penis to do the job you want it to do.

CHAPTER 30

WHAT TO EAT . . .

When You Want to Improve Fertility

O ne of life's great joys is bringing a child into the world. But it's not just about all the day-to-day craziness that ensues—the diapers and coloring books, the first steps, the coos, the toots, the school send-offs, and everything in between. It's also about the monumental responsibility, raw emotion, and awe that come with the absolute miracle that happens from conception to graduation.

We also know that in the field of reproductive health, one of life's great frustrations is not being able to conceive a child. In the scope of this book, we can't cover the complexity of most medical issues, especially that of infertility and reproductive health, because so many factors are involved. For this chapter, we will look at just one factor: sperm health.

Men are most likely to be fertile if their ejaculate—the semen discharged in one ejaculation—contains at least 15 million sperm a milliliter. Quantity is important; simple math dictates that the more sperm, the better the chance that one of them can fertilize an egg. But here's the problem: Sperm counts are going down, according to recent research out of Hebrew

University in Jerusalem.[9] Some four decades ago, sperm counts in North America, Europe, and Australia averaged 30 million sperm a milliliter, compared with an average of 15 million a milliliter today. Experts in this field do not know why this reduction has occurred, but believe food choices, reduction in physical activity, increased stress, and toxins in the environment have all played a role in this decline.

Sperm count is considered the best measure of male fertility, so this decrease is alarming for many folks. But it's not the only factor. You need more than just numbers. You need sperm that can move, known as motility. As you can imagine, motility is about having enough sperm that are strong and fast enough to travel through a woman's cervix, uterus, and fallopian tubes to reach an egg.

That may not seem like such a major task, but here's why it may be complicated: Some sperm don't give a hoot about getting to an egg. Turns out that some of them serve as biological blockers: counterpoints to help other sperm achieve fertilization. And some sperm even try to do both: get to an egg and block other sperm (an action thought to evolve from the animal kingdom, where sperm from multiple partners made it important to block sperm from competing males).

So how can food play a role? For one, weight gain and sleep apnea (often caused by the former) seem to play a role in sperm counts.[10,11,12] Therefore, men who reduce their weight through better eating may improve their fertility. In addition, some nutrients have been shown to help sperm count and motility, whereas others can harm them. We certainly cannot say that if you eat X, you'll automatically start producing a gaggle of thumb suckers. But if you want to improve the chances that you and your partner will conceive a child, some dietary decisions can help:

MVPs: Walnuts and certain fish. These foods are the best sources of ALA and DHA omega-3 fatty acids, which have been shown to have an important effect on improving the quality and quantity of sperm.[13,14] Snack on walnuts, and have plenty of fish for dinner, lunch, or breakfast—especially ocean trout and salmon. Do make sure to choose low-mercury fish, and vary from where the fish come. You can also supplement with fish oil that has a purified form of the key fat DHA omega-3.[15] Why walnuts? They seem to help decrease the chances that sperm will be damaged by a process that hurts the membranes of sperm cells, which are made up of polyunsaturated fats.[16] Walnuts are the only tree nuts with a significant amount of ALA, and data show that eating about a handful of walnuts a day is associated with increased sperm quality and motility.[17]

Key Players: Many other nutrients, including zinc, selenium, folic acid, and vitamins C and E, have been shown to be important for maintaining a healthy sperm count. One of the best choices here are tomatoes, which contain the flavonoid lycopene. Lycopene appears to help increase sperm motility.[18] It's best to receive lycopene from cooked sources, so tomato sauce is better than raw tomatoes. Add a little extra-virgin olive oil to improve your body's ability to absorb it.

Cut From the Team: Saturated fat, which comes in red meat and dairy. Multiple studies have shown that saturated fat is associated with reduced semen quality.[19,20] As a general rule you should cut down on the saturated fat (yes, that includes coconut oil). But if you're trying to have a baby, you should be especially in tune with reducing this food from your diet.

The Sub Shop: Foods for Fertility

SUB OUT...	SUB IN...
Chips	Pumpkin seeds. They're high in zinc, which plays a role in the development of sperm and production of testosterone.
Corn	Lentils, which have some of the highest amounts of folate. Men with lower intake of folate have higher rates of genetic abnormalities in their sperm.[21]
Milk	Water. Besides getting a boost because you will have cut the saturated fat, water can help. Semen is water based, and increasing your H_2O intake can help increase your ejaculate and thus your sperm production.
Cookies	A bowl of pomegranates and blueberries. Blueberries have quercetin, which in animal studies helps sperm swim.[22] And pomegranates have been found to increase testosterone levels,[23] which may improve sperm quality.

| CHAPTER 31 |

WHAT TO EAT . . .

When You Need to
Shrink Your Prostate

"**B**igger is better" may apply to paychecks, TV screens, and bear hugs. But it doesn't always apply to the body. Not bellies. Not swollen ankles. Not open wounds. (In these cases, bigger is, uh, badder.) Same is true for the prostate, the walnut-shaped gland in men that controls the speed, strength, and frequency of urination and ejaculation.

It may seem like a bigger prostate means a stronger one as well. But the opposite is true: Docs do rectal exams to actually feel if the prostate has grown, especially with nodules that may indicate cancer. Even when it grows uniformly, it squeezes down on your urethra, slowing the flow of urine and semen.

This noncancerous enlargement is called benign prostatic hyperplasia (BPH) and affects about 10 percent of men by the age of 30 and up to 90 percent of men as they get older.[24] Men who have this condition may first notice it when they have trouble at the toilet or in bed. That can mean feeling pain or just having trouble moving fluid from inside the body to out. As it worsens, you can find yourself getting up frequently during the night, and it may feel like you're never able to get it all out. Worst case: The squeeze on the urethra is so bad, it's like clamping a hose. This can cause fluid to back up into the kidneys and result in infection, or kidney dysfunction.

Symptoms related to the function of the prostate can also be a sign of prostate cancer (a common disease that will affect nearly every man who lives long enough). Its aggressiveness is related to age; slower-growing cancers tend to occur in older men, whereas aggressive forms are more frequently found in younger generations. The point: If you experience any irregularity in the function of your penis, you need to see a doctor to get a clear diagnosis.

Certain medications can decrease the swelling of the prostate and relax the muscle that clamps the urethra. There are also very minor interventions and a more invasive surgery that can remove parts of the prostate (this comes with risks, as it's close to the nerves that help control erections and urine, too).

In addition, you can—and should—use food to help control the swelling as much as you can. You want to maintain a healthy When Way diet, have at least four servings of vegetables a day, and maintain a regular level of physical activity. But here's how your plate should look if you want to keep stepping up to bat:

MVP: Though there's no evidence (thank goodness) to suggest that Popeye's prostate was as strong as his biceps, it's not a bad theory. Zinc is an important vitamin for normal prostate function. In a study of Swedish men diagnosed with prostate cancer, those who ate foods with the most zinc were the least likely to die from the cancer.[25] But a recent lab-based study found that high levels of zinc can make prostate cancer cells resistant to treatment.[26] This suggests you should get your zinc from food instead of supplements, so make spinach a regular part of your diet. Eat it raw in salads, sneak it into smoothies, or sauté it.

Key Players: Nuts, seeds, legumes, and beans have been shown to have pro-prostate effects.[27,28] Specifically, kidney and lima beans, chickpeas, peanuts, and pumpkin and sesame seeds are all good choices. In addition, cooked tomatoes contain lycopene, a known prostate fortifier.[29]

Cut From the Team: You'll want to reduce saturated fats—especially ones that are associated with red meat. One study linked diets high in saturated fats to aggressive prostate cancer, and found that men who ate more polyunsaturated fats like those found in fish and nuts had a lower risk of aggressive prostate cancer.[30] In addition, experiment with cutting down on your caffeine, which can make the symptoms of BPH worse.

The Sub Shop: Grub for Your Gland

SUB OUT...	SUB IN...
Coffee	Green tea. In one study, men who drank green and black tea had improved urine flow and decreased inflammation.[31] Teas also have less caffeine than coffee, which can help lessen BPH symptoms.
Corn	Cruciferous vegetables like cabbage and Brussels sprouts contain the compound sulforaphane, which has been shown to help play a role in lowering the risk of cancer.[32]
Orange juice	Pomegranate juice, according to some research, may help to slow the progression of prostate cancer.[33]

WHAT TO EAT . . .

When You Have a Family History of Cancer

Whenyou're in the health profession, as we are, you learn that every medical issue is equally as important as another. If you're suffering from condition X, then that's your priority: It's what influences your world and that of those around you. Although we can cite statistics for prevalence and severity, we also know that it's a dangerous game to imply that any one disease is more significant than any other. Some are life-threatening, some are not. But all diseases are life-*changing*. And that's why we have chosen to cover so many topics, situations, and conditions in this book: because living in the biological cocktail of our bodies, a lot of different things can happen at different stages of our lives.

That said, we know full well that cancer is a hot-button medical issue. It's an ugly, hard, and potentially deadly disease that has affected just about every single person in some form or fashion. And it's a scary one. We have all seen—or lived with—the effects of cancer, and have borne witness to how it can very quickly or very slowly change our lives.

Cancer is a complex disease, very much dependent on the type, stage, location, treatment methods, and how those factors interact with each person's body. So please understand this chapter is not meant to imply that eating certain foods can cure or all-out prevent cancer. It's also not to say that you can stave off the nastiness of the disease by swigging down daily doses of spinach smoothies.

That's because, like many diseases, so many factors play a role in the development of cancer, from genetic predispositions to lifestyle choices (smoking and excessive sun are two of the biggies, of course). And it certainly should go without saying that staying up on your diagnostics (like colon and breast cancer screenings) can help with early detection. This won't prevent cancer per se, but can help thwart its development via early treatment.

But we are here to say that you can take steps to help decrease your risk of developing cancer through nutrition. Many foods and nutrients have been linked to lower cancer rates because of the role they play in the body. In fact, an analysis of research by Cancer Research UK indicates just a few lifestyle changes—including maintaining a healthy body weight, eating a healthy diet (similar to the When Way), cutting back on alcohol, not smoking, enjoying the sun safely, and keeping active—can prevent 4 in 10 cancers.[1] And according to a 2018 study, more than 40 percent of cancers in the United States are preventable, while at least a third of preventable cancer deaths can be avoided through changes in diet and physical activity.[2]

The simple addition of these two lifestyle changes can really radically reduce the risk of death in people with cancer.

For example, for those with breast cancer, eating five or more servings a day of fruits and veggies and getting 30 minutes of physical activity six days a week reduces the risk of death by about 50 percent over 10 years.[3] Yes, you read that right.

A quick look at how this works: A couple systems can help fortify your body against the development of cancer cells. The main driver: the efficiency and power of your immune system. Your body is filled with immune cells that work like a security system; their job is to identify any foreign cells that can appear in your body.

The immune system works in ways that you probably already understand. When you have a cold or are sick from a virus, your immune cells recognize some nasty stuff causing problems and send in other immune cells to fight them. The result of that fight is what you see or feel—coughing, runny nose, inflammation, fever, and things of that sort. You also might see it when you cut yourself or twist an ankle. Redness or swelling are a result of those immune cells identifying a problem and sending in cells to heal the area.

Cancer cells come from normal cells that mutate as a result of environmental and genetic stressors. If your immune cells can recognize cancer or a protein the cancer cell has on its surface as foreign—like a virus—it can attack and kill it. A strong immune system may be able to kill off cancerous cells, but that's not always the case; some cancer cells are able to hide their proteins from the immune system while they grow and spread quickly. One way to keep your immune system in top form is to make sure your vitamin D levels stay high. Although it's most known for maintaining strong bones, vitamin D plays a crucial role in your immune system's ability to identify and root out harmful cells in your body.[4]

Another thing that can lead to cancer is the development of free radicals in the body. Free radicals are formed when oxygen interacts with certain molecules. They set off a chain reaction of damage affecting your DNA and cells. To fight these free radicals, your body needs inside-the-cell antioxidants, which bind to free radicals and then rid them from your body to stop damage from developing. Antioxidants we consume can increase the amount of that binding power inside your cells, and can be found in a variety of foods and nutrients, especially fruits and vegetables. Part of this power comes from inside-the-cell antioxidants (superoxide dismutase [SOD], catalase,

At a Glance: Why You Need More Fruits and Veggies

The Produce	Produces . . .
Kiwi	They're power-packed with many anti-cancer compounds, such as vitamin C, vitamin E, lutein, and copper.
Berries	They're ranked highest in increasing in-the-cell antioxidant power.
Apples	Studies suggest that people who have diets rich in apples have a lower risk of cancer. One reason may be that when apples ferment in the colon, chemicals that can fight the formation of cancer cells are produced.[21]

Tomatoes (especially cooked)	They contain lycopene, a powerful polyphenol that seems to have anticancer properties.
Citrus fruits	They have been shown to cut the risk of mouth and throat cancers by half in people who eat them daily.[22]
Garlic	It may inhibit tumor growth, and studies suggest that it can reduce the incidence of some cancers by a factor of two.[23,24,25]
Cruciferous veggies	One study showed that women who ate the most cruciferous veggies (cabbage, broccoli, cauliflower, watercress, arugula, and Brussels sprouts) had a 50 percent lower risk of breast cancer than those who ate the least.[26] But don't microwave your broccoli: A Spanish study found that doing so may destroy 97 percent of its flavonoids.[27] Sprouts, like broccoli sprouts, contain sulforaphane, an anticancer compound, in up to 50 times the quantity found in mature plants. But sprouts can become contaminated with bacteria, so scientists are still figuring out how to get the benefits without the risks.
Mushrooms	They're good sources of selenium, which is linked to lower rates of cancer in some studies.

and glutathione are major ones). Blueberries, blackberries, raspberries, and pomegranates are the fruits that are best at directly increasing in-the-cell antioxidants.[5]

MVPs: Vegetables are nature's best protective medicine. They're fortified with so many good-for-you compounds and nutrients that we could write about each one of them for pages and pages. When it comes to preventing or fighting cancer, it's best to eat them raw or lightly cooked (sautéed in extra-virgin olive oil is our favorite). The best types for fighting cancer include allium vegetables (like garlic, onions, and leeks), carrots, cruciferous veggies (think broccoli and cauliflower), and cooked tomatoes. They're all packed with substances such as isoflavones, lycopene, selenium, sulfur-containing compounds, flavonoids—and that's not even mentioning the vitamins! See the chart on pages 246–247 for the specific effect each has on cancer rates. If there's one thing you can do to help reduce your risk, it's to make a conscious effort to cover more of your plate with veggies (and fruits are excellent as well!).

Key Players: Coffee *and* tea may be helpful in fending off cancer; both are full of antioxidants, polyphenols, and flavonoids that have been linked with lower risk of the disease. In fact, research links coffee consumption with decreased rates of both liver and endometrial cancer.[6] Researchers at the National Cancer Institute found that those who drink four or more cups of coffee a day (regular or decaf, black please, and through a filter) have a 15 percent lower risk of colon cancer than those who do not drink coffee.[7] And other studies showed that women who drank at least two cups of black tea a day had a 32 percent lower risk of ovarian cancer than those who drank one or none.[8]

Cut From the Team: Red and processed meat (ham, bacon, salami, sausage). There may be several reasons why evidence links red and processed meats (pork is considered red meat) to big-time increases in rates of cancer. But scientists tend to point to the chemicals within them. For example, red meat contains a naturally occurring red pigment called heme, which could damage cells in the body that may be linked to development of cancer. And chemicals called nitrates (used to preserve processed meat) can be converted to potentially cancer-causing chemicals. Many red meats are also cooked at high temperatures when they're grilled or barbecued. This process can spark the production of cancerous chemicals, like acrylamide and heterocyclic amines.[9] (Cooking in or marinating with olive oil, beer, or wine may help inhibit the development of these chemicals.[10,11,12]) The World Health Organization (WHO) lists red meat as probably carcinogenic to humans.[13]

By the way, unprocessed cooked white meats like chicken and fish are not linked to an increase in cancer. Eggs, which are rich in choline, on the other hand, have been linked to prostate cancer, and researchers hypothesize that the pro-inflammatory chemical trimethylamine N-oxide (TMAO, made by gut bacteria from choline and lecithin in eggs and carnitine in meat) may be partly responsible.[14,15] So cutting both red meat and eggs may be a good idea. We may get a probiotic or substance that reduces bacterial production of TMAO.

The Sub Shop: Cancer Fighters

SUB OUT...	SUB IN...
Sprinkling sugar on your cereal	Simple sugars feed cancer growth. Instead, top cereal (or better yet, oatmeal) with blueberries, which provide sweetness as well as healthy antioxidants.
White flour crackers	Carrots, which contain beta-carotene and other compounds associated with a decreased risk of brain and neck cancers.[16] Or sliced cucumbers. Or any cruciferous veggie—the more you eat, the less your cancer likelihood.
Red and processed meats like beef, pork, and sausage	White meat like chicken and fish.
Sugar in your tea	A slice of ginger as tea brews. A number of studies show that gingerroot has cancer-fighting properties.[17,18]
Bacon breakfast sandwiches	Bran cereal. It's one of the richest sources of fiber, which can help reduce the risk of colon cancer.[19] Or avocado slices on 100 percent whole wheat toast, which has healthy fat and fiber.
Processed salad dressing	Balsamic vinegar and extra-virgin olive oil. In a study of 4,000 women, those on a Mediterranean diet (rich in olive oil) had 68 percent lower rates of breast cancer than those on a low-fat diet (with saturated fat as the main fat).[20]

CHAPTER 33

WHAT TO EAT . . .

When You Want
to Protect Your Heart

You can skip a song on your playlist. You can skip stones across a pond. Heck, skip around the block if you like. But—please—do not skip this chapter.

Although some of the conditions in this book may not apply to you (and we encourage flipping around to find the ones that do), protecting your heart applies to everyone, whether or not you think you're at risk of heart disease.

That's because heart disease and stroke are the number one causes of death in the United States and in the world.[28] So this is a must-read chapter if you're a prime candidate for heart disease, that is, if you've either already suffered some sort of heart issue or you eat the standard American diet. But here's something that will surprise you more than a *Game of Thrones* cliff-hanger: Even if you think you've done everything right— from diet to exercise to ohm'ing with the best of 'em—heart disease is still a threat. That means we all have room to improve the way our tickers work.

You probably already know that your heart is your body's workaholic organ; 24/7, it's pumping blood to deliver the oxygen your organs and muscles need to do their jobs. Your heart needs blood, too, and it gets it from the tiny coronary arteries that cover its surface. When the inner surfaces of these arteries become damaged, the body attempts to repair them with a mix of cholesterol, fats, and clotting factors. Think of it like spackling that small hole in your wall to get your deposit back when you move out of your apartment. In your heart, we don't know exactly what causes the damage in the first place. But we do have some good suspects, like high blood pressure, high blood sugar, smoking, or just generalized inflammation. Researchers at the Cleveland Clinic have also found that animal products, including meat and eggs, contain carnitine, choline, and lecithin, which can be metabolized by bacteria in the gut to create a substance that causes injury to your arteries.[29,30,31]

These plaques can start building up in childhood, and can affect all your arteries, including those of your heart, brain, kidneys, gonads, and skin. That's why impotence or wrinkles are often the first sign of arterial aging. These plaques tend to increase more rapidly after your 30s. As they grow, they can start to limit the amount of blood that is able to flow through your blood vessels.

That, you may suspect, is a problem. Your hardworking and hungry heart needs oxygen to pump blood to the rest of your bod. When it can't, you may feel that as chest pain. And when it gets really bad, it can cause a heart attack.

In addition, as plaques grow, the repair process can be sloppy (like unlicensed contractors cutting corners). As a result, these plaques can become unstable. That means that when a wave of inflammation hits, either after that big pulled pork platter or the flu, they can break or rupture.

When this happens, the tissue underneath the plaque becomes exposed and the body needs to rapidly repair the raw surface (after all, a damaged vessel could start leaking blood). In these circumstances, a clot rapidly forms. This clot can cause a blood vessel to completely close off, leaving the portion of the heart muscle typically served by that vessel completely without blood. That scenario usually results in a heart attack.

Now, it's true that some heart disease risk is genetic. But the majority is related to lifestyle choices. Hypertension (high blood pressure), type 2 diabetes (high blood sugar), a high blood LDL cholesterol, and smoking all greatly increase your risk. These risk factors (assuming you don't smoke) are all attributable to diet, stress, and other lifestyle changes. But diet is the big factor here. So although we have procedures that can help address clogged arteries, you can also reverse arterial disease with food.

Where you fall on the spectrum for heart disease risk can help determine the best way to eat. To find out your status, answer the questions in the following quiz and add up your points.

1. **Have you ever had a heart attack?**
   a. No (0)
   b. Yes (16)

2. **Has your doctor diagnosed you with angina (chest pain on exertion or at rest)?**
   a. No (0)
   b. Yes (16)

3. Are you overweight?
    a. No (0)
    b. Yes (2)

4. Do you have high blood pressure?
    a. No (0)
    b. Yes (4)

5. Do you have diabetes?
    a. No (0)
    b. Yes (4)

6. Do you have high (lousy) LDL cholesterol (greater than 190)?
    a. No (0)
    b. Yes (3)

7. Have you had your flu shot every year for the last 10 years? (A recent bout of influenza has been determined to be a risk factor.)
    a. Yes (0)
    b. No (3)

8. Have you ever smoked regularly within the past 15 years?
    a. No (0)
    b. Yes (5)

9. Does heart disease run in your family?
    a. No (0)
    b. Yes (3)

If you scored: 16 points or more: Follow the **When Way Diet Plus**
If you scored: 11 to 15 points: Follow the **When Way Diet Hybrid**
If you scored: 10 or fewer points: Follow the **When Way Diet**

When Way Diet: The When Way is a modification of a Mediterranean style diet, but with just as much focus on the time you are eating as the what. It's based on getting most of your calories from plants, healthy plant-based fats (like extra-virgin olive oil, avocados, and nuts), and a few fish choices like salmon and ocean trout. It's also very low in both sugar and saturated fats (found in red meat, dairy, and egg yolks). These are the main culprits in raising your lousy LDL cholesterol and increasing inflammation—two important contributors to heart and arterial disease risks. The filling high-fiber vegetables, lack of added sugar, and focus on plant-based proteins, rather than animal proteins, should meet all of your nutritional needs. This choice is also key because it helps you feel full and maintain a healthy weight, which can reduce the risk of type 2 diabetes, hypertension, and inflammation.

Compared with a low-fat diet, Mediterranean diets rich in olive oil and nuts have been shown to reduce the risk of high blood pressure, high lousy cholesterol, and diabetes.[32,33] An important study of the Mediterranean diet published in the prestigious *New England Journal of Medicine* also found that it could reduce the combined risk of heart attacks, stroke, and death from cardiovascular disease (heart disease, stroke, and other arterial diseases) by up to 30 percent.[34] Another study showed that this kind of diet improved health outcomes for people already on medications for heart-related problems, and who are judged optimally managed with medications.[35] Without a diet discussion and change, you aren't optimally managed.

When Way Diet Plus: The low-fat diet that became somewhat of medical dogma in the 1980s was based on the fact that a diet rich in saturated fat was a major risk for heart disease. Unfortunately, the low-fat diet oversimplified the concept and led to treating all fats the same, both the good (such as omega-9s in extra-virgin olive oil and those omega-3s from walnuts, flaxseeds, and salmon) and the not-so-good (animal) fats. In addition, with the major focus on fat, people also tended to focus less on another important culprit in chronic disease: sugar and foods that quickly turn into sugar in your body like carbs stripped of their fiber. Eating the When Way is not a low-fat diet, but for those at the highest risk of heart disease, you're going to want to cut fats from about 35 percent down to about 10 percent.

Why? A low-fat vegetarian diet is probably the healthiest diet you can be on and has been shown in studies to reverse heart disease in people with proven pathology and multiple risk factors.[36,37] Admittedly, it can be harder to enjoy as you need a lot of cooking education to add spices that keep the flavors exciting. But if you're at a high risk, you owe it to yourself and your loved ones to try. Dean Ornish and Caldwell Esselstyn pioneered the following guidelines:

EAT: Vegetables, fruits, legumes, soy, whole grains, one to two tablespoons of ground flaxseeds or chia seeds, or an ounce of walnuts a day for omega-3s.

DON'T EAT: Meat, poultry, dairy, eggs, and fish (basically avoid anything with a face or a mother), as well as oils and sugar.

We know, we know, this plan looks tougher than a hockey puck-cooked steak. But we know lots of people who've been on this diet (including a few close relatives of Dr. C's). Once you get used to it, it becomes much easier. We also like to think it's better than the alternatives: getting cut open or death. Think of oil in cooking as the ingredient that adds moisture and keeps foods from burning when heated. With that in mind you can substitute wine, vegetable broth, vinegar, or even water in the initial cooking steps for many dishes, including soups, braises, roasted and grilled vegetables, and even sautés. Salads and vegetable-based sandwiches can be dressed with vinegar or other acids like lemon and lime instead of oil.

When Way Diet Hybrid: The hybrid plan is to eat the When Way Plus Diet four days a week and the standard When Way for the other three. This allows you a little flexibility, but also helps you take advantage of a plant-based diet for the majority of the week.

CHAPTER 34

WHAT TO EAT . . .

When You Need to Fortify Your Skeleton

S keletons are fun at Halloween and in anatomy classes—but maybe not so much when your joints creak like a 19th-century farmhouse floor when you get out of bed.

Our skeletal system, as you know, is our biological hanger, providing the literal backbone for our bodies. When we're younger, we typically don't give our skeleton much thought, unless we flip off a bike or slam a finger in a door. But as we get a little older, we become a little more aware of how we move— and what hurts. Usually those issues either have to do with muscles (strains, pains, or weakness) or with joints—that is, the spaces *between* the bones. Knees hurt, hips ache, ankles don't quite move the way they used to.

Our movement (which we so often take for granted) is a complex orchestra of bones, joints, muscles, tendons, and other soft tissues; our brain is the conductor. Compromises between any of those body parts can certainly play a role in how easily you move, and whether pain is involved. For these purposes, though, we're going to deal specifically with bones and joints.

The Luscious Lube

Your cartilage contains a complex molecule called aggrecan. It makes up 10 percent of the dry weight of cartilage (the rest is mostly water). Aggrecan molecules help hydrate the cartilage, which is a key component for helping it function well. When you switch between standing and sitting, cartilage works like an accordion, squeezing water in and out. The more aggrecan you have, the better your body is able to handle this switch.

Oils made from avocado and soybeans can improve the function of aggrecan, and may even help slow down damage or help repair damaged joints. The downside is that it requires a specific extract of those oils, not the ones you can get easily from the foods. Although the jury is still out on its effectiveness, you could try a daily 300-milligram avocado soybean unsaponifiables (ASU) supplement. The French government has tracked its safety for 15 years, with no significant problems documented.[41]

Though problems associated with your skeleton—osteoporosis (bones) and osteoarthritis (joints)—sound similar, that doesn't mean they're the same. Let's review the big picture of how your biological bag of bones looks and works.

Bones: Although they serve the role of holding us up and protecting our vital organs (thank you, rib cage!), they also serve vital chemical roles in that they store nutrients and help produce blood and stem cells. Bones are living organs that, among other things replenish and regenerate new organs in the place of old ones, in this case, bones.

To stay hard and dense, bones store minerals like calcium—but that doesn't mean they're solid. They're actually built in a honeycomb-like structure. As you age, that supporting structure gets weaker and more porous, meaning that when your bones are compromised, they're more susceptible to breaking. And when that density becomes really compromised—that is, the process of recycling bone matter and calcium deposits can't keep up with the thinning—you develop osteoporosis.

For the record, a break itself isn't the bad part; it's what happens afterward that is. Breaks can trigger a series of events that can lead to all kinds of health problems, including clots in your vascular system and a compromised immune system. Vitamins D and K, as well as calcium, are some of the nutrients you need to help strengthen your bone structures.

Joints: For many, joints present more of a day-to-day problem than bones. Because of the degeneration of material that cushions the area between them, we can feel that pain every day. Joints act like door hinges: They allow our bones to move (try to imagine typing, running, or sitting with one solid bone structure). Composed of ligaments and cartilage, joints get their cushioning from a couple of areas. Soft tissue provides some of it: The knee, for example, has a meniscus, which acts as a shock absorber, taking the brunt of the weight from the upper body. (This is also one of the reasons why weight control is so important: It eases that impact.) Cushioning also comes from lubrication; healthy joints have their own version of WD-40 that allows the entire structure to glide.

When joints degenerate, you lose that cushioning, and the glide changes to a grind. Grinding your knees or hips or any joint means you'll end up grinding your teeth in pain and frustration. Without the cushioning, you have more chance that bone (hard and dense, remember?) can rub against the soft tissue—or, as it progresses, against its opposing bones. That friction creates an inflammatory response, which often creates an expletive-filled response.

It's not fun, but sadly, it's one of life's inevitable outcomes brought on by the wear and tear of age. Some 85 percent of us will have osteoarthritis by the time we reach 85. But at the same time, many of us will feel the effects much earlier. We're sure you know some 50-year-olds who have already had knee or hip replacements, right?

So how does food influence your intricate system of movement? First and foremost, eating the When Way will help you control inflammation as well as your weight; that will take some of the burden off your joints. But the When Way is also important when it comes to bones. With the right nutrients, you can send in reinforcements to increase their density, which will make them stronger as you get older (and heal better if they're broken).

To be clear, bones and joints are related—but like stepsiblings. They're part of the same family, but aren't really constructed the same way or serve the same functions. So to keep your system moving well and staying strong, you'll need to think about the nutrients you take in, as well as keeping control of inflammation. By eating the When Way, you can have plenty of meals that will help you fortify your anatomical suit of armor.

MVP: You may have expected us to push milk mustaches here—and yes, dairy contains calcium and vitamins D and K, the building blocks of bones. But we prefer you get these essential vitamins from dark green vegetables—think broccoli, collard greens, kale, spinach, and bok choy, which are good sources of calcium and vitamin K. You can get D from our favorite fish—yes, salmon! In addition, these veggies are also anti-inflammatory, so they will help with joint issues as well.

Key Players: There are plenty of stealthy ways to get calcium, including spinach, okra, artichokes, and figs (which also contain potassium and magnesium, both good for your bones). Healthy fats also help improve bone density. Foods that contain polyphenols—coffee, avocados, walnuts, tomatoes—will help keep inflammation down. A recent study also suggests that certain types of probiotics (good bacteria) can help prevent bone density loss. [38]

Cut From the Team: That grab-and-go sandwich. Besides processed meats having a negative effect on your body, the white bread is an inflammation fire starter. Sub in 100 percent whole grain bread and eat with a fatty fish, avocado, or a chicken breast.

The Sub Shop: Movement Makers

SUB OUT...	SUB IN...
White potatoes	Sweet potatoes, which contain magnesium and potassium, important minerals in the formation of bone matter. Remember, it's even better if you eat them cold.

SUB OUT...	SUB IN...
Shrimp	Salmon and sardines. These fatty fish have bone-healthy vitamin D.
Butter	Extra-virgin olive oil. It is packed with phyto-nutrients that have antioxidant power, and studies suggest it can protect bones.[39]
Juice	Whole citrus fruits. They have vitamin C, which is linked to helping prevent bone loss.[40]
Cheese dip	Guacamole. Avocados have healthy fats and polyphenols, both of which are good for joint health.

CHAPTER 35

WHAT TO EAT . . .

When You Don't Want
to Lose Your Mind

O K, pop quiz. Do you remember what happens to food when it enters the small intestine (page 44)? Or where the two of us now work (pages 9–10)? If you do, great! If not, don't worry—we weren't trying to trick you; it was just a fun exercise to grease your neurons a bit.

Our brains—as big, powerful, and wondrous as they are— can't be expected to remember everything we read, see, notice, hear, and learn. We bet many of you can remember one of your elementary school teachers (hi, Mrs. Judd!), but it would take you 10 minutes to recall what you had for dinner three nights ago.

And maybe that's why brain-related issues are such a burden. As a group, we have a wide range of abilities when it comes to intellect, memory, and critical thinking skills. But brains aren't as easy to measure for health as bones or blood vessels.

That's why it gets tricky when we start talking about age-related cognitive ability. There's brain fog and brain farts. And then there's the kind of memory problems that may seem innocuous at first, but are actually the beginning of one form of dementia or another (there are many types; Alzheimer's is just one). Perhaps you cannot remember where you placed your keys. Or maybe you can't remember a person's face. Sometimes you forget what you just said. And sometimes you forget what you just said.

The truth, as we know, is that memory problems are no joke. When someone experiences serious cognitive decline, it's a major health threat and a major health burden for caregivers—logistically, physically, and emotionally. About a third of Americans will suffer cognitive problems at the age of 85 or older.[42] And that deadline can weigh heavily on our minds. In fact, 72 percent of people over 30 say they are worried about losing their memory as they grow older.[43]

Making matters more complex is that we haven't even scratched the surface of what we know about the brain: a biological, chemical, and electrical universe that controls decisions, organs, hormones, emotions, heart rhythms, breathing, and so much more. But we do know a bit about how our memory declines as we age.

Basically, it works like this: To recall information, neurons need to communicate with each other. One sends a message to another, the receiver gets the message, and that connection builds bridges of information that you can use and recall whenever you need to.

What breaks down those bridges? For one, lack of use. If you don't constantly send and receive messages, those bridges won't get traveled on, nobody will maintain them, and they'll eventually crumble and fall apart. (This is the main reason for the "use it or lose it" mantra you hear so much. When you stop using your brain, your neural "muscles" atrophy.)

Here's the other thing about those bridges: They are built and solidified with information. But they can also become enhanced—or compromised—by all kinds of elements and influences. That's where food comes in.

The wrong kind of food, as you might imagine, works as extreme weather (or gargantuan comic book villains) coming to rust the bridge girders; as a result, inflammatory mediators tear the bridges down. That wrong food makes it much harder for information to travel from neuron to neuron.

The right kinds of food, as you might imagine, work as bridge builders, bridge cleaners (helping to remove rusty inflammation), and bridge protectors (like two coats of paint covering the structures). In other words, they keep that pathway between neurons spotless and easily navigable.

We want to be clear here: We're not suggesting that an apple a day will prevent Alzheimer's (there are genetic predispositions, of course). But you can, and should, leverage food in your favor. In this case—and especially if you have a family history of memory problems—food is a great opportunity to allow what goes into your mouth to influence what goes on between your ears.

MVP: Eating the When Way means you're already fortifying your brain. But for extra reinforcements, get used to eating a lot of salmon salads. Salmon (as well as ocean trout) is filled with DHA, the healthy fat that makes up most of your brain. A great deal of research links a steady diet of healthy fat to slower rates of decline in the brain.[44] (It's one of the main reasons why Dr. R's nickname is Grizzly; he eats more salmon than an Alaskan bear.)

Also, don't leave out the salad part of the equation: A healthy dose of leafy greens every day is important to maintaining high cognitive function. Some research, in fact, looked at people who ate at least one serving of leafy greens daily over a five-year period and found they had remarkably lower rates of cognitive decline. This is especially important when you consider that the researchers took into account factors like age, gender, exercise, and other variables.[45]

Key Players: While you're at it, sprinkle some walnuts onto your salad, or have a handful as a snack. They're filled with the healthy fats that all nuts are. But walnuts are also one of the best sources of (and only nut with a significant source of) sources of alpha-linolenic acid, which is a plant-based form of omega-3 fatty acids. Low levels of omega-3 have been associated with a higher likelihood of cognitive problems in adults.[46] Walnuts also have compounds that have been shown to help protect cells against some of the junk (called amyloid plaque) that has been associated with Alzheimer's and that accumulates on brain bridges.[47]

It's also worth considering eating only when the sun shines and shortening the number of hours you eat in a day (one form of intermittent fasting, see page 66). In epidemiologic studies, early eating is associated with less development of cognitive decline, and in animal studies, time-restricted feeding has been shown to prevent cognitive decline. Researchers hypothesize that frequent switching of a body's fuel sources from glucose to ketones may underlie the mechanism for this latter observation.[48]

Cut From the Team: Sugar, sugar, sugar. Refined and processed foods are the hurricanes to your brain bridges that can make those roadways impassable. And a lot of it? Well, that's essentially a Category 5 storm that just hovers over the bridges and never leaves. Think of that next time you have the urge to pour a milk shake down the old chute.

The Sub Shop: Don't Mind If I Do

SUB OUT...	SUB IN...
Soda	Coffee. Among its many health benefits, coffee has also been linked to higher cognitive function and lower risk of decline.[49,50] Tea is also a good choice, as it's been shown to have positive cognitive effects.[51]
Vegetable oil	Olive oil is a better choice because of the ratio of fats it contains.
Cereal	A bowl of blueberries. Berries have anti-inflammatory nutrients that have been suggested to improve brain function.[52] As a bonus, sprinkle on some ground flaxseed, which will give you an extra dose of healthy fats.

CHAPTER 36

WHAT TO EAT . . .

When You Want to Prevent Type 2 Diabetes

Think about the way our modern media world works. You are flooded with information, videos, links, tweets, and everything else at a hyperfast pace. It comes from your phone, your computer, your TV, your gabbing coworkers, and on and on. Many of us breathe in that info like oxygen—constantly needing to be plugged in—and it's very difficult to shut off. Our brains often feel as if they're at capacity, and it's overwhelming.

The same type of thing has been happening in our bodies for decades. But instead of being steamrolled by a social media feed, our bodies have been walloped by, well, the original kind of feed: a trough of excess calories, easy-to-grab junk food, drive-through fat bombs, and a steady stream of "treats."

This collective change in our dietary habits (as well as more readily available processed foods) is one of the main reasons why this country has been fighting an obesity epidemic. With more than 70 percent of Americans overweight, we're not just putting pressure on our scales; we're also burdening our health care systems (and our lives!) with all the downsides that come with excess belly fat.[53]

One of the main effects of excess weight and inches around your waist: development of type 2 diabetes, the condition that comes with elevated levels of blood glucose from increased insulin resistance. About 9 percent of Americans have type 2 diabetes, with at least another third of us at risk of developing the disease.[54] This condition—the seventh leading cause of death in the United States—has plenty of problems associated with it, including eye, nerve, and kidney damage.[55] But it is also scary because of the increased risk of heart and brain-functioning problems.

Now, if you remember our discussion from earlier in the book, you'll recall the biology of the problem: When you eat too much food or focus on the wrong kinds of foods, you have more circulating glucose in your blood. Your pancreas, which produces insulin, cannot keep up with the excess. And that's a problem, because insulin is what hauls the glucose out of your blood and into your muscles and organs to use for energy. The remaining blood sugar—with nowhere to go—then circulates in your blood, combining with your proteins and causing them to become less functional. This in turn weakens cellular bonds in your arteries and damages them, and also creates all other kinds of unstable environments in your body.

The way to prevent diabetes comes down to losing some inches around your waist and extra weight by eating healthier, and by moving your body. Losing waist size and weight helps decrease insulin resistance. Also, because you'll be eating better quality foods, you'll be reducing the excess sugar and saturated fat that needs to be processed.

Managing stress works the same way: Your brain won't try to comfort you by demanding excess or poor-quality calories.

Activity also works to help you lose weight, making your muscles work harder and thereby improving their ability to use insulin and absorb glucose. Some research even shows that exercise and a healthy diet have a greater effect on reducing diabetes risk than diabetes medication.[56] You don't need to sweat like a first-time public speaker to see the effects. Walking—10,000 steps a day seems to be the number that really breaks down insulin resistance[57]—and doing some resistance exercises can reduce the risk.[58]

Without question, the best thing you can do to prevent diabetes is follow the When Way approach to eating well, which will help you maintain a healthy weight. For reinforcements, here's how you can focus your plan of attack:

MVP: Have a cup of coffee. Or two. Or more! Four cups of coffee (300 milligrams of caffeine) has been suggested to reduce the risk of type 2 diabetes by about 25 percent (it's similar with decaffeinated coffee). It's not totally clear why it has this effect, but some speculate that the nutrients in coffee help reduce insulin resistance and improve metabolism.[59] Others think it's because coffee and caffeine decrease your desire for food. Just don't mistake coffee for a milk shake and fill it with cream and sugar. If you want to add something to take the bitter edge off, try some almond milk and sprinkle in some cinnamon, which has been shown in small studies to help control blood sugar.[60]

Key Players: Healthy fats and healthy grains are key not just for controlling weight, but also for their role in reducing risk. Research shows that increased intake of polyunsaturated fats from vegetables, nuts, and seeds—for example, those found in olive oil, avocados, walnuts—may reduce the risk of type 2 diabetes.[61] Same goes for whole grains and fiber. Women who average about two servings of whole grains a day are around 30 percent less likely to develop diabetes than those who don't.[62] (Simple carbs—white bread, white rice, some cereals—don't have the same effect because they have a high glycemic index, which causes higher spikes in blood sugar.) Those healthy fats and grains, of course, are staples of a well-balanced diet and should be part of your "what to eat anytime" way of eating. Eating diverse, fiber-rich foods helps improve glucose control; research has shown that by-products of some gut bacteria reduce potentially harmful bacteria that increase insulin.[63]

Cut From the Team: Red meats, processed meats, and all processed food (especially those loaded with sugar) are the main villains here. Research has found that just one small serving of red meat a day increases risk of developing type 2 diabetes by 20 percent, while small amounts of processed meats (yes, that means bacon) increase the risk by more than 50 percent. The theory is that a substance found in red and processed meats may damage the cells that produce insulin, making it harder to handle blood glucose. But researchers have also uncovered some good news: If you swap those meats with a serving of nuts or whole grains, you could lower the risk of diabetes by 35 percent.[64] You'll also want to avoid foods that are high in simple sugars. These are those refined carbohydrates (found in most forms of packaged and processed foods) that give an immediate blood sugar jolt to your system. Your body cannot handle those fast influxes the way it can handle slower-digesting foods.

The Sub Shop: Down With Diabetes

SUB OUT...	SUB IN...
Soda	Black coffee or unsweetened green tea. Studies show these beverages can reduce your risk of diabetes.[65,66]
Chips	Crunchy vegetables with sea salt. You'll get that satisfying crunch you crave, without the grease, fat, and carb bomb.
Fries	Baked potato skins with olive oil and garlic or roasted asparagus. Delicious, and better than deep-fried white potatoes, which are just sugar and fat that help increase the risk of diabetes.
Delivery pizza	Do-it-yourself pizza with 100 percent whole grain crust, marinara, and lots of veggies (you can use a little low-fat or skim mozzarella). If you make it yourself, you control the carbs, sugar, salt, and fat.
Burgers	Salmon burgers or veggie burgers with your favorite spices, topped with grilled onions and peppers. These are loaded with good fat and fiber, respectively, instead of bad saturated fats and lack of fiber in a traditional burger.
Desserts	Berries mixed with a few chunks or sprinkles of dark chocolate (to satisfy your sweet cravings, but with fiber and antioxidants to keep your blood sugar from spiking). Pair with a glass of red wine (moderate alcohol consumption can help with prevention).

The Spice of Your Life

One fear as you transition from junk foods to more healthful options is the thought of sacrificing taste. After all, those processed foods are infused with fat, sugar, and artificial flavors to make your tongue do the "wow" dance and get you hooked. The secret to combating that scenario is hidden in your spice rack. The possibilities for new flavors are endless: garlic, coriander, dill, cilantro, curry powder, you name it. There's a zillion combinations and ways to make our food fun, flavorful, and different—and appeal to our inherent desire to enjoy what we eat. When you make the spice aisle one of your favorites, your senses will thank you—and so will your body.

| CHAPTER 37 |

WHAT TO EAT . . .

When You Want
Healthy Lungs

G et two doctors in a room, bring up the word "lungs," and you can guess what the first words out of our mouths are going to be: Ditch the damn cigarettes. But we're not going to go on an antismoking tirade, because, well, you already know this and don't need us slapping your wrists for inhaling mini-death sticks. (If you want help quitting, see *This Is Your Do-Over* or *YOU: The Owner's Manual,* revised edition, for a plan that works.)

What we will say is that lung health is largely dependent on what in the world people are exposed to. On the downside, there's smoke and other environmental toxins; on the upside, there's deep breathing and intense exercise, which improves function. What you give to your lungs, you will get back.

Here's the problem: Breathing is like toilet paper. Some-times, you take it for granted—and you don't realize there's a problem until it's no longer there.

Although you may not think about your lungs too much (except maybe after climbing eight flights of stairs), you do know the importance of them. They are working all the time, pulling in air. This happens as your diaphragm moves down to allow them to expand. That inhale is what pulls in the oxygen you need to live, along with any other microscopic gunk and the occasional bug that may be in your path. When you exhale, your lung tissue gets rid of carbon dioxide and other dangerous substances. Most of us don't perform this inhale-exhale process correctly as we age or sleep; therefore, a warm-up period is needed to avoid the shortness of breath and feeling of breathlessness that comes from sudden need for more oxygen—as when you climb a hill or bike 15 miles.

Your lungs also serve an important function when it comes to your immune system, protecting your body from the outside world—specifically, with little brushes in your tubes (think of your lungs as upside-down trees with an intricate branch system leading down from your airway). These brushes, called cilia, clean up the pollutants that you breathe in. But they can also be damaged (by smoke, for instance), making them less effective at protecting your lungs for the long term.

Without question, following the lifestyle of no to smoking and yes to exercising is paramount to healthy lung function and prevention of lung diseases. In addition, you can use foods to help bolster their function, too.

MVP: Gulp it on up. As well as providing hydration, water helps keep blood flowing to and from the lungs. This is important because it allows the mucus collected there to move freely and get dispelled, rather than to allow a buildup. Because mucus is removed along with toxins, pollutants, and microbes, you need it to be thin and easy to move through your system of waste disposal (that's your lymph system). You should make water your primary hydration choice anyway, but we can see the effects very tangibly when it comes to having high-quality lung function.

Key Players: Spice up your food. Why? Many spices help reduce inflammation throughout the body. That's important to lung function because foreign invaders can enter the lungs, which become battlegrounds for wars between the immune system and those invaders. Too much inflammation creates free radicals, which can permanently damage the delicate tissues of the lungs where the gas exchange occurs, decreasing your ability to take in oxygen. That's why spices can help. For example, garlic, onions, and turmeric have been shown to reduce inflammation,[67,68] and ginger has properties that may help the small lung tubes relax (which is important in lung disease like asthma).[69] Add in some tomatoes: Research suggests that people who eat more than two tomatoes a day had a slower decline in lung function.[70]

Cut From the Team: Fried foods. Not that they should ever be on your roster. When you gain weight, that extra fat in your belly restricts deep breaths and can put undue pressure on your lungs, forcing them to work harder with every breath. Over time, that wear and tear takes its toll. The best functioning lungs are well hydrated and can operate freely without fat working against them. So sorry: no funnel cake at the fair.

The Sub Shop: Eating to Exhale

SUB OUT...	SUB IN...
Pretzel sticks	Celery sticks. Celery has been linked to reduced inflammation, which may help decrease the chance of tumor development.[71]
Corn	Cabbage, cauliflower, broccoli, and kale may help cut the risk of developing lung cancer by about half in people who never smoked and 40 percent in people who quit.[72]
A bite-size piece of candy	Harmless enough every once in a while, but why not go for an apple? Apples contain quercetin and vitamins E and C, which have been shown to help protect lung function.[73,74,75] Oranges and grapefruit are also good choices.
Carbonated drinks	Go for the still water here. Bubbles aren't the best for lung health because they can cause gas and bloating, which pushes your abdomen up and adds undue pressure on your lungs.

CHAPTER 38

WHAT TO EAT . . .

When You Want to
Reduce Inflammation

Plenty of health concepts are easy to visualize even if you cannot see them: a broken bone, a clogged artery, a torn muscle. But at the chemical level, it gets a little trickier to *see* your anatomical world working. Because of this, it can be harder to grasp the scale and importance of certain health events.

That's really the case when it comes to inflammation. You hear the word all the time, and likely know it's not good (nobody goes around thinking, "gotta get me some of that inflammation today"). But perhaps you don't really understand what it is and why it's such a threat to your body. It's not like the cupcake that you can imagine going directly to your hips or the tobacco charring your lungs. Those effects are powerful because we can easily understand them. For many people, inflammation feels like quantum physics: You know it sounds serious, but have no idea what the heck it actually means.

Yet inflammation in its most chronic form ranks as one of the most important health concepts with which you should familiarize yourself. That's because—unlike the kind that comes with a sore throat or a pounding headache—inflammation can be chronic, persistent, and put your body under attack day after day after day. In the end, it's a key domino in many healthy fails. So let's look at what exactly this means.

In the beginning, inflammation serves as a positive process in your body; it signals that you're fighting off something that shouldn't be there. This is the case when you have a cold or an allergy or a stubbed toe (or even a reaction to an inhaled toxin like those found in many cleaning products). The body knows to identify an injury or insult, then sounds the anatomical alarm to send immune cells into the area to repair it. In the repair process, immune cells tangle with invader cells. The result of this fight—the debris, shrapnel, chaos—is inflammation. This inflammation is why throats inflame, ankles swell, and bloody scrapes scab. In acute situations, the inflammation subsides, your immune system gobbles up the bacteria or virus, and the area heals. Scabs turn to scars, and ankles go from cantaloupe-size to plum-size.

Now take that same line of thinking and apply it to the chronic pounding that can happen to your cells when they're constantly under attack. Such is the case when you have too much blood sugar circulating, or consume too much saturated fat or animal protein. Your body sends signals that it needs help, so it calls for reinforcements. Now it is in constant fight mode and constant inflammation mode—a recipe for constant duress.

Inflammation is kind of like trying to clean up the streets after a snowstorm. The snow is the invader (or unhealthy lifestyle) and the plows and salt are the immune system. When it snows, the city deploys the plows and salt machines to clear the roads. They are effective at getting rid of snow, but also are hard on the roads and nearby vegetation, causing potholes and killing plants. Still, this damage is worthwhile to ensure that you can drive on a clear road. And after the snow stops, the city sends repair crews to fill in the potholes and replant the landscape. But if it keeps snowing, the snow-clearing crew is always working and slowly damaging the roads more and more. The repair crew cannot keep up. And if the potholes aren't ever repaired, the chances of more damage increase.

The fact of the matter is that your immune system is ready 24/7 to protect your body from invaders—but sometimes its cells can get caught in the cross fire. Your body needs time to repair itself, but when your security cells have to work all the time, the body is not able to continually do so.

The result: more inflammation, which puts your body at risk of continuing a vicious cycle that contributes to even more inflammation. For example, having high triglycerides increases inflammation, which damages your blood vessels, which makes it more likely to increase your lousy LDL cholesterol. This creates plaques in your blood vessels as your body attempts to heal itself. That cycle happens all over your body with all kinds of organs, cells, and systems. And the endgame? You've put yourself at higher risk of developing heart disease, stroke, cancer, arthritis, memory issues, pain, hormonal issues, organ damage, and more.

That's why getting a handle on inflammation is so vital to having a strong, healthy body. Above all, the things you can do to quiet inflammation contain a whole lot of "don'ts." That's why not smoking, not eating processed foods, and not eating processed meats are high on the anti-inflammatory list of directives.

You can also do a lot to help quiet inflammation by eating foods that will help shush the immune response.

When You Eat: When you're moving, your body can slow down inflammation. When you're at rest, it's more likely that sparks will start flying. That's why it's especially bad to eat inflammatory foods—those that are processed or have added sugars—at night. The pro-inflammatory effect can be magnified once you turn in for the night. In addition, eating these kinds of foods during high-stress times will also magnify the effect of inflammation. That's why it's important to have an antistress eating strategy (see page 113).

What You Eat: If you eat the When Way, you'll already be choosing anti-inflammatory foods. That's because fruits and vegetables, as well as the healthy fats found in fish and nuts, are considered some of the strongest nutritional firepower in the fight against inflammation. The following are your anti-inflammatory all-stars:

Fruits and vegetables. Mix in foods of all colors to get a wide range of vitamins and nutrients. Make sure to get plenty of citrus fruits, which contain immune-supporting vitamin C.

Prebiotic fiber. It turns out that all those bacteria in your gut play a big role in inflammation. These bacteria actually start digesting your food before you do and help create a barrier between the cells that make up your GI tract and the food traveling through it. If you're eating the standard American diet, you probably have limited diversity in your gut bacteria compared with people eating the When Way. To give the good guys a boost, make sure you are eating plenty of prebiotic fiber. These are foods that you cannot necessarily digest, but that feed healthy gut bacteria: whole grains, beans, and vegetables, especially leafy greens and artichokes. As a bonus, you can get both prebiotics and probiotics from fermented vegetables like kimchi or unpasteurized sauerkraut.

Fish, nuts, oils. Healthy fats are some of the strongest foods that reduce inflammation. This is one of the reasons why a salad with salmon, a little extra-virgin olive oil, and a few walnuts may be the most powerful meal that your body can have.

Yogurt. Cultured Greek or Icelandic yogurt contains bacteria that help replenish healthy gut bacteria, especially if you are taking antibiotics, which can deplete your good gut bacteria.

Oats. Choose long-to-digest whole grains, which will help slow processes that contribute to inflammation.

What Not to Eat: Added sugars, syrups, simple or stripped carbs, and foods with saturated or trans fats all stimulate inflammation. And anyone who says eating egg yolks (which contain choline) doesn't also contribute should be banned from writing books, columns, and blogs, IMHO! Egg whites are fine.

CHAPTER 39

WHAT TO EAT . . .

When You Have
Hormonal Issues

The body is the world's most fascinating ecosystem. Here, system A influences system B and organ C interacts with chemical D to force system A to change the way it works, and so on. It's why the body is beautiful. It's why the body is enigmatic. And it's also why simplifying complex topics is not always easy.

The area where that is most certainly the case is the hormonal system. For us to break down "hormones" into one simple chapter is like saying you can learn to build a car engine with a three-minute YouTube video. The reality is that hormones ooze throughout this whole book *(ewww!)*. We've addressed hormonal issues in a variety of areas, such as hot flashes (page 227) and sex drive (page 231) and the prostate (page 239).

That said, we do think it's worth addressing some uber-hormone issues—which is to say that many people have dysfunctional hormonal systems that are frustrating, complex, and difficult to treat. Some of those treatments involve medication, and some of them involve lifestyle changes.

Those treatment methods are far too complex for this book—and yet it is worth exploring some more common hormonal issues and how you can address them with dietary choices.

Hormones—chemical messengers made in your endocrine glands and sent throughout the body—play a role in how you feel every day. Your metabolism, your body temperature, your heart rate, your libido, your mood, and more are all affected. The pituitary gland, located deep in your brain, acts as the main controller; some have compared it to the conductor of an orchestra. Other glands—for example, the thyroid and adrenal gland—receive signals from hormones released by your pituitary and then send out a second group of hormones to your body. How they interact with various organs, systems, and chemicals plays a role in how you feel via the symptoms and body functions mentioned previously.

Here's why hormones are trickier than a street performer's card game: There's so much subjectivity when it comes to reading hormonal levels and figuring out how to control them. Although we have blood tests to show levels of a hormone, the same "number" doesn't always mean the same thing for everyone. It's not like clogged arteries, where we can see specific percentages of blockages. It's nuanced, and good endocrinologists can help you figure out if and how your symptoms can be treated with medical interventions.

Our job here is to help you figure out how food can help your hormone systems stabilize—that is, what you can eat to optimize how your hormones function. As you may have guessed, that depends on which hormones need to be addressed.

Thyroid: The hormones produced by the thyroid are associated with symptoms like increased heart rate, anxiety, weight gain or loss, insomnia, and more. You can have an overactive thyroid (that's called hyperthyroid) or an underactive one (that's hypo). As you might imagine, those would manifest themselves in opposite ways—typically, you gain weight with hypothyroidism as everything slows, but can have heart palpitations and insomnia with hyperthyroidism as everything revs up. Here's a simplified version of how to tweak your When Way of eating, based on thyroid issues:

Hyperthyroidism. In hyperthyroidism, the gland pumps out more hormones than you need, which revs up your metabolism. Although some people might want the weight loss that comes along with this, it also means that many of your body's cells are turning over so quickly that you need to maximize your nutrients to support your skin, bones, hair, heart, and other organs. And the condition can damage some of those organs, as with hyperthyroid heart disease or eye disease. If you suffer from hyperthyroidism, you want to make sure to eat the When Way, getting lots of plant-based proteins that help build new cell components, as well as cruciferous vegetables like kale and broccoli, which are high in calcium to help protect bones. Cruciferous vegetables also contain a substance that can potentially interfere with the production of thyroid hormones, though there is likely not enough to make a difference if you have hyperthyroidism.[76] One thing you may not need more of is iodine, so your doc may suggest avoiding iodine-rich foods like iodized salt, seafood, and iodine-enriched grains.

Hypothyroidism. The thyroid needs iodine to make hormones, so a small amount is required to ramp up a slowed thyroid that has been deprived. The best food source is low-mercury fish or algae, as well as iodized salt. You may also be able to help your thyroid by avoiding processed meats, which contain nitrates. (Nitrates block the thyroid from taking in iodine, therefore decreasing thyroid hormones.) One study found that people with higher dietary intake of nitrates had an increased risk for thyroid cancer.[77] If you're taking hormones for a low thyroid, don't wash them down with soy milk or other soy products; studies suggest soy can block absorption. But it's OK to eat them later in the day.[78]

Adrenal: The adrenal hormones consist of an inner adrenal that releases epinephrine or adrenalin and norepinephrine or noradrenaline, as well as an outer adrenal that produces cortisol. Together, they orchestrate many functions of the body, including metabolism, energy, stress response, blood pressure, digestion, and immune functions.

For these purposes, we're most concerned with the adrenal production of cortisol—the stress hormone. Too much cortisol circulating in your bloodstream may increase hunger, which can lead to overeating, and this hormone can also increase storage of abdominal fat.[79] That fat is dangerous because it's so close to your vital organs and puts you at risk of developing heart problems among a number of other disorders. That's one of the reasons you want to avoid high-sugar and simple-carb foods when you're stressed; they make everything worse. Your body tends to crave sugary foods when you're stressed because these foods can help lower cortisol levels.[80] Although that might help in the short term, in the long run stress eating leads to the fat we just explained.

So when you're experiencing stress, what to eat when is actually *nothing*. Instead of reaching for a snack (even a healthy one), you may be better off trying to divert the emotional reflex to grab food by trying a quick meditation session that helps control your breathing and instead divorce yourself from the eating-as-a-stress-fix reaction. You can practice meditation with the help of a variety of apps, or just experiment yourself: Sit in a quiet room with your eyes closed and no distractions. Pick a mantra, a phrase, or some guttural sound (like *ohm*), and repeat it over and over, breathing slow and controlled breaths.

Skin: You probably don't think of your skin as a gland or even as an organ. But in fact, it is the body's largest of both! The skin is responsible for production of vitamin D, which is actually a hormone. Vitamins technically aren't made by the body, but "vitamin D" is. The skin uses the power of the ultraviolet B rays from the sun to convert a form of cholesterol, 7-dehydrocholesterol, into vitamin D_3.

This inactive form of vitamin D then travels in the blood to the liver, where oxygen and hydrogen are added, and on to the kidney, where it is finally converted to its active form, known as calcitriol. Active vitamin D helps the gut absorb the calcium needed to support strong bones, regulates cell growth to help prevent cancer, protects from heart disease, and serves many other functions throughout the body.[81]

But let's face it: In this day and age, many of us probably aren't spending the 15 or more minutes a day in the sun, especially in the winter. Also because of skin cancer concerns (sun exposure is a big risk factor), the American Academy of

Dermatology actually recommends against getting vitamin D from the sun, suggesting that we turn to other natural sources.[82] Many of those sources are foods you're probably not eating much of anymore if you're eating the When Way: fortified milk, cheese, and egg yolks. But you can find a lot of vitamin D in When Way–approved foods like salmon or leafy greens. If you're not eating salmon just about every day like Dr. R, you may want to consider a supplement.

WHAT TO EAT . . .

When You Have
Other Health Issues

The headlines on the front page or at the top of your Twitter feed are there to do the following job: tell you what's important and what you should care about. In various forms of health communication, we tend to follow the same algorithm: A whole host of headliner diseases and conditions continue to garner the most attention, either because they affect the most people or have the most damaging effects. That's why this book—and many other health resources—focus most often on obesity, heart disease, diabetes, cancer, and brain issues, because they tend to top the list of issues you most want to treat and prevent.

That said, it's also important to remember that the smaller stories are equally important—especially if you suffer from them. Although gout and cataracts may not be front and center in media coverage, millions experience them. That's why we've put together this chapter: to show you how food can help alleviate a range of problems you may encounter in the future—or are experiencing today.

As we've observed, any medical problem requires a holistic approach to treatment. In many cases, specific medication(s), surgery, exercise, stress management, toxin avoidance, or other interventions may be the best answer for the most immediate, effective, and long-term relief. Still, food can play a huge role both in the treatment of some issues, as well as in their prevention. For example, just eating a Mediterranean diet enhanced with extra-virgin olive oil as the predominant fat can decrease the risk of breast cancer by more than 60 percent, according to one large study.[83]

In the following list of diseases, you may not find your typical click-bait headlines ("23 Surefire Ways to Shrink Your Goiter Now!"). But you will find smart eating tips that can change the way you feel and the way you live. In addition, just adopting the When Way can help mitigate many health problems.

CATARACTS

Clouds may be wonderful to encounter in a beautiful blue sky—but not so much when they're in your beautiful blue (or green or brown) eyes. Cataracts—a cloudy or opaque area on the lens of an eye—can be removed and replaced with an artificial lens through surgery. But food choices can increase or decrease your risk of developing them in the first place. Typically associated with aging, cataracts also can occur in people who have experienced trauma or some metabolic conditions like diabetes.

What to Eat: Several nutrients have been linked to a decreased risk for developing cataracts, including polyunsaturated fats, protein, vitamin A, antioxidants like vitamin C and

E, and several minerals or vitamins (like manganese, niacin, thiamine, and riboflavin).[84,85,86,87,88] That's why the optimum cataract-preventing meal would be salmon or ocean trout with broccoli or spinach (both high in the carotenoids linked to decreased risk of cataracts). Unsurprisingly, research shows that people with diets high in simple carbs and salt have a higher risk of developing cataracts.[89,90]

GALLSTONES

A lot of stones are entertaining. The Rolling Stones. Oliver. Sharon. But gallstones? Not so much. Gallstones form when hardened substances in your digestive fluid stick together to form little nuggets in your digestive ducts. When these stones try to move through the bile ducts to help digest fat, they end up blocking the ducts, increasing pressure in the gallbladder. This inability to empty the gallbladder risks the formation of infections—or even blocking the ducts completely and bringing the digestive process to a halt. (By the way, one way to determine whether you have gallstones is by noting whether you experience pain when eating a fatty food like a piece of fried chicken; if you do, a gallstone could be the culprit.) Although women are twice as likely as men to develop gallstones, there is also a relationship between gallstones and diets high in fat and low in fiber.

What to Eat: Eating the When Way will go a long way toward preventing the formation of gallstones. For extra protection, caffeinated coffee, moderate amounts of alcohol, and nuts (preferably not at the same time) have also been linked to lower risk.[91,92,93,94] Diets high in fiber are also crucial, because fiber helps move fat through your system more easily. Focus on fruits, veggies, and just about any bean.

GOUT

A form of arthritis, gout is best known for its quick onset, characterized by intense pain that typically starts in one joint (often the big toe). It's an uncomfortable condition—one that happens when uric acid crystallizes in the joints. Uric acid is a product of a chemical compound found in food and drinks called purines.

What to Eat: The When Way basics do more for you than just shrink your waistline. A diet composed of all three macronutrients—lean or plant-based protein, healthy fats, and whole grain carbs—are linked to lower levels of uric acid and reduced risk of gout.[95,96] You should drink lots of water, which has been linked to a lower amount of gout attacks as well.[97] And you can focus on a few other things, like increasing the consumption of coffee and cherries, both of which have been associated with keeping gout attacks at bay.[98,99] In general, you should avoid food with purine, which can contribute to gout attacks. This includes organ meats like liver and kidneys—but you were probably already avoiding these super-bad-for-you foods. However, fruit and vegetables with purine—for example, asparagus and peas—are OK, as they have not been shown to increase gout.[100]

KIDNEY STONES

Kidney stones, you may have heard, are often described as the most painful acute condition a person can experience (unless you count having to sit in day-before-Thanksgiving traffic or delivering a child without anesthesia). Anyone who's had a stone may describe the intensity of the pain—felt in the lower back as the stone tries to move through your system—as a 432 on a scale of 1 to 10. (Unfortunately, if you've already had one, you're at a higher risk of developing another.)

Kidney stones form when your urine cannot dilute crystals that result from constituents like calcium, uric acid, and oxalate. When these crystals come together, a hard stone substance is formed; your body tries to pass it through your urinary tract. But squeezing a stone through a tube and hole that's smaller than the actual stone—well, that's where the grit-your-teeth, call-your-mama pain comes from.

What to Eat: Contrary to popular belief, cutting back on calcium won't prevent stones. What will: water, water, water. Staying hydrated helps dilute your urine to break up those crystals. In addition, you can try drinking diet limeade or lemonade (without extra sugar), because fruits and juices high in citrate have been shown to help prevent the development of stones.[101,102,103] Another tactic: Drink and eat foods that are high in calcium and high in oxalate at the same time instead of separately (oxalate-rich foods include peanuts, beets, chocolate, spinach, sweet potatoes). These two substances are more likely to bind together in the stomach and intestines, instead of in the kidneys, where stones form.

RESTLESS LEG SYNDROME

Ah, the blissful bed. You snuggle in under toasty blankets, in a dark room, with the soothing sounds of white noise lulling you into a dreamy sleep. And then . . . your legs fire off like you're performing with the Rockettes. Not even counting how many bruises you may have given your bedmate, restless leg syndrome—or the ohmygawd leg cramps—can really disrupt sleep patterns, which is a problem not only because of associated fatigue, but also because sleep disturbances are associated with all sorts of long-term and serious health problems, including cognitive decline and infertility.

What to Eat: Lots of websites say that the easiest solution is to drink some diet tonic water because it contains quinine, an ingredient shown to decrease cramping. But the FDA has warned that this research is out of date, and there isn't nearly enough quinine in tonic to help, so we don't recommend it.[104] The truth is, you may be deficient in certain vitamins and minerals like D_3 or potassium, which have been linked to cramps. If this is the case, eating spinach and fish is a must to get your dose of these important nutrients.

Restless leg also may be an indication of a more serious problem: low iron. Spinach, seafood, most beans, and whole grain bread offer this crucial nutrient without some of the potential detrimental qualities of other iron-rich options like red meat (which is filled with carnitine). You also can try adding folate and magnesium to your diet, which have been shown in small studies to help some with restless leg syndrome.[105,106] Find these in lentils, beans, dark leafy greens, almonds, and edamame.

Finally, one of the big keys to solving restless leg is to avoid alcohol and caffeine before bed. These can disrupt your sleep and make the symptoms worse.

More Ways to Fix Your Body With Food

If you want to improve your night vision... As you get older, you may find that seeing at night is more difficult. Try eating more oranges, kale, and spinach, all of which contain nutrients linked to preserving eye function over time.[107]

If you live in an area with a lot of air pollution... Bulk up on olive oil and salmon, which have been shown to be anti-inflammatory and help mitigate the effects of air pollution.[108,109] Extra-virgin oil is especially good, as it contains a vitamin that helps lung function as well as healthy fat, which reduces inflammation.

If you're a prime target for bugs... Some people seem to attract bugs like they're rock stars and mosquitoes are groupies. Bugs are attracted to certain people by the smells they emit. How you smell isn't just a function of your deodorant use, but also what foods you eat and how you emit them in your sweat and through your skin. Tip: Mosquitoes are suckers, quite literally, for Limburger cheese and alcohol[110,111]—so plan to avoid these if you're the constant subject of bugs' affection.

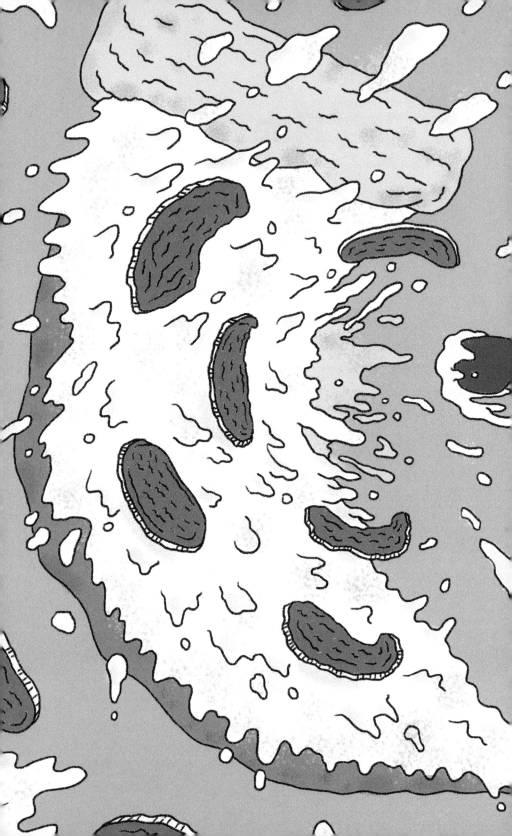

| PART 4 |

The Final Word: What to Eat When

CHAPTER 41

HOW TO WIN THE WHEN WAY

Managing Temptation

With all due respect to the rest of the (amazing) information in this (life-changing) book about the (new) way you're going to eat, much of the struggle when it comes to eating right has traditionally revolved around one word: temptation. Anybody who has ever battled with weight or food-related health issues—or cannot walk by a checkout counter without giving in to a Snickers—knows exactly what we're talking about. The allure of foods around us is strong. We're drawn in by sugar and fat and all the processed concoctions that may taste great, but that also act like shrapnel to our vital organs, tissues, and systems.

Making the When Way your new foundation of eating includes knowing how to deal with the constant bombardment of food choices that we encounter in stores, on street corners, in the office, and everywhere we turn.

A lot of research has been done on temptation—the psychological state of being lured in to perform an action, perhaps against our better judgment. And the truth is that this is one of the most difficult aspects of eating to manage. How do you avoid giving in to temptation and instead learn to handle it? It's not as simple as digging your feet into the sand and screaming "NO!" every time a cheese block passes under your nose. It's much more nuanced than that. To best resist tempting treats you'll encounter one or a hundred times a day, be aware of the following four principles:

It's not your fault. Remember when we talked about the emotional side and executive functions of your brain? We are wired to react emotionally first; this is the reptilian response that ensured our survival. Rather than sitting around and thinking about whether we should run from a forest fire, our instincts and emotions tell us to hightail it. The same principle is at play here. You see a doughnut. It has pink glaze. And sprinkles. And damn, does that thing shine. You're attracted to it, and the reptilian side of your brain wants you to act upon that attraction. It draws you to the doughnut before your executive side has a chance to make a smart decision. Now, that doesn't mean you can't override the reptilian side (more on that in a moment). But it does mean this: Handling temptation can be an uphill battle, because our bodies are designed to give in to impulses. That doesn't mean you throw up your hands and funnel a can of Spaghetti-O's down your throat. Instead, just knowing that your instant reaction is to eat first allows you to come up with strategies to beat your biology.

The food industry intensified the problem. Think about what life was like back when the sweetest dessert options were berries on bushes. If our biology told us to give in to temptation, so what if you gorged on a whole bush of them after feasting on a wild hog you caught that day? These days, processed, packaged foods with high amounts of sugar, chemicals, and refined ingredients are widely available, and have been shown to disturb the biological beauty of the way the body is supposed to work. This has made the repercussions of giving in to temptation that much worse. So it's no coincidence that our rates of obesity, diabetes, and metabolic syndrome have risen at the same time as options for high-sugar and high-processed foods have grown. That doesn't mean you can't beat the system. But it does mean you have more edible enemies to plot against.

Willpower is overrated. Must be strong. Must resist enchiladas. Must spend happy hour being unhappy. That's what willpower is, right? It's all about your ability to override strong, biological urges to satisfy your tastes, increase your energy, or alleviate hunger. No. Willpower—when it comes to eating food—is sort of a misnomer. As we said, your biology drives you to eat: When you're tired, you want sugar; when you're tempted by something that looks and smells delicious, you want to give in. Somehow we've managed to place blame on people for not being *strong* enough to resist.

But eating strategically isn't about strength. Eating strategically is about, well, strategy. That is, knowing what you will do in the face of any number of temptations you may experience allows you to eat the When Way and not give in to cream-filled pastries. The antidote to temptation is preparation.

Create your environment. If you work in an office where everyone brings in doughnuts three days a week, that's tough (unless you have a plan). If you live in a home where nine bags of chips are always sitting in the pantry, that's tough (unless you have a plan). If you make it a habit to eat drive-through food several times a week, that's tough (unless you have a plan).

Get the point? But fear not! You can do two things to manage temptation:

- *Create environments that allow you to make smart choices.* To deal with Doughnut Dave, you need to keep a stash of When Way snacks (like walnuts and dark chocolate discs) at the ready so you have something to turn to when you're tempted by the maple glazed. In environments you control, get rid of temptation. If you don't keep chips in your pantry, there's no easy way to gorge on them in the heat of the moment.
- *Plan ahead.* People get into the most trouble when they have no blueprint for tough situations. So if you're out for happy hour and someone orders nachos, you may partake because they look delicious. But what if you knew beforehand that this might happen? You eat a hearty and fiber-filled snack before heading to the bar, so the pile of chips doesn't look all that appealing. You can do the same thing for just about any temptation-filled situation. This takes a little planning, as well as some self-reflection. If you know your vulnerabilities, you can use the When Way principles to come up with solutions for handling them. That becomes your blueprint—and when the time comes, you simply follow the directions. You can also employ this strategy by looking at menus beforehand and making decisions before you sit down. That's how new habits form, and that's how you beat your reptilian biology.

This is why stocking your home with When Way foods is

the greatest gift you can give yourself. It means you'll always have healthy foods (see page 72 for our YES foods) on standby when temptation strikes, as well as options for on-the-go strategies (a bag of nuts in your purse or car is a classic). The When Way is easy when you make it so.

Bonus tip: Enlist a buddy or two (or three). It can be easier to plan and conquer temptation when you have support. Your partner or team can hold each other accountable and/or enjoy the healthy snacks together at happy hour.

The Best Tactics for Temptation

Following the When Way is half the battle in reaching your health goals. The other part: learning appropriate swaps and cooking techniques to make eating the When Way even easier. Here are three temptation-fighting principles that have helped us reach our goals:

Crunch with spice: We're not going to pretend that it's easy to contend with a bag of chips—especially if you're stressed, tired, or angry. There's a reason: Food manufacturers have pumped up these processed bags of artery cloggers with salt, fat, and other chemicals to make your mouth say "yes" even if your innards say "get the hell out." The best way to counteract a hankering is to make your own chip. Do it with raw veggies (carrots, celery, cauliflower, radishes, cucumbers, kale, you name it), but be creative about how you liven them up: a sprinkle of sea salt, Old Bay, curry powder, or another favorite spice can go a long way. That allows you to crunch away and fill your belly up enough (hello fiber!) to keep you satisfied, so that you can take the edge off.

Make stealth desserts: If you have more of a sweet tooth (like Dr. C), you may be drawn to shakes, pies, or pie-flavored shakes. And when you're craving some kind of dessert, you'll do just about anything to get your lips around a triple-decker cookie creation. What to do? Try this: In a bowl, mix up some almond butter and Greek yogurt (experiment with the ratio for a creamy consistency, but for starters, try a teaspoon almond butter in three tablespoons of yogurt; even add cocoa powder for extra flavor). Pop in a few walnuts and a spoonful of dark chocolate chips or cocoa nibs. It's a healthy alternative to sweet treats. But best of all, it's filling, luxurious, and has a *touch* of sweet, so you'll be satisfied and won't need to fall face-first into a pool of pudding.

Be mindful: You already know the laundry list of foods that you're tempted by. So when it comes to these, strive to eliminate the habit of the infinite feast. That is, when you do occasionally give in to consuming your favorite sinful delights, manage the intake. No need to order the XXL, no need to eat right out of the bag, no need to go back to have more and more and more. When you do indulge, control your portion size, eat slowly, savor the flavor, and then move on. As our friend Dr. Oz says, it's not the first or second bite that will do you in; it's the

15th and 16th and 150th bite. For example, just have one bite of that blueberry pie and don't worry about wasting the rest—you can share it with friends or family or just toss it. This, more than anything, will help you control your cravings. And it's OK to give in every once in a while—especially on special occasions.

THE 10 COMMANDMENTS OF THE WHEN WAY

As you've probably noticed, eating the When Way isn't about following orders; it's about setting in motion a slight shift—in "when" and "what" you eat. For the big picture, that shift means rethinking the traditional definitions and timing of meals. It also means knowing how to adapt your food choices to whatever circumstances you find yourself in.

There are no complicated rules or portions in the When Way; it's a means of thinking, of feeling, of eating. So as you embark on your new journey—and as you start to feel your body shifting with these new decisions and habits—we want to help make it simple. The 10 commandments of the When Way are our meal-to-mouth mantras. Post them on your fridge, pantry, bathroom mirror, or deeply in your hippocampus so you can always remember what to eat when.

1. **Eat when the sun is out.** Research shows that your body will perform best and be healthier when you limit the window you eat in to align with your circadian rhythm.

2. **More early, less later.** Stack your meals so that three quarters (or more) of what you eat comes before 2 p.m., the rest between then and sundown.

3. **Stop stereotyping foods.** Salads or salmon make for a great breakfast, and an egg-white frittata with veggies can be an awesome dinner.

4. **Balance your nutrients.** Don't get hung up on exact ratios of protein, fat, and carbohydrates. If you're eating When Way foods, you'll be getting the right mix of each, and the high-fiber vegetables and whole grains should keep you from overeating. (Just don't overdo it on the fats by doing shots of oil or downing entire bowls of guac or nuts.)

5. **You can eat well in any situation.** Life can throw you curveballs, but you don't have to swing and miss if you have strategies for dealing with whatever it brings you.

6. **Mistakes shouldn't derail you.** Don't worry if you eat a big dinner or stop eating the When Way for a day or two. Just pick things back up tomorrow.

7. **Be social.** Encourage your friends and family to join you in your quest to eat the When Way. Community is the best side dish you can have.

8. **Stay hydrated.** Water will not only make you healthier; it will also make you more satisfied.

9. **Make a plan.** Planning and preparation are temptation's kryptonite.

10. **Love what you eat.** Experiment with spices, flavors, and new ways of preparing healthy foods. A whole new world of eating—and a whole new body to go with it—await.

ACKNOWLEDGMENTS

FROM THE AUTHORS

With the publication of any book, those of us with our names on the cover tend to get all the attention. But the reality is that the sausage-making process (wait, that's not a When Way food) is what makes a book come to life. The team at National Geographic has been more than just a pleasure to work with. They have made this book a reality—from the early stages to the chef's-knife-sharp editing that made every chapter and sentence stronger. In particular, we want to thank Susan Goldberg, chief content officer of National Geographic Partners, and Lisa Thomas, editorial director and publisher of National Geographic Books, for having the vision to understand that this was a book that the world needed. Deputy Editor Hilary Black and Senior Editorial Project Manager Allyson Johnson helped sharpen our vision, from the big picture of the book to the very last detail of our message. Thanks to the exceptional art team who made the book a visual treat: Creative Director Melissa Farris, Senior Photo Editor Moira Haney, and the very talented illustrator Michael Shen. And we appreciate those who worked to get the book out and in your hands: Senior Director of Marketing Daneen Goodwin; Senior Director of Global Communications Ann Day; Communications Manager Kelly Forsythe; Director of Managing Editorial Jennifer Thornton; and Senior Production Editor Judith Klein. We are proud to be part of the National Geographic family that inspires and educates the world.

FROM MICHAEL F. ROIZEN, M.D.

There are few things more important to your health than (1) your food choices and (2) achieving an optimal physiology—whether you're facing a job interview, avoiding menopausal hot flashes, or implementing best practices to live longer. Imparting this philosophy to the world has been achieved through the 17 books I've written—none of which would have happened without super editor, thought leader, and agent Candice Fuhrman. She helped us articulate the vision for *What to Eat When* and provided much critical feedback along the way. Thank you for so much, Candice.

I've had the benefit of enormous help in developing recommendations for tasty food and want to thank the many coworkers, clinicians, scientists, and experts at the Cleveland Clinic, as well as coworkers in the Wellness Institute, who have made this possible. But prior to that I had many teachers. John La Puma, M.D., is a super doc and super chef who taught me how to cook and how to enjoy food more (and how to teach medical students to do the same, in such a fun way). He deserves much of my applause. Donna Szymanski and Dan Zakri helped him impart his extensive knowledge.

I am fortunate to work with many caregivers who have broken traditional molds to make the Cleveland Clinic the best place to work and to receive care—especially those who seek wellness as a culture and a long-term outcome. Both former CEO Dr. Toby Cosgrove and new CEO Dr. Tom Mihaljevic have stated that although the clinic is known as one of the best for treating disease, wellness (or extending your warranty) is what the clinic excels at for every employee and every patient we touch.

I am greatly indebted to wellness institute executive chef Jim Perko and chief nutritionist Kristin Kirkpatrick, who have created healthy, delicious food your body will love. And I have been fortunate to work over the past few years with the talented and creative Dr. Martin Harris, Dr. Bridget Duffy, Dr. Mike O'Donnell, Dennis Kenny, Dr. Rich Lang, Dr. Raul Seballos, Dr. Steven Feinleib, Dr. Barbara Messinger-Rapport, Dr. Roxanne Sukol, Mira Ilic, Sarah Balser, Karen Tabor, Karen Jones, Dr. Jim Young, and the Canyon Ranch experts, including former surgeon general Dr. Rich Carmona, who run the gamut from inner-city schoolteachers (thank you, Rosalind Strickland, the Reverend Otis Moss, and those who inspire) to executive coaches.

Our family was fully engaged in the process of creating this book: my son, Jeff Roizen, our M.D./Ph.D. endocrinologist at Children's Hospital of Pennsylvania; his M.D./Ph.D. wife, Sydney Shaffer; and mother-in-law Jill. Jennifer Roizen, our daughter and Ph.D. chemist at Duke, made great contributions including on the cover. And thanks to my wife's mother, Marion, who made great soups. To my wife, Nancy; my sister, Marsha; and brother-in-law, Richard Lowry, thank you for serving as critical readers.

These direct family members were joined at times by the "enlarged family" of the Katzes, Unobskeys, and Campodonicos. I also need to thank Mehmet and Lisa Oz, and their family, including master chef Daphne Oz, John Mauldin, Zack Wasserman, and others for encouraging and critiquing the concepts here.

The list of those who contributed scientifically is long, but a special thanks to Keith Roach and Anita Shreve, and to the many gerontologists and internists who read sections of the book for accuracy. And thanks to others on the RealAge team who validated and verified the health content and contributed their expertise to this book.

My administrative associates Beth Grubb and especially Jackie Frey made this work possible. My prior associate, Anne-Marie Prince, deserves special thanks, as does Diane Reverand—she started this process by telling me not to worry about offending medical colleagues. As long as the science was solid, they would understand that we were trying to motivate *you* to understand that you can control your genes.

And, of course, my co-authors Ted Spiker and Dr. Michael Crupain made the science, foods, and writing much more accurate and enjoyable—I'm sure you'll see what I mean.

Having a great partner to alleviate stress daily is clearly a magnificent way to make your RealAge younger and extend your warranty. Nancy, just looking at you is a joy and makes my telomeres grow nightly, I'm sure.

Finally, thanks to all of you for believing in this book, which will help you love healthful food, make great choices, be in optimal shape for every condition, and live younger and longer. To see fewer people needing the illness part of our medical system for many more years would be the best reward any physician could want.

FROM MICHAEL J. CRUPAIN, M.D.

There are lots of "secrets to success": putting yourself in the right place at the right time, being persistent, keeping your eyes open for opportunity, and taking calculated risks. Having a little bit of luck helps too. These all came into play a few years ago when I was at a fund-raiser for HealthCorps (a charity started by Mehmet and Lisa Oz to teach teens about nutrition, physical fitness, and mental resilience) and told Mike R. that I had some extra time and would love to work on a project with him. The next thing I knew we were writing a book! Mike R. is one of the smartest, most passionate, generous, and just about nicest guys around, and I'm very thankful to him for bringing me on to this project and having the opportunity to become friends and co-authors—and of course, to learn from him about the world of books and TMAO. And of course, a big shout-out to Ted Spiker, who is both a great partner and smart and clever writer who knew just how to keep us organized and find our collective voice.

Of course, I have to acknowledge Mehmet Oz, who I have had the privilege of working with for many years now. First, I'm sorry for stealing your writing partner. Second, I'm appreciative of what I've learned from you about questioning dogma and keeping an open mind. When Mike and I first started working on this project, I was skeptical about the role of "when" in health—but I kept an open mind and was amazed about just how important it was. Also, thanks to Mehmet for introducing me to Mike and always encouraging me to do more. I also want to thank all of the people at the *Dr. Oz Show:* Amy, Stacy, Kathy, Christine, Ali, Tina, Cheryl, Jacqueline, Jessica, Lisa, Nicole, Ann, Marty, and everyone else who taught me so much about how to talk to real people about complex medical topics. And finally, thanks to Michael Shen, who is currently an awesome internist-in-training but formerly a researcher in my department, and the artist behind this book's clever and illuminating illustrations.

Before joining the *Dr. Oz Show,* I spent about three years at *Consumer Reports.* There, Dr. Urvashi Rangan taught me to be a rigorous researcher and good communicator. One of the most important skills I learned from Urvashi was how to look at research and make a good decision (even in the face of imperfect information) to improve public health. That came in handy on this project. I'd also like to acknowledge all the other folks at CR who taught me how to be a better writer and advocate for consumer health: Jen Schecter, Jean Halloran, Michael Hansen, Andrea Rock, and Trisha Calvo.

Dr. Miriam Alexander, the program director during my preventive medicine residency at the Johns Hopkins Bloomberg School of Public Health, is a formative figure in my life. Miriam took a chance on an unusual candidate, which has allowed me to realize my dream of combining food and medicine. She has also been a great friend and mentor, and her encouragement and guidance laid the path to this project. I'd like to thank my other mentor from the school of public health, Dr. Bob Lawrence, along with all of my colleagues at the Center for a Livable Future. Bob is a true visionary leader in medicine and public health and was the first person to show me how food and agriculture fell into the domain of medicine.

I have to also thank Walter Luque, an amazing pastry chef who helped me find my passion for food and cooking, and showed me how to take it to the next level. I also owe a great debt of gratitude to my friend Silvestro Silvestori, who taught me what the Mediterranean diet is really about—and the importance of following your dreams. Thanks to my other favorite chefs Sue Torres and Björn Böttcher, who let me cook with them in their kitchens. And of course, I am grateful to my closest friends and family, who have learned to accept that I'm either going to be cooking or taking them on a culinary adventure.

Finally, thanks to my parents, Diane and Daniel Crupain, who not only gave me life but the love and support I need, no matter what. It was they who inspired my love of food and health, and for that I will be forever grateful.

GLOSSARY

anti-inflammatory: A substance that decreases inflammation in the body.

antioxidant: An anti-inflammatory substance.

cholesterol: A molecule that helps our bodies function. LDL is the bad kind, HDL, the healthy kind.

chrononutrition: The idea that eating habits should align with optimum times in your 24-hour cycle for optimum health.

circadian rhythm: Your body's clock, which operates in a 24-hour cycle and sends signals to help you sleep, wake, eat, and so on.

glucose: Blood sugar; the main energy source for your body to operate. But excess in your blood is bad for your body and brain.

glycemic index: A ranking of foods with carbohydrates in terms of how they influence blood glucose levels when eaten.

glycogen: A form of stored energy (converted from glucose) that your body can use if no glucose is available.

high-glycemic food: A food with a high score on the glycemic index, so it causes a rapid rise in blood sugar when eaten.

inflammation: A defense mechanism in the body designed to prevent harm that can do the opposite when present chronically.

insulin: Hormone secreted by the pancreas to shuttle sugar (glucose) from blood into your cells so it can be used for energy.

insulin resistance: When the body's cells do not react normally to the presence of insulin.

insulin sensitivity: A measure of how reactive to insulin the body's cells are.

macronutrients: The major nutritional building blocks in your body that you need in large quantities. These are protein, fat, and carbohydrates.

metabolic syndrome: A cluster of conditions marked by insulin resistance, high blood pressure, overweight, high blood lipids associated with heart disease, and diabetes.

microbiome: The bacteria in your body's ecosystem, including those in your gut. This network is in constant motion, because the makeup of the bacteria is influenced by a number of complex factors, including what you eat.

micronutrients: These compounds are essential for optimal body function. You need less of these than macronutrients. Think vitamins and minerals.

phytonutrient: Chemical in plants believed to be beneficial for health.

salmon: Mike R's favorite food (but if you're reading the glossary you already knew that!).

suprachiasmatic nucleus: The area of the brain that controls your circadian rhythm.

SOURCES

INTRODUCTION

1. Cardenas, Diana. "Let Not Thy Food Be Confused With Thy Medicine: The Hippocratic Mis-quotation." *European Society for Clinical Nutrition and Metabolism* 8, no. 6 (2013): e262. doi:// doi.org/10.1016/j.clnme.2013.10.002.
2. Sawyer, Bradley, and Cynthia Cox. "How Does Health Spending in the U.S. Compare to Other Countries?" Peterson-Kaiser, accessed July 28, 2018. www.healthsystemtracker.org/chart -collection/health-spending-u-s-compare-countries/.
3. Meisler, Laurie. "Americans Die Younger Despite Spending the Most on Health Care." Bloomberg .com, Aug. 2, 2017. www.bloomberg.com/graphics/2017-health-care-spending/.
4. Choi, Sang-Woon, and Simonetta Friso. "Epigenetics: A New Bridge Between Nutrition and Health." *Advances in Nutrition* 1, no. 1 (Nov. 2010): 8–16. doi:10.3945/an.110.1004.
5. Micha, Renata, Jose L. Peñalvo, Frederick Cudhea, Fumiaki Imamura, Colin D. Rehm, and Dariush Mozaffarian. "Association Between Dietary Factors and Mortality From Heart Disease, Stroke, and Type 2 Diabetes in the United States." *JAMA* 317, no. 9 (Mar. 7, 2017): 912–24. doi:10.1001/jama.2017.0947.
6. American Cancer Society. "Lifetime Risk of Developing or Dying From Cancer." Accessed July 28, 2018. www.cancer.org/cancer/cancer-basics/lifetime-probability-of-developing -or-dying-from-cancer.html.
7. Anand, Preetha, Ajaikumar Kunnumakara, Chitra Sundaram, Kuzhuvelil Harikumar, Sheeja Tharakan, Oiki Lai, Bokyung Sung, and Bharat Aggarwal. "Cancer Is a Preventable Disease That Requires Major Lifestyle Changes." *Pharmaceutical Research* 25, no. 9 (Sept. 2008): 2097–116. doi:10.1007/s11095-008-9661-9.

CHAPTER 1

1. Mohawk, Jennifer A., Carla B. Green, and Joseph S. Takahashi. "Central and Peripheral Circa-dian Clocks in Mammals." *Annual Review of Neuroscience* 35, no. 1 (2012): 445–62. doi:10.1146/ annurev-neuro-060909-153128.
2. Herculano-Houzel, Suzana. "The Human Brain in Numbers: A Linearly Scaled-Up Primate Brain." *Frontiers in Human Neuroscience* 3 (Nov. 9, 2009). doi:10.3389/neuro.09.031.2009.
3. Freeman, G. Mark, Rebecca M. Krock, Sara J. Aton, Paul Thaben, and Erik D. Herzog. "GABA Networks Destabilize Genetic Oscillations in the Circadian Pacemaker." *Neuron* 78, no. 5 (June 5, 2013): 799–806. doi:10.1016/j.neuron.2013.04.003.
4. Hastings, Michael H., Akhilesh B. Reddy, and Elizabeth S. Maywood. "A Clockwork Web: Circa-dian Timing in Brain and Periphery, in Health and Disease." *Nature Reviews Neuroscience* 4, no. 8 (Aug. 2003): 649–61. doi:10.1038/nrn1177.
5. NIOSH. "CDC—Work Schedules: Shift Work and Long Hours: NIOSH Workplace Safety and Health Topic." Accessed July 28, 2018. www.cdc.gov/niosh/topics/workschedules/default .html.
6. Givens, Marjory L., Kristen C. Malecki, Paul E. Peppard, Mari Palta, Adnan Said, Corinne D. Engelman, Matthew C. Walsh, and F. Javier Nieto. "Shiftwork, Sleep Habits, and Metabolic

Disparities: Results From the Survey of the Health of Wisconsin." *Sleep Health* 1, no. 2 (June 2015): 115–20. doi:10.1016/j.sleh.2015.04.014.

7. Zhao, Isabella, Fiona Bogossian, and Catherine Turner. "Does Maintaining or Changing Shift Types Affect BMI? A Longitudinal Study." *Journal of Occupational and Environmental Medicine* 54, no. 5 (May 2012): 525–31. doi:10.1097/JOM.0b013e31824e1073.

8. McHill, Andrew W., Edward L. Melanson, Janine Higgins, Elizabeth Connick, Thomas M. Moehlman, Ellen R. Stothard, and Kenneth P. Wright. "Impact of Circadian Misalignment on Energy Metabolism During Simulated Nightshift Work." *Proceedings of the National Academy of Sciences of the United States of America* 111, no. 48 (Dec. 2, 2014): 17302–307. doi:10.1073/pnas.1412021111.

9. Mosendane, T., and F. J. Raal. "Shift Work and Its Effects on the Cardiovascular System." *Cardiovascular Journal of Africa* 19, no. 4 (July–Aug., 2008): 210–15.

10. Bechtold, David A., and Andrew S. I. Loudon. "Hypothalamic Clocks and Rhythms in Feeding Behaviour." *Trends in Neurosciences* 36, no. 2 (Feb. 2013): 74–82. doi:10.1016/j.tins.2012.12.007.

11. Scheer, Frank A. J. L., Christopher J. Morris, and Steven A. Shea. "The Internal Circadian Clock Increases Hunger and Appetite in the Evening Independent of Food Intake and Other Behaviors." *Obesity* (Silver Spring, MD) 21, no. 3 (Mar. 2013): 421–23. doi:10.1002/oby.20351.

12. Mendoza, J. "Circadian Clocks: Setting Time by Food." *Journal of Neuroendocrinology* 19, no. 2 (Feb. 2007): 127–37. doi:10.1111/j.1365-2826.2006.01510.x.

13. Shi, Shu-qun, Tasneem S. Ansari, Owen P. McGuinness, David H. Wasserman, and Carl Hirschie Johnson. "Circadian Disruption Leads to Insulin Resistance and Obesity." *Current Biology: CB* 23, no. 5 (Mar. 4, 2013): 372–81. doi:10.1016/j.cub.2013.01.048.

14. Saad, Ahmed, Chiara Dalla Man, Debashis K. Nandy, James A. Levine, Adil E. Bharucha, Robert A. Rizza, Rita Basu, et al. "Diurnal Pattern to Insulin Secretion and Insulin Action in Healthy Individuals." *Diabetes* 61, no. 11 (Nov. 2012): 2691–700. doi:10.2337/db11-1478.

15. Morgan, L. M., F. Aspostolakou, J. Wright, and R. Gama. "Diurnal Variations in Peripheral Insulin Resistance and Plasma Non-Esterified Fatty Acid Concentrations: A Possible Link?" *Annals of Clinical Biochemistry* 36 (Pt. 4) (July 1999): 447–50. doi:10.1177/000456329903600407.

16. Bandín, C., F. A. J. L. Scheer, A. J. Luque, V. Ávila-Gandía, S. Zamora, J. A. Madrid, P. Gómez-Abellán, and M. Garaulet. "Meal Timing Affects Glucose Tolerance, Substrate Oxidation and Circadian-Related Variables: A Randomized, Crossover Trial." *International Journal of Obesity* (2005) 39, no. 5 (May 2015): 828–33. doi:10.1038/ijo.2014.182.

17. Van Cauter, E., K. S. Polonsky, and A. J. Scheen. "Roles of Circadian Rhythmicity and Sleep in Human Glucose Regulation." *Endocrine Reviews* 18, no. 5 (Oct. 1997): 716–38. doi:10.1210/edrv.18.5.0317.

18. Carrasco-Benso, Maria P., Belen Rivero-Gutierrez, Jesus Lopez-Minguez, Andrea Anzola, Antoni Diez-Noguera, Juan A. Madrid, Juan A. Lujan, et al. "Human Adipose Tissue Expresses Intrinsic Circadian Rhythm in Insulin Sensitivity." *FASEB Journal: Official Publication of the Federation of American Societies for Experimental Biology* 30, no. 9 (Sept. 2016): 3117–123. doi:10.1096/fj.201600269RR.

19. Bray, M. S., W. F. Ratcliffe, M. H. Grenett, R. A. Brewer, K. L. Gamble, and M. E. Young. "Quantitative Analysis of Light-Phase Restricted Feeding Reveals Metabolic Dyssynchrony in Mice." *International Journal of Obesity* (2005) 37, no. 6 (June 2012): 843–52. doi:10.1038/ijo.2012.137.

20. Bray, M. S., J. -Y Tsai, C. Villegas-Montoya, B. B. Boland, Z. Blasier, O. Egbejimi, M. Kueht, and M. E. Young. "Time-of-Day-Dependent Dietary Fat Consumption Influences Multiple Cardiometabolic Syndrome Parameters in Mice." *International Journal of Obesity* (2005) 34, no. 11 (Nov. 2010): 1589–98. doi:10.1038/ijo.2010.63.

21. Garaulet, M., P. Gómez-Abellán, J. J. Alburquerque-Béjar, Y. -C Lee, J. M. Ordovás, and F. A. J. L. Scheer. "Timing of Food Intake Predicts Weight Loss Effectiveness." *International Journal of Obesity* (2005) 37, no. 4 (Apr. 2013): 604–11. doi:10.1038/ijo.2012.229.

22. Bandín et al. "Meal Timing Affects Glucose Tolerance, Substrate Oxidation and Circadian-Related Variables."

23. Thaiss, Christoph A., David Zeevi, Maayan Levy, Gili Zilberman-Schapira, Jotham Suez, Anouk C.

Sources

Tengeler, Lior Abramson, et al. "Transkingdom Control of Microbiota Diurnal Oscillations Promotes Metabolic Homeostasis." *Cell* 159, no. 3 (Oct. 23, 2014): 514–29. doi:10.1016/j.cell.2014.09.048.

24. Thaiss et al. "Transkingdom Control of Microbiota Diurnal Oscillations."
25. Ibid.

CHAPTER 2

1. Sacks, Frank M., Alice H. Lichtenstein, Jason H. Y. Wu, Lawrence J. Appel, Mark A. Creager, Penny M. Kris-Etherton, Michael Miller, et al. "Dietary Fats and Cardiovascular Disease: A Presidential Advisory From the American Heart Association." *Circulation* 136, no. 3 (July 18, 2017): e23. doi:10.1161/CIR.0000000000000510.

2. Devkota, Suzanne, Yunwei Wang, Mark W. Musch, Vanessa Leone, Hannah Fehlner-Peach, Anuradha Nadimpalli, Dionysios A. Antonopoulos, et al. "Dietary-Fat-Induced Taurocholic Acid Promotes Pathobiont Expansion and Colitis in Il10-/- Mice." *Nature* 487, no. 7405 (July 5, 2012): 104–08. doi:10.1038/nature11225.

3. Hernández, Elisa Álvarez, Sabine Kahl, Anett Seelig, Paul Begovatz, Martin Irmler, Yuliya Kupriyanova, Bettina Nowotny, et al. "Acute Dietary Fat Intake Initiates Alterations in Energy Metabolism and Insulin Resistance." *The Journal of Clinical Investigation* 127, no. 2 (Feb. 1, 2017): 695–708. doi:10.1172/JCI89444.

4. Devore, Elizabeth E., Meir J. Stampfer, Monique M. B. Breteler, Bernard Rosner, Jae Hee Kang, Olivia Okereke, Frank B. Hu, and Francine Grodstein. "Dietary Fat Intake and Cognitive Decline in Women With Type 2 Diabetes." *Diabetes Care* 32, no. 4 (Apr. 2009): 635–40. doi:10.2337/dc08-1741.

5. Okereke, Olivia I., Bernard A. Rosner, Dae H. Kim, Jae H. Kang, Nancy R. Cook, JoAnn E. Manson, Julie E. Buring, et al. "Dietary Fat Types and 4-Year Cognitive Change in Community-Dwelling Older Women." *Annals of Neurology* 72, no. 1 (July 2012): 124–34. doi:10.1002/ana.23593.

6. Brennan, Sarah F., Jayne V. Woodside, Paula M. Lunny, Chris R. Cardwell, and Marie M. Cantwell. "Dietary Fat and Breast Cancer Mortality: A Systematic Review and Meta-Analysis." *Critical Reviews in Food Science and Nutrition* 57, no. 10 (July 3, 2017): 1999–2008. doi:10.1080/10408398.2012.724481.

7. Yang, Jae Jeong, Danxia Yu, Yumie Takata, Stephanie A. Smith-Warner, William Blot, Emily White, Kim Robien, et al. "Dietary Fat Intake and Lung Cancer Risk: A Pooled Analysis." *Journal of Clinical Oncology: Official Journal of the American Society of Clinical Oncology* 35, no. 26 (Sept. 10, 2017): 3055–64. doi:10.1200/JCO.2017.73.3329.

8. Sacks et al. "Dietary Fats and Cardiovascular Disease."

9. Paniagua, J. A., A. Gallego de la Sacristana, I. Romero, A. Vidal-Puig, J. M. Latre, E. Sanchez, P. Perez-Martinez, et al. "Monounsaturated Fat-Rich Diet Prevents Central Body Fat Distribution and Decreases Postprandial Adiponectin Expression Induced by a Carbohydrate-Rich Diet in Insulin-Resistant Subjects." *Diabetes Care* 30, no. 7 (July 2007): 1717–23. doi:10.2337/dc06-2220.

10. Mozaffarian, Dariush, and Jason H. Y. Wu. "Omega-3 Fatty Acids and Cardiovascular Disease: Effects on Risk Factors, Molecular Pathways, and Clinical Events." *Journal of the American College of Cardiology* 58, no. 20 (Nov. 8, 2011): 2047–67. doi:10.1016/j.jacc.2011.06.063.

11. Lukaschek, Karoline, Clemens von Schacky, Johannes Kruse, and Karl-Heinz Ladwig. "Cognitive Impairment Is Associated With a Low Omega-3 Index in the Elderly: Results From the KORA-Age Study." *Dementia and Geriatric Cognitive Disorders* 42, no. 3–4 (2016): 236–45. doi:10.1159/000448805.

12. Pasiakos, Stefan M., Sanjiv Agarwal, Harris R. Lieberman, and Victor L. Fulgoni. "Sources and Amounts of Animal, Dairy, and Plant Protein Intake of US Adults in 2007–2010." *Nutrients* 7, no. 8 (Aug. 21, 2015): 7058–69. doi:10.3390/nu7085322.

13. Le, Michael H., Pardha Devaki, Nghiem B. Ha, Dae Won Jun, Helen S. Te, Ramsey C. Cheung, and Mindie H. Nguyen. "Prevalence of Non-Alcoholic Fatty Liver Disease and Risk Factors for Advanced Fibrosis and Mortality in the United States." *PloS One* 12, no. 3 (2017): e0173499. doi:10.1371/journal.pone.0173499.

14. Centers for Disease Control and Prevention. National Diabetes Statistics Report, 2017. Atlanta, GA: Centers for Disease Control and Prevention, U.S. Department of Health and Human Services, 2017.

15. Lee, Jane J., Alison Pedley, Udo Hoffmann, Joseph M. Massaro, and Caroline S. Fox. "Association of Changes in Abdominal Fat Quantity and Quality With Incident Cardiovascular Disease Risk Factors." *Journal of the American College of Cardiology* 68, no. 14 (Oct. 4, 2016): 1509–21. doi:10.1016/j.jacc.2016.06.067.

16. Wang, Fei, Liyuan Liu, Shude Cui, Fuguo Tian, Zhimin Fan, Cuizhi Geng, Xuchen Cao, et al. "Distinct Effects of Body Mass Index and Waist/Hip Ratio on Risk of Breast Cancer by Joint Estrogen and Progestogen Receptor Status: Results From a Case-Control Study in Northern and Eastern China and Implications for Chemoprevention." *The Oncologist* 22, no. 12 (Dec. 2017): 1431–43. doi:10.1634/theoncologist.2017-0148.

17. von Hafe, Pedro, Francisco Pina, Ana Pérez, Margarida Tavares, and Henrique Barros. "Visceral Fat Accumulation as a Risk Factor for Prostate Cancer." *Obesity Research* 12, no. 12 (Dec. 2004): 1930–35. doi:10.1038/oby.2004.242.

18. Swainson, Michelle G., Alan M. Batterham, Costas Tsakirides, Zoe H. Rutherford, and Karen Hind. "Prediction of Whole-Body Fat Percentage and Visceral Adipose Tissue Mass From Five Anthropometric Variables." *PloS One* 12, no. 5 (2017): e0177175. doi:10.1371/journal.pone.0177175.

CHAPTER 3

1. Melkani, Girish C., and Satchidananda Panda. "Time-Restricted Feeding for Prevention and Treatment of Cardiometabolic Disorders." *The Journal of Physiology* 595, no. 12 (June 15, 2017): 3691–3700. doi:10.1113/JP273094.

2. Hatori, Megumi, Christopher Vollmers, Amir Zarrinpar, Luciano DiTacchio, Eric A. Bushong, Shubhroz Gill, Mathias Leblanc, et al. "Time-Restricted Feeding Without Reducing Caloric Intake Prevents Metabolic Diseases in Mice Fed a High-Fat Diet." *Cell Metabolism* 15, no. 6 (June 6, 2012): 848–60. doi:10.1016/j.cmet.2012.04.019.

3. Gill, Shubhroz, and Satchidananda Panda. "A Smartphone App Reveals Erratic Diurnal Eating Patterns in Humans That Can Be Modulated for Health Benefits." *Cell Metabolism* 22, no. 5 (Nov. 3, 2015): 789–98. doi:10.1016/j.cmet.2015.09.005.

4. St-Onge, Marie-Pierre, Jamy Ard, Monica L. Baskin, Stephanie E. Chiuve, Heather M. Johnson, Penny Kris-Etherton, and Krista Varady. "Meal Timing and Frequency: Implications for Cardio-vascular Disease Prevention: A Scientific Statement From the American Heart Association." *Circulation* 135, no. 9 (Feb. 28, 2017): e121. doi:10.1161/CIR.0000000000000476.

5. Scully, T. *The Art of Cookery in the Middle Ages.* Suffolk, UK: The Boydell Press, 1995.

6. Rupp, Rebecca. "Cereal: How Kellogg Invented a 'Better' Breakfast." *National Geographic,* Jan. 26, 2015.

7. Nicklas, T. A., L. Myers, C. Reger, B. Beech, and G. S. Berenson. "Impact of Breakfast Consump-tion on Nutritional Adequacy of the Diets of Young Adults in Bogalusa, Louisiana: Ethnic and Gender Contrasts." *Journal of the American Dietetic Association* 98, no. 12 (Dec. 1998): 1432–38. doi:10.1016/S0002-8223(98)00325-3.

8. Bi, Huashan, Yong Gan, Chen Yang, Yawen Chen, Xinyue Tong, and Zuxun Lu. "Breakfast Skip-ping and the Risk of Type 2 Diabetes: A Meta-Analysis of Observational Studies." *Public Health Nutrition* 18, no. 16 (Nov. 2015): 3013–19. doi:10.1017/S1368980015000257.

9. Lee, Tae Sic, Jai Soon Kim, Yoo Jung Hwang, and Yon Chul Park. "Habit of Eating Breakfast Is

Sources

Associated With a Lower Risk of Hypertension." *Journal of Lifestyle Medicine* 6, no. 2 (Sept. 2016): 64-67. doi:10.15280/jlm.2016.6.2.64.

10. Cahill, Leah E., Stephanie E. Chiuve, Rania A. Mekary, Majken K. Jensen, Alan J. Flint, Frank B. Hu, and Eric B. Rimm. "Prospective Study of Breakfast Eating and Incident Coronary Heart Disease in a Cohort of Male US Health Professionals." *Circulation* 128, no. 4 (July 23, 2013): 337-43. doi:10.1161/CIRCULATIONAHA.113.001474.

11. Cho, Sungsoo, Marion Dietrich, Coralie J. P. Brown, Celeste A. Clark, and Gladys Block. "The Effect of Breakfast Type on Total Daily Energy Intake and Body Mass Index: Results From the Third National Health and Nutrition Examination Survey (NHANES III)." *Journal of the American College of Nutrition* 22, no. 4 (Aug. 2003): 296-302.

12. Wennberg, Maria, Per E. Gustafsson, Patrik Wennberg, and Anne Hammarström. "Poor Breakfast Habits in Adolescence Predict the Metabolic Syndrome in Adulthood." *Public Health Nutrition* 18, no. 1 (Jan. 2015): 122-29. doi:10.1017/S1368980013003509.

13. Schlundt, D. G., J. O. Hill, T. Sbrocco, J. Pope-Cordle, and T. Sharp. "The Role of Breakfast in the Treatment of Obesity: A Randomized Clinical Trial." *The American Journal of Clinical Nutrition* 55, no. 3 (Mar. 1992): 645-51. doi:10.1093/ajcn/55.3.645.

14. Farshchi, Hamid R., Moira A. Taylor, and Ian A. Macdonald. "Deleterious Effects of Omitting Breakfast on Insulin Sensitivity and Fasting Lipid Profiles in Healthy Lean Women." *The American Journal of Clinical Nutrition* 81, no. 2 (Feb. 2005): 388-96. doi:10.1093/ajcn.81.2.388.

15. Jakubowicz, Daniela, Julio Wainstein, Bo Ahren, Zohar Landau, Yosefa Bar-Dayan, and Oren Froy. "Fasting Until Noon Triggers Increased Postprandial Hyperglycemia and Impaired Insulin Response After Lunch and Dinner in Individuals With Type 2 Diabetes: A Randomized Clinical Trial." *Diabetes Care* 38, no. 10 (Oct. 2015): 1820-26. doi:10.2337/dc15-0761.

16. Chowdhury, Enhad A., Judith D. Richardson, Geoffrey D. Holman, Kostas Tsintzas, Dylan Thompson, and James A. Betts. "The Causal Role of Breakfast in Energy Balance and Health: A Randomized Controlled Trial in Obese Adults." *The American Journal of Clinical Nutrition* 103, no. 3 (Mar. 2016): 747-56. doi:10.3945/ajcn.115.122044.

17. Betts, James A., Judith D. Richardson, Enhad A. Chowdhury, Geoffrey D. Holman, Kostas Tsintzas, and Dylan Thompson. "The Causal Role of Breakfast in Energy Balance and Health: A Randomized Controlled Trial in Lean Adults." *The American Journal of Clinical Nutrition* 100, no. 2 (Aug. 2014): 539-47. doi:10.3945/ajcn.114.083402.

18. Kobayashi, Fumi, Hitomi Ogata, Naomi Omi, Shoichiro Nagasaka, Sachiko Yamaguchi, Masanobu Hibi, and Kumpei Tokuyama. "Effect of Breakfast Skipping on Diurnal Variation of Energy Metabolism and Blood Glucose." *Obesity Research & Clinical Practice* 8, no. 3 (May–June 2014): 201. doi:10.1016/j.orcp.2013.01.001.

19. Baron, Kelly G., Kathryn J. Reid, Andrew S. Kern, and Phyllis C. Zee. "Role of Sleep Timing in Caloric Intake and BMI." *Obesity* 19, no. 7 (July 2011): 1374-81. doi:10.1038/oby.2011.100.

20. Bo, Simona, Giovanni Musso, Guglielmo Beccuti, Maurizio Fadda, Debora Fedele, Roberto Gambino, Luigi Gentile, et al. "Consuming More of Daily Caloric Intake at Dinner Predisposes to Obesity. A 6-Year Population-Based Prospective Cohort Study." *PloS One* 9, no. 9 (2014): e108467. doi:10.1371/journal.pone.0108467.

21. Jakubowicz, Daniela, Maayan Barnea, Julio Wainstein, and Oren Froy. "High Caloric Intake at Breakfast vs. Dinner Differentially Influences Weight Loss of Overweight and Obese Women." *Obesity* 21, no. 12 (Dec. 2013): 2504-12. doi:10.1002/oby.20460.

22. Garaulet, M., P. Gómez-Abellán, J. J. Alburquerque-Béjar, Y. -C Lee, J. M. Ordovás, and F. A. J. L. Scheer. "Timing of Food Intake Predicts Weight Loss Effectiveness." *International Journal of Obesity* (2005) 37, no. 4 (Apr. 2013a): 604-11. doi:10.1038/ijo.2012.229.

23. Leidy, Heather J., Mandi J. Bossingham, Richard D. Mattes, and Wayne W. Campbell. "Increased Dietary Protein Consumed at Breakfast Leads to an Initial and Sustained Feeling of Fullness During Energy Restriction Compared to Other Meal Times." *The British Journal of Nutrition* 101, no. 6 (Mar. 2009): 798-803.

24. Foley, Nicholas C., David C. Jangraw, Christopher Peck, and Jacqueline Gottlieb. "Novelty Enhances Visual Salience Independently of Reward in the Parietal Lobe." *The Journal of Neuroscience: The Official Journal of the Society for Neuroscience* 34, no. 23 (June 4, 2014): 7947–57. doi:10.1523/JNEUROSCI.4171-13.2014.

25. Pot, G. K., R. Hardy, and A. M. Stephen. "Irregular Consumption of Energy Intake in Meals Is Associated With a Higher Cardiometabolic Risk in Adults of a British Birth Cohort." *International Journal of Obesity* (2005) 38, no. 12 (Dec. 2014): 1518–24. doi:10.1038/ijo.2014.51.

26. Farshchi, H. R., M. A. Taylor, and I. A. Macdonald. "Regular Meal Frequency Creates More Appropriate Insulin Sensitivity and Lipid Profiles Compared With Irregular Meal Frequency in Healthy Lean Women." *European Journal of Clinical Nutrition* 58, no. 7 (July 2004): 1071–77. doi:10.1038/sj.ejcn.1601935.

27. Farshchi, Hamid R., Moira A. Taylor, and Ian A. Macdonald. "Beneficial Metabolic Effects of Regular Meal Frequency on Dietary Thermogenesis, Insulin Sensitivity, and Fasting Lipid Profiles in Healthy Obese Women." *The American Journal of Clinical Nutrition* 81, no. 1 (Jan. 2005): 16–24. doi:10.1093/ajcn/81.1.16.

28. Longo, Valter D., and Mark P. Mattson. "Fasting: Molecular Mechanisms and Clinical Applications." *Cell Metabolism* 19, no. 2 (Feb. 4, 2014): 181–92. doi:10.1016/j.cmet.2013.12.008.

29. Brandhorst, Sebastian, In Young Choi, Min Wei, Chia Wei Cheng, Sargis Sedrakyan, Gerardo Navarrete, Louis Dubeau, et al. "A Periodic Diet That Mimics Fasting Promotes Multi-System Regeneration, Enhanced Cognitive Performance, and Healthspan." *Cell Metabolism* 22, no. 1 (July 7, 2015): 86–99. doi:10.1016/j.cmet.2015.05.012.

30. Soeters, Maarten R., Peter B. Soeters, Marieke G. Schooneman, Sander M. Houten, and Johannes A. Romijn. "Adaptive Reciprocity of Lipid and Glucose Metabolism in Human Short-Term Starvation." *American Journal of Physiology—Endocrinology and Metabolism* 303, no. 12 (Dec. 15, 2012): 1397. doi:10.1152/ajpendo.00397.2012.

31. Klein, S., Y. Sakurai, J. A. Romijn, and R. M. Carroll. "Progressive Alterations in Lipid and Glucose Metabolism During Short-Term Fasting in Young Adult Men." *The American Journal of Physiology* 265, no. 5 Pt. 1 (Nov. 1993): 801. doi:10.1152/ajpendo.1993.265.5.E801.

32. Mattson, Mark P., Keelin Moehl, Nathaniel Ghena, Maggie Schmaedick, and Aiwu Cheng. "Intermittent Metabolic Switching, Neuroplasticity and Brain Health." *Nature Reviews Neuroscience* 19, no. 2 (Feb. 2018): 63–80. doi:10.1038/nrn.2017.156.

CHAPTER 4

1. Keenan, Michael J., June Zhou, Maren Hegsted, Christine Pelkman, Holiday A. Durham, Diana B. Coulon, and Roy J. Martin. "Role of Resistant Starch in Improving Gut Health, Adiposity, and Insulin Resistance." *Advances in Nutrition* 6, no. 2 (Mar. 2015): 198–205. doi:10.3945/an.114.007419.

2. Neale, Elizabeth P., Linda C. Tapsell, Allison Martin, Marijka J. Batterham, Cinthya Wibisono, and Yasmine C. Probst. "Impact of Providing Walnut Samples in a Lifestyle Intervention for Weight Loss: A Secondary Analysis of the HealthTrack Trial." *Food & Nutrition Research* 61, no. 1 (2017): 1344522. doi:10.1080/16546628.2017.1344522.

3. Estruch, Ramón, Emilio Ros, Jordi Salas-Salvadó, Maria-Isabel Covas, Dolores Corella, Fernando Arós, Enrique Gómez-Gracia, et al. "Primary Prevention of Cardiovascular Disease With a Mediterranean Diet Supplemented With Extra-Virgin Olive Oil Or Nuts." *The New England Journal of Medicine* 378, no. 25 (June 21, 2018): e34. doi:10.1056/NEJMoa1800389.

4. Guasch-Ferré, Marta, Mònica Bulló, Miguel Ángel Martínez-González, Emilio Ros, Dolores Corella, Ramon Estruch, Montserrat Fitó, et al. "Frequency of Nut Consumption and Mortality Risk in the PREDIMED Nutrition Intervention Trial." *BMC Medicine* 11, (July 16, 2013): 164. doi:10.1186/1741-7015-11-164.

5. Holscher, Hannah D., Heather M. Guetterman, Kelly S. Swanson, Ruopeng An, Nirupa R.

Sources

Matthan, Alice H. Lichtenstein, Janet A. Novotny, and David J. Baer. "Walnut Consumption Alters the Gastrointestinal Microbiota, Microbially Derived Secondary Bile Acids, and Health Markers in Healthy Adults: A Randomized Controlled Trial." *The Journal of Nutrition* 148, no. 6 (June 1, 2018): 861–67. doi:10.1093/jn/nxy004.

6. United States Department of Agriculture Economic Research Service. "Food Availability and Consumption." www.ers.usda.gov/data-products/ag-and-food-statistics-charting-the -essentials/food-availability-and-consumption/.

7. Vinjé, Sarah, Erik Stroes, Max Nieuwdorp, and Stan L. Hazen. "The Gut Microbiome as Novel Cardio-Metabolic Target: The Time Has Come!" *European Heart Journal* 35, no. 14 (Apr. 2014): 883–87.

8. Zhu, Weifei, Jill C. Gregory, Elin Org, Jennifer A. Buffa, Nilaksh Gupta, Zeneng Wang, Lin Li, et al. "Gut Microbial Metabolite TMAO Enhances Platelet Hyperreactivity and Thrombosis Risk." *Cell* 165, no. 1 (Mar. 24, 2016): 111–24. doi:10.1016/j.cell.2016.02.011.

9. Fogelman, Alan M. "TMAO Is Both a Biomarker and a Renal Toxin." *Circulation Research* 116, no. 3 (Jan. 30, 2015): 396–97. doi:10.1161/CIRCRESAHA.114.305680.

10. Xu, Rong, QuanQiu Wang, and Li Li. "A Genome-Wide Systems Analysis Reveals Strong Link Between Colorectal Cancer and Trimethylamine N-Oxide (TMAO), a Gut Microbial Metabolite of Dietary Meat and Fat." *BMC Genomics* 16 Suppl. 7, (2015): S4. doi:10.1186/ 1471-2164-16-S7-S4.

11. Li, Hao, Tao Qi, Zhan-Sen Huang, Ying Ying, Yu Zhang, Bo Wang, Lei Ye, Bin Zhang, Di-Ling Chen, and Jun Chen. "Relationship Between Gut Microbiota and Type 2 Diabetic Erectile Dysfunction in Sprague-Dawley Rats." *Journal of Huazhong University of Science and Technology* [Medical Sciences] 37, no. 4 (Aug. 2017): 523–30. doi:10.1007/s11596-017-1767-z.

12. Reicks, Marla, Satya Jonnalagadda, Ann M. Albertson, and Nandan Joshi. "Total Dietary Fiber Intakes in the US Population Are Related to Whole Grain Consumption: Results From the National Health and Nutrition Examination Survey 2009 to 2010." *Nutrition Research* 34, no. 3 (Mar. 2014): 226–34. doi:10.1016/j.nutres.2014.01.002.

CHAPTER 5

1. Carrière, K., B. Khoury, M. M. Günak, and B. Knäuper. "Mindfulness-Based Interventions for Weight Loss: A Systematic Review and Meta-Analysis." *Obesity Reviews: An Official Journal of the International Association for the Study of Obesity* 19, no. 2 (Feb. 2018): 164–77. doi:10.1111/ obr.12623.

2. Dunn, C., O. Olabode-Dada, L. Whetstone, C. Thomas, and S. Aggarwal. "Mindful Eating and Weight Loss, Results From a Randomized Trial." *Journal of Family Medicine and Community Health* 5, no. 3 (2018): 1152.

3. Dunn, Carolyn. "Study Suggests Using a Mindfulness Approach Helps Weight Loss." Accessed July 28, 2018. www.eurekalert.org/pub_releases/2017-05/eaft-ssu051717.php.

4. Yamaji, Takayuki, Shinsuke Mikami, Hiroshi Kobatake, Koichi Tanaka, Yukihito Higashi, and Yasuki Kihara. "Abstract 20249: Slow Down, You Eat Too Fast: Fast Eating Associate With Obesity and Future Prevalence of Metabolic Syndrome." *Circulation* 136, no. A20249 (June 9, 2018).

5. Kokkinos, Alexander, Carel W. le Roux, Kleopatra Alexiadou, Nicholas Tentolouris, Royce P. Vincent, Despoina Kyriaki, Despoina Perrea, et al. "Eating Slowly Increases the Postprandial Response of the Anorexigenic Gut Hormones, Peptide YY and Glucagon-Like Peptide-1." *The Journal of Clinical Endocrinology and Metabolism* 95, no. 1 (Jan. 2010): 333–37. doi:10.1210/ jc.2009-1018.

6. Patel, Zara M. "The Evidence for Olfactory Training in Treating Patients With Olfactory Loss." *Current Opinion in Otolaryngology & Head and Neck Surgery* 25, no. 1 (Feb. 2017): 43–46. doi:10.1097/MOO.0000000000000328.

7. Temmel, Andreas F. P., Christian Quint, Bettina Schickinger-Fischer, Ludger Klimek, Elisabeth Stoller, and Thomas Hummel. "Characteristics of Olfactory Disorders in Relation to Major Causes of Olfactory Loss." *Archives of Otolaryngology—Head & Neck Surgery* 128, no. 6 (June 2002): 635–41.

8. Schubert, Carla R., Karen J. Cruickshanks, David M. Nondahl, Barbara E. K. Klein, Ronald Klein, and Mary E. Fischer. "Association of Exercise With Lower Long-Term Risk of Olfactory Impairment in Older Adults." *JAMA Otolaryngology—Head & Neck Surgery* 139, no. 10 (Oct. 2013): 1061–66. doi:10.1001/jamaoto.2013.4759.

SECTION: AT ODDS

CHAPTERS 6-9

1. Nassauer, Sarah. "Using Scent as a Marketing Tool, Stores Hope It—and Shoppers—Will Linger." *Wall Street Journal,* May 21, 2014. www.wsj.com/articles/using-scent-as-a-marketing-tool-stores-hope-it-and-shoppers-will-linger-1400627455.

2. Albrecht, Leslie. "How McDonald's Uses Interior Design Tricks to Keep Customers Wanting More." MarketWatch, April 30, 2018. Accessed Jul 29, 2018. www.marketwatch.com/story/how-mcdonalds-uses-interior-design-tricks-to-keep-customers-wanting-more-2018-03-23.

3. Avant, Mary. "Mind Over Matter." *QSR Magazine,* June 20, 2014.

4. Bushman, Brad J., C. Nathan Dewall, Richard S. Pond, and Michael D. Hanus. "Low Glucose Relates to Greater Aggression in Married Couples." *Proceedings of the National Academy of Sciences of the United States of America* 111, no. 17 (Apr. 29, 2014): 6254–57. doi:10.1073/pnas.1400619111.

5. MacCormack, Jennifer. "Feeling 'Hangry': When Hunger Is Conceptualized as Emotion." Thesis. University of North Carolina at Chapel Hill.

6. Jenkins, David J. A., Cyril W. C. Kendall, Livia S. A. Augustin, Sandra Mitchell, Sandhya Sahye-Pudaruth, Sonia Blanco Mejia, Laura Chiavaroli, et al. "Effect of Legumes as Part of a Low Glycemic Index Diet on Glycemic Control and Cardiovascular Risk Factors in Type 2 Diabetes Mellitus: A Randomized Controlled Trial." *Archives of Internal Medicine* 172, no. 21 (Nov. 26, 2012): 1653–60. doi:10.1001/2013.jamainternmed.70.

7. Li, Siying S., Cyril W. C. Kendall, Russell J. de Souza, Viranda H. Jayalath, Adrian I. Cozma, Vanessa Ha, Arash Mirrahimi, et al. "Dietary Pulses, Satiety and Food Intake: A Systematic Review and Meta-Analysis of Acute Feeding Trials." *Obesity* 22, no. 8 (Aug. 2014): 1773–80. doi:10.1002/oby.20782.

8. Kristensen, Marlene D., Nathalie T. Bendsen, Sheena M. Christensen, Arne Astrup, and Anne Raben. "Meals Based on Vegetable Protein Sources (Beans and Peas) Are More Satiating Than Meals Based on Animal Protein Sources (Veal and Pork)—A Randomized Cross-Over Meal Test Study." *Food & Nutrition Research* 60 (2016): 32634.

9. Carvalho, A. C., R. S. Lees, R. A. Vaillancourt, R. B. Cabral, and R. W. Colman. "Activation of the Kallikrein System in Hyperbetalipoproteinemia." *The Journal of Laboratory and Clinical Medicine* 91, no. 1 (Jan. 1978): 117–22.

10. Markus, C. R., G. Panhuysen, A. Tuiten, H. Koppeschaar, D. Fekkes, and M. L. Peters. "Does Carbohydrate-Rich, Protein-Poor Food Prevent a Deterioration of Mood and Cognitive Performance of Stress-Prone Subjects When Subjected to a Stressful Task?" *Appetite* 31, no. 1 (Aug. 1998): 49–65. doi:10.1006/appe.1997.0155.

11. Cherian, Laurel, Yamin Wang, Thomas Holland, Puja Agarwal, Neelum Aggarwal, and Martha Clare Morris. "Dietary Approaches to Stop Hypertension (DASH) Diet Associated With Lower Rates of Depression." Abstract, AAN 70th ANNUAL MEETING (February 25, 2018).

12. "DASH-Style Diet Associated With Reduced Risk of Depression." Accessed July 29, 2018. www.rush.edu/news/press-releases/dash-style-diet-associated-reduced-risk-depression.

Sources

13. Grosso, Giuseppe, Fabio Galvano, Stefano Marventano, Michele Malaguarnera, Claudio Bucolo, Filippo Drago, and Filippo Caraci. "Omega-3 Fatty Acids and Depression: Scientific Evidence and Biological Mechanisms." *Oxidative Medicine and Cellular Longevity* 2014 (2014): 313570. doi:10.1155/2014/313570.

14. Kimura, Kenta, Makoto Ozeki, Lekh Raj Juneja, and Hideki Ohira. "L-Theanine Reduces Psychological and Physiological Stress Responses." *Biological Psychology* 74, no. 1 (Jan. 2007): 39–45. doi:10.1016/j.biopsycho.2006.06.006.

15. Norton, Michael I., and Francesca Gino. "Rituals Alleviate Grieving for Loved Ones, Lovers, and Lotteries." *Journal of Experimental Psychology General* 143, no. 1 (Feb. 2014): 266–72. doi:10.1037/a0031772.

SECTION: AT HOME

CHAPTERS 10-14

1. National Heart, Lung, and Blood Institute. "Sleep Deprivation and Deficiency—Why Is Sleep Important?" National Heart, Lung, and Blood Institute. Accessed July 29, 2018. www.nhlbi.nih.gov/node/4605.

2. Xie, Lulu, Hongyi Kang, Qiwu Xu, Michael J. Chen, Yonghong Liao, Meenakshisundaram Thiyagarajan, John O'Donnell, et al. "Sleep Drives Metabolite Clearance From the Adult Brain." *Science* 342, no. 6156 (Oct. 18, 2013): 373–77. doi:10.1126/science.1241224.

3. Irwin, Michael R. "Why Sleep Is Important for Health: A Psychoneuroimmunology Perspective." *Annual Review of Psychology* 66 (Jan. 3, 2015): 143–72. doi:10.1146/annurev-psych-010213-115205.

4. Wilson, Stephanie J., Lisa M. Jaremka, Christopher P. Fagundes, Rebecca Andridge, Juan Peng, William B. Malarkey, Diane Habash, et al. "Shortened Sleep Fuels Inflammatory Responses to Marital Conflict: Emotion Regulation Matters." *Psychoneuroendocrinology* 79, (May 2017): 74–83. doi:10.1016/j.psyneuen.2017.02.015.

5. St-Onge, Marie-Pierre, Amy Roberts, Ari Shechter, and Arindam Roy Choudhury. "Fiber and Saturated Fat Are Associated With Sleep Arousals and Slow Wave Sleep." *Journal of Clinical Sleep Medicine* 12, no. 1 (Jan. 2016): 19–24. doi:10.5664/jcsm.5384.

6. St-Onge et al. "Fiber and Saturated Fat Are Associated With Sleep Arousals and Slow Wave Sleep."

7. Hansen, Anita L., Lisbeth Dahl, Gina Olson, David Thornton, Ingvild E. Graff, Livar Frøyland, Julian F. Thayer, and Staale Pallesen. "Fish Consumption, Sleep, Daily Functioning, and Heart Rate Variability." *Journal of Clinical Sleep Medicine* 10, no. 5 (May 15, 2014): 567–75. doi:10.5664/jcsm.3714.

8. Bravo, R., S. Matito, J. Cubero, S. D. Paredes, L. Franco, M. Rivero, A. B. Rodríguez, and C. Barriga. "Tryptophan-Enriched Cereal Intake Improves Nocturnal Sleep, Melatonin, Serotonin, and Total Antioxidant Capacity Levels and Mood in Elderly Humans." *Age* 35, no. 4 (Aug. 2013): 1277–85. doi:10.1007/s11357-012-9419-5.

9. Abbasi, Behnood, Masud Kimiagar, Khosro Sadeghniiat, Minoo M. Shirazi, Mehdi Hedayati, and Bahram Rashidkhani. "The Effect of Magnesium Supplementation on Primary Insomnia in Elderly: A Double-Blind Placebo-Controlled Clinical Trial." *Journal of Research in Medical Sciences* 17, no. 12 (Dec. 2012): 1161–69.

10. St-Onge, Marie-Pierre, Anja Mikic, and Cara E. Pietrolungo. "Effects of Diet on Sleep Quality." *Advances in Nutrition* 7, no. 5 (Sept. 2016): 938–49. doi:10.3945/an.116.012336.

11. Martin, Vincent T., and Brinder Vij. "Diet and Headache: Part 1." *Headache* 56, no. 9 (Oct. 2016): 1543–52. doi:10.1111/head.12953.

12. Zaeem, Zoya, Lily Zhou, and Esma Dilli. "Headaches: A Review of the Role of Dietary Factors." *Current Neurology and Neuroscience Reports* 16, no. 11 (Nov. 2016): 101. doi:10.1007/s11910-016-0702-1.

13. Menon, Saras, Rodney A. Lea, Sarah Ingle, Michelle Sutherland, Shirley Wee, Larisa M. Haupt, Michelle Palmer, and Lyn R. Griffiths. "Effects of Dietary Folate Intake on Migraine Disability and Frequency." *Headache* 55, no. 2 (Feb. 2015): 301–09. doi:10.1111/head.12490.

14. Lea, Rod, Natalie Colson, Sharon Quinlan, John Macmillan, and Lyn Griffiths. "The Effects of Vitamin Supplementation and MTHFR (C677T) Genotype on Homocysteine-Lowering and Migraine Disability." *Pharmacogenetics and Genomics* 19, no. 6 (June 2009): 422–28. doi:10.1097/FPC.0b013e32832af5a3.

15. Martin, Vincent T., and Brinder Vij. "Diet and Headache: Part 2." *Headache* 56, no. 9 (Oct. 2016): 1553–62. doi:10.1111/head.12952.

16. Schoenen, J., J. Jacquy, and M. Lenaerts. "Effectiveness of High-Dose Riboflavin in Migraine Prophylaxis. A Randomized Controlled Trial." *Neurology* 50, no. 2 (Feb. 1998): 466–70.

17. Food Composition Database: Egg, White, Raw, Fresh. Accessed July 29, 2018. https://ndb.nal.usda.gov/ndb/foods/show/01124?fgcd=&manu=&format=&count=&max=25&offset=&sort=default&order=asc&qlookup=egg+white&ds=&qt=&qp=&qa=&qn=&q=&ing=.

18. "Riboflavin Fact Sheet for Health Professionals." Accessed July 29, 2018. https://ods.od.nih.gov/factsheets/Riboflavin-HealthProfessional/.

19. Mauskop, Alexander, and Jasmine Varughese. "Why all Migraine Patients Should Be Treated With Magnesium." *Journal of Neural Transmission* 119, no. 5 (May 2012): 575–79. doi:10.1007/s00702-012-0790-2.

20. Peikert, A., C. Wilimzig, and R. Köhne-Volland. "Prophylaxis of Migraine With Oral Magnesium: Results From a Prospective, Multi-Center, Placebo-Controlled and Double-Blind Randomized Study." *Cephalalgia: An International Journal of Headache* 16, no. 4 (June 1996): 257–63. doi:10.1046/j.1468-2982.1996.1604257.x.

21. Teigen, Levi, and Christopher J. Boes. "An Evidence-Based Review of Oral Magnesium Supplementation in the Preventive Treatment of Migraine." *Cephalalgia: An International Journal of Headache* 35, no. 10 (Sept. 2015): 912–22. doi:10.1177/0333102414564891.

22. Krymchantowski, Abouch Valenty, and Carla da Cunha Jevoux. "Wine and Headache." *Headache* 54, no. 6 (June 2014): 967–75. doi:10.1111/head.12365.

23. Ramsden, Christopher E., Keturah R. Faurot, Daisy Zamora, Chirayath M. Suchindran, Beth A. Macintosh, Susan Gaylord, Amit Ringel, et al. "Targeted Alteration of Dietary N-3 and N-6 Fatty Acids for the Treatment of Chronic Headaches: A Randomized Trial." *Pain* 154, no. 11 (Nov. 2013): 2441–51. doi:10.1016/j.pain.2013.07.028.

24. Lea et al. "The Effects of Vitamin Supplementation and MTHFR (C677T) Genotype."

25. van den Brink, Gijs R., Daniëlle E. M. van den Boogaardt, Sander J. H. van Deventer, and Maikel P. Peppelenbosch. "Feed a Cold, Starve a Fever?" *Clinical and Diagnostic Laboratory Immunology* 9, no. 1 (Jan. 2002): 182–83.

26. Wang, Andrew, Sarah C. Huen, Harding H. Luan, Shuang Yu, Cuiling Zhang, Jean-Dominique Gallezot, Carmen J. Booth, and Ruslan Medzhitov. "Opposing Effects of Fasting Metabolism on Tissue Tolerance in Bacterial and Viral Inflammation." *Cell* 166, no. 6 (Sept. 8, 2016): 1525.e12. doi:10.1016/j.cell.2016.07.026.

27. Saketkhoo, K., A. Januszkiewicz, and M. A. Sackner. "Effects of Drinking Hot Water, Cold Water, and Chicken Soup on Nasal Mucus Velocity and Nasal Airflow Resistance." *Chest* 74, no. 4 (Oct. 1978): 408–10.

28. Rennard, B. O., R. F. Ertl, G. L. Gossman, R. A. Robbins, and S. I. Rennard. "Chicken Soup Inhibits Neutrophil Chemotaxis in Vitro." *Chest* 118, no. 4 (Oct. 2000): 1150–57.

29. Lavine, J. B. "Chicken Soup or Jewish Medicine." *Chest* 119, no. 4 (Apr. 2001): 1295.

30. Lissiman, Elizabeth, Alice L. Bhasale, and Marc Cohen. "Garlic for the Common Cold." *The Cochrane Database of Systematic Reviews*, no. 11 (Nov. 11, 2014): CD006206. doi:10.1002/14651858.CD006206.pub4.

31. Chang, Jung San, Kuo Chih Wang, Chia Feng Yeh, Den En Shieh, and Lien Chai Chiang. "Fresh Ginger *(Zingiber officinale)* Has Anti-Viral Activity Against Human Respiratory Syncytial Virus

Sources

in Human Respiratory Tract Cell Lines." *Journal of Ethnopharmacology* 145, no. 1 (Jan. 9, 2013): 146–51. doi:10.1016/j.jep.2012.10.043.

32. Dai, Xiaoshuang, Joy M. Stanilka, Cheryl A. Rowe, Elizabethe A. Esteves, Carmelo Nieves, Samuel J. Spaiser, Mary C. Christman, et al. "Consuming *Lentinula edodes* (Shiitake) Mushrooms Daily Improves Human Immunity: A Randomized Dietary Intervention in Healthy Young Adults." *Journal of the American College of Nutrition* 34, no. 6 (2015): 478–87. doi:10.1080/07315724.2014.950391.

33. Hemilä, Harri. "Zinc Lozenges May Shorten the Duration of Colds: A Systematic Review." *The Open Respiratory Medicine Journal* 5 (2011): 51–58. doi:10.2174/1874306401105010051.

34. Hemilä, Harri, and Elizabeth Chalker. "Vitamin C for Preventing and Treating the Common Cold." *The Cochrane Database of Systematic Reviews,* no. 1 (Jan. 31, 2013): CD000980. doi:10.1002/14651858.CD000980.pub4.

35. Hemilä, Harri. "Zinc Lozenges May Shorten the Duration of Colds."

36. Veronese, Nicola, Brendon Stubbs, Marianna Noale, Marco Solmi, Claudio Luchini, Toby O. Smith, Cyrus Cooper, et al. "Adherence to a Mediterranean Diet Is Associated With Lower Prevalence of Osteoarthritis: Data From the Osteoarthritis Initiative." *Clinical Nutrition* 36, no. 6 (Dec. 2017): 1609–14. doi:10.1016/j.clnu.2016.09.035.

37. Beauchamp, Gary K., Russell S. J. Keast, Diane Morel, Jianming Lin, Jana Pika, Qiang Han, Chi-Ho Lee, Amos B. Smith, and Paul A. S. Breslin. "Phytochemistry: Ibuprofen-Like Activity in Extra-Virgin Olive Oil." *Nature* 437, no. 7055 (Sept. 1, 2005): 45-46. doi:10.1038/437045a.

38. Terry, Rohini, Paul Posadzki, Leala K. Watson, and Edzard Ernst. "The Use of Ginger *(Zingiber officinale)* for the Treatment of Pain: A Systematic Review of Clinical Trials." *Pain Medicine* 12, no. 12 (Dec. 2011): 1808–18. doi:10.1111/j.1526-4637.2011.01261.x.

39. Rayati, Farshid, Fatemeh Hajmanouchehri, and Elnaz Najafi. "Comparison of Anti-Inflammatory and Analgesic Effects of Ginger Powder and Ibuprofen in Postsurgical Pain Model: A Randomized, Double-Blind, Case-Control Clinical Trial." *Dental Research Journal* 14, no. 1 (Jan–Feb, 2017): 1–7.

40. Wilson, Patrick B. "Ginger *(Zingiber officinale)* as an Analgesic and Ergogenic Aid in Sport: A Systemic Review." *Journal of Strength and Conditioning Research* 29, no. 10 (Oct. 2015): 2980–95. doi:10.1519/JSC.0000000000001098.

41. Bartels, E. M., V. N. Folmer, H. Bliddal, R. D. Altman, C. Juhl, S. Tarp, W. Zhang, and R. Christensen. "Efficacy and Safety of Ginger in Osteoarthritis Patients: A Meta-Analysis of Randomized Placebo-Controlled Trials." *Osteoarthritis and Cartilage* 23, no. 1 (Jan. 2015): 13–21. doi:10.1016/j.joca.2014.09.024.

42. Chainani-Wu, N. "Safety and Anti-Inflammatory Activity of Curcumin: A Component of Turmeric *(Curcuma longa)*." *The Journal of Alternative and Complementary Medicine* 9 no. 1 (Feb. 2003): 161–68.

43. Dickinson, Scott, Dale P. Hancock, Peter Petocz, Antonio Ceriello, and Jennie Brand-Miller. "High-Glycemic Index Carbohydrate Increases Nuclear Factor-kappaB Activation in Mononuclear Cells of Young, Lean Healthy Subjects." *The American Journal of Clinical Nutrition* 87, no. 5 (May 2008): 1188–93. doi:10.1093/ajcn/87.5.1188.

44. Jameel, Faizan, Melinda Phang, Lisa G. Wood, and Manohar L. Garg. "Acute Effects of Feeding Fructose, Glucose and Sucrose on Blood Lipid Levels and Systemic Inflammation." *Lipids in Health and Disease* 13 (Dec. 16, 2014): 195. doi:10.1186/1476-511X-13-195.

45. Buyken, Anette E., Victoria Flood, Marianne Empson, Elena Rochtchina, Alan W. Barclay, Jennie Brand-Miller, and Paul Mitchell. "Carbohydrate Nutrition and Inflammatory Disease Mortality in Older Adults." *The American Journal of Clinical Nutrition* 92, no. 3 (Sept. 2010): 634–43. doi:10.3945/ajcn.2010.29390.

46. Baratloo, Alireza, Alaleh Rouhipour, Mohammad Mehdi Forouzanfar, Saeed Safari, Marzieh Amiri, and Ahmed Negida. "The Role of Caffeine in Pain Management: A Brief Literature Review." *Anesthesiology and Pain Medicine* 6, no. 3 (June 2016): e33193. doi:10.5812/aapm.33193.

47. Vitale, Kenneth C., Shawn Hueglin, and Elizabeth Broad. "Tart Cherry Juice in Athletes:

A Literature Review and Commentary." *Current Sports Medicine Reports* 16, no. 4 (Jul/Aug, 2017): 230–39. doi:10.1249/JSR.0000000000000385.

48. Whitehead, Anne, Eleanor J. Beck, Susan Tosh, and Thomas M. S. Wolever. "Cholesterol-Lowering Effects of Oat β-Glucan: A Meta-Analysis of Randomized Controlled Trials." *The American Journal of Clinical Nutrition* 100, no. 6 (Dec. 2014): 1413–21. doi:10.3945/ajcn.114.086108.

49. Hu, Ming-Luen, Christophan K. Rayner, Keng-Liang Wu, Seng-Kee Chuah, Wei-Chen Tai, Yeh-Pin Chou, Yi-Chun Chiu, et al. "Effect of Ginger on Gastric Motility and Symptoms of Functional Dyspepsia." *World Journal of Gastroenterology* 17, no. 1 (Jan. 7, 2011): 105–10. doi:10.3748/wjg .v17.i1.105.

SECTION: AT WORK

CHAPTERS 15-19

1. Micha, Renata, Peter J. Rogers, and Michael Nelson. "Glycaemic Index and Glycaemic Load of Breakfast Predict Cognitive Function and Mood in School Children: A Randomised Controlled Trial." *The British Journal of Nutrition* 106, no. 10 (Nov. 2011): 1552–61. doi:10.1017/ S0007114511002303.

2. Nehlig, A. "Are We Dependent upon Coffee and Caffeine? A Review on Human and Animal Data." *Neuroscience and Biobehavioral Reviews* 23, no. 4 (Mar. 1999): 563–76.

3. Paiva, C. L. R. S., B. T. S. Beserra, C. E. G. Reis, J. G. Dorea, T. H. M. Da Costa, and A. A. Amato. "Consumption of Coffee or Caffeine and Serum Concentration of Inflammatory Markers: A Systematic Review." *Critical Reviews in Food Science and Nutrition* (Oct. 2, 2017): 1–12. doi:10.1080/10408398.2017.1386159.

4. Chacko, Sabu M., Priya T. Thambi, Ramadasan Kuttan, and Ikuo Nishigaki. "Beneficial Effects of Green Tea: A Literature Review." *Chinese Medicine* 5 (Apr. 6, 2010): 13. doi:10.1186/ 1749-8546-5-13.

5. Leone, María Juliana, Diego Fernandez Slezak, Diego Golombek, and Mariano Sigman. "Time to Decide: Diurnal Variations on the Speed and Quality of Human Decisions." *Cognition* 158, (Jan. 2017): 44–55. doi:10.1016/j.cognition.2016.10.007.

SECTION: AT PLAY

CHAPTERS 20-24

1. McKay, Gretchen. "PNC Park Takes Crazy Foods to New Level With Cracker Jack & Mac Dog." *Pittsburgh Post-Gazette,* April 2, 2016. www.post-gazette.com/life/food/2016/ 04/02/PNC-Park-takes-crazy-foods-to-new-level-with-Cracker-Jack-Mac-Dog/stories/ 201604020027.

2. Tal, Aner, Scott Zuckerman, and Brian Wansink. "Watch What You Eat: Action-Related Television Content Increases Food Intake." *JAMA Internal Medicine* 174, no. 11 (Nov. 2014): 1842–43. doi:10.1001/jamainternmed.2014.4098.

3. Pase, Matthew P., Andrew B. Scholey, Andrew Pipingas, Marni Kras, Karen Nolidin, Amy Gibbs, Keith Wesnes, and Con Stough. "Cocoa Polyphenols Enhance Positive Mood States but Not Cognitive Performance: A Randomized, Placebo-Controlled Trial." *Journal of Psychopharmacology* 27, no. 5 (May 2013): 451–58. doi:10.1177/0269881112473791.

4. Bennard, Patrick, and Eric Doucet. "Acute Effects of Exercise Timing and Breakfast Meal Glycemic Index on Exercise-Induced Fat Oxidation." *Applied Physiology, Nutrition, and Metabolism* 31, no. 5 (Oct. 2006): 502–11. doi:10.1139/h06-027.

5. De Bock, K., E. A. Richter, A. P. Russell, B. O. Eijnde, W. Derave, M. Ramaekers, E. Koninckx,

Sources

B. Léger, J. Verhaeghe, and P. Hespel. "Exercise in the Fasted State Facilitates Fibre Type-Specific Intramyocellular Lipid Breakdown and Stimulates Glycogen Resynthesis in Humans." *The Journal of Physiology* 564, no. Pt. 2 (Apr. 15, 2005): 649–60. doi:10.1113/jphysiol.2005.083170.

6. Rederstorff, M., A. Krol, and A. Lescure. "Understanding the Importance of Selenium and Selenoproteins in Muscle Function." *Cellular and Molecular Life Sciences: CMLS* 63, no. 1 (Jan. 2006): 52–59. doi:10.1007/s00018-005-5313-y.

7. Kamanna, Vaijinath S., and Moti L. Kashyap. "Mechanism of Action of Niacin." *The American Journal of Cardiology* 101, no. 8A (Apr. 17, 2008): 26B. doi:10.1016/j.amjcard.2008.02.029.

8. Paulsen, Gøran, Kristoffer T. Cumming, Geir Holden, Jostein Hallén, Bent Ronny Rønnestad, Ole Sveen, Arne Skaug, et al. "Vitamin C and E Supplementation Hampers Cellular Adaptation to Endurance Training in Humans: A Double-Blind, Randomised, Controlled Trial." *The Journal of Physiology* 592, no. 8 (Apr. 15, 2014): 1887–1901. doi:10.1113/jphysiol.2013.267419.

9. Bryer, S. C., and A. H. Goldfarb. "Effect of High Dose Vitamin C Supplementation on Muscle Soreness, Damage, Function, and Oxidative Stress to Eccentric Exercise." *International Journal of Sport Nutrition and Exercise Metabolism* 16, no. 3 (June 2006): 270–80.

10. Ding, Eric L., Susan M. Hutfless, Xin Ding, and Saket Girotra. "Chocolate and Prevention of Cardiovascular Disease: A Systematic Review." *Nutrition & Metabolism* 3 (Jan. 3, 2006): 2. doi:10.1186/1743-7075-3-2.

SECTION: FOR WOMEN

CHAPTERS 25-28

1. Vutyavanich, T., S. Wongtra-ngan, and R. Ruangsri. "Pyridoxine for Nausea and Vomiting of Pregnancy: A Randomized, Double-Blind, Placebo-Controlled Trial." *American Journal of Obstetrics and Gynecology* 173, no. 3 Pt. 1 (Sept. 1995): 881–84.

2. Gaskins, Audrey J., and Jorge E. Chavarro. "Diet and Fertility: A Review." *American Journal of Obstetrics and Gynecology* 218, no. 4 (Apr. 2018): 379–89. doi:10.1016/j.ajog.2017.08.010.

3. Nehra, Deepika, Hau D. Le, Erica M. Fallon, Sarah J. Carlson, Dori Woods, Yvonne A. White, Amy H. Pan, et al. "Prolonging the Female Reproductive Lifespan and Improving Egg Quality With Dietary Omega-3 Fatty Acids." *Aging Cell* 11, no. 6 (Dec. 2012): 1046–54. doi:10.1111/acel.12006.

4. Lazzarin, Natalia, Elena Vaquero, Caterina Exacoustos, Elena Bertonotti, Maria Elisabetta Romanini, and Domenico Arduini. "Low-Dose Aspirin and Omega-3 Fatty Acids Improve Uterine Artery Blood Flow Velocity in Women With Recurrent Miscarriage Due to Impaired Uterine Perfusion." *Fertility and Sterility* 92, no. 1 (July 2009): 296–300. doi:10.1016/j.fertnstert.2008.05.045.

5. Al-Safi, Zain A., Huayu Liu, Nichole E. Carlson, Justin Chosich, Mary Harris, Andrew P. Bradford, Celeste Robledo, et al. "Omega-3 Fatty Acid Supplementation Lowers Serum FSH in Normal Weight but Not Obese Women." *The Journal of Clinical Endocrinology and Metabolism* 101, no. 1 (Jan. 2016): 324–33. doi:10.1210/jc.2015-2913.

6. Robbins, Wendie A., Lin Xun, Leah Z. FitzGerald, Samantha Esguerra, Susanne M. Henning, and Catherine L. Carpenter. "Walnuts Improve Semen Quality in Men Consuming a Western-Style Diet: Randomized Control Dietary Intervention Trial." *Biology of Reproduction* 87, no. 4 (Oct. 2012): 101. doi:10.1095/biolreprod.112.101634.

7. Attaman, Jill A., Thomas L. Toth, Jeremy Furtado, Hannia Campos, Russ Hauser, and Jorge E. Chavarro. "Dietary Fat and Semen Quality Among Men Attending a Fertility Clinic." *Human Reproduction* 27, no. 5 (May 2012): 1466–74. doi:10.1093/humrep/des065.

8. U.S. Food and Drug Administration. *A Quantitative Assessment of the Net Effects on Fetal Neurodevelopment From Eating Commercial Fish (as Measured by IQ and also by Early Age Verbal Development in Children)*, 2014.

WHAT TO EAT WHEN

9. Chavarro, J. E., J. W. Rich-Edwards, B. Rosner, and W. C. Willett. "A Prospective Study of Dairy Foods Intake and Anovulatory Infertility." *Human Reproduction* 22, no. 5 (May 2007): 1340–47. doi:10.1093/humrep/dem019.

10. Choy, Christine M. Y., Christopher W. K. Lam, Lorena T. F. Cheung, Christine M. Briton-Jones, L. P. Cheung, and Christopher J. Haines. "Infertility, Blood Mercury Concentrations and Dietary Seafood Consumption: A Case-Control Study." *BJOG: An International Journal of Obstetrics and Gynaecology* 109, no. 10 (Oct. 2002): 1121–25.

11. *Consumer Reports.* "Which Fish Are Safe for Pregnant Women?" *Consumer Reports,* January 27, 2017.

12. Chavarro, Jorge E., Janet W. Rich-Edwards, Bernard A. Rosner, and Walter C. Willett. "Diet and Lifestyle in the Prevention of Ovulatory Disorder Infertility." *Obstetrics and Gynecology* 110, no. 5 (Nov. 2007): 1050–58. doi:10.1097/01.AOG.0000287293.25465.e1.

13. Hester, James M., and Francisco Diaz. "Growing Oocytes Need Zinc: Zinc Deficiency in the Preantral Ovarian Follicle." *The FASEB Journal* 32, no. 1_supplement (Apr. 20, 2018): 882.1. doi:10.1096/fasebj.2018.32.1_supplement.882.1.

14. Duncan, Francesca E., Emily L. Que, Nan Zhang, Eve C. Feinberg, Thomas V. O'Halloran, and Teresa K. Woodruff. "The Zinc Spark Is an Inorganic Signature of Human Egg Activation." *Scientific Reports* 6 (Apr. 26, 2016): 24737. doi:10.1038/srep24737.

15. Akinboro, A., M. A. Azeez, and A. A. Bakare. "Frequency of Twinning in Southwest Nigeria." *Indian Journal of Human Genetics* 14, no. 2 (2008): 41–47. doi:10.4103/0971-6866.44104.

16. Chavarro et al. "Diet and Lifestyle in the Prevention of Ovulatory Disorder Infertility."

17. Xia, Wei, Yu-Han Chiu, Paige L. Williams, Audrey J. Gaskins, Thomas L. Toth, Cigdem Tanrikut, Russ Hauser, and Jorge E. Chavarro. "Men's Meat Intake and Treatment Outcomes Among Couples Undergoing Assisted Reproduction." *Fertility and Sterility* 104, no. 4 (Oct. 2015): 972–79. doi:10.1016/j.fertnstert.2015.06.037.

18. Weiser, Michael J., Christopher M. Butt, and M. Hasan Mohajeri. "Docosahexaenoic Acid and Cognition Throughout the Lifespan." *Nutrients* 8, no. 2 (Feb. 17, 2016): 99. doi:10.3390/nu8020099.

19. Martin, Camilia R., Pei-Ra Ling, and George L. Blackburn. "Review of Infant Feeding: Key Features of Breast Milk and Infant Formula." *Nutrients* 8, no. 5 (May 11, 2016): 279. doi:10.3390/nu8050279.

20. American College of Obstetricians and Gynecologists. "Frequently Asked Questions FAQ 29 Labor Delivery and Postpartum Care." Accessed July 29, 2018. www.acog.org/-/media/For-Patients/faq029.pdf.

21. Scholey, Andrew, and Lauren Owen. "Effects of Chocolate on Cognitive Function and Mood: A Systematic Review." *Nutrition Reviews* 71, no. 10 (Oct. 2013): 665–81. doi:10.1111/nure.12065.

22. Martin, Francois-Pierre J., Serge Rezzi, Emma Peré-Trepat, Beate Kamlage, Sebastiano Collino, Edgar Leibold, Jürgen Kastler, et al. "Metabolic Effects of Dark Chocolate Consumption on Energy, Gut Microbiota, and Stress-Related Metabolism in Free-Living Subjects." *Journal of Proteome Research* 8, no. 12 (Dec. 2009): 5568–79. doi:10.1021/pr900607v.

23. Massolt, Elske T., Paul M. van Haard, Jens F. Rehfeld, Eduardus F. Posthuma, Eveline van der Veer, and Dave H. Schweitzer. "Appetite Suppression Through Smelling of Dark Chocolate Correlates With Changes in Ghrelin in Young Women." *Regulatory Peptides* 161, no. 1–3 (Apr. 9, 2010): 81–86. doi:10.1016/j.regpep.2010.01.005.

24. Zarei, Somayeh, Sakineh Mohammad-Alizadeh-Charandabi, Mojgan Mirghafourvand, Yousef Javadzadeh, and Fatemeh Effati-Daryani. "Effects of Calcium-Vitamin D and Calcium-Alone on Pain Intensity and Menstrual Blood Loss in Women With Primary Dysmenorrhea: A Randomized Controlled Trial." *Pain Medicine* 18, no. 1 (Jan. 1, 2017): 3–13. doi:10.1093/pm/pnw121.

25. Penland, J. G., and P. E. Johnson. "Dietary Calcium and Manganese Effects on Menstrual Cycle Symptoms." *American Journal of Obstetrics and Gynecology* 168, no. 5 (May 1993): 1417–23.

26. Walker, A. F., M. C. De Souza, M. F. Vickers, S. Abeyasekera, M. L. Collins, and L. A. Trinca. "Magnesium Supplementation Alleviates Premenstrual Symptoms of Fluid Retention." *Journal of Women's Health* 7, no. 9 (Nov. 1998): 1157–65.

27. Ebrahimi, Elham, Shiva Khayati Motlagh, Sima Nemati, and Zohreh Tavakoli. "Effects of Magnesium and Vitamin B$_6$ on the Severity of Premenstrual Syndrome Symptoms." *Journal of Caring Sciences* 1, no. 4 (Dec. 2012): 183–89. doi:10.5681/jcs.2012.026.

28. Penland and Johnson. "Dietary Calcium and Manganese Effects on Menstrual Cycle Symptoms."

29. Chen, Chen X., Bruce Barrett, and Kristine L. Kwekkeboom. "Efficacy of Oral Ginger *(Zingiber officinale)* for Dysmenorrhea: A Systematic Review and Meta-Analysis." *Evidence-Based Complementary and Alternative Medicine: eCAM* 2016 (2016): Article 6295737. doi:10.1155/2016/6295737.

30. Chiaffarino, F., F. Parazzini, C. La Vecchia, L. Chatenoud, E. Di Cintio, and S. Marsico. "Diet and Uterine Myomas." *Obstetrics and Gynecology* 94, no. 3 (Sept. 1999): 395–98.

31. Shen, Yang, Yanting Wu, Qing Lu, and Mulan Ren. "Vegetarian Diet and Reduced Uterine Fibroids Risk: A Case-Control Study in Nanjing, China." *The Journal of Obstetrics and Gynaecology Research* 42, no. 1 (Jan. 2016): 87–94. doi:10.1111/jog.12834.

32. Atkinson, Charlotte, Johanna W. Lampe, Delia Scholes, Chu Chen, Kristiina Wähälä, and Stephen M. Schwartz. "Lignan and Isoflavone Excretion in Relation to Uterine Fibroids: A Case-Control Study of Young to Middle-Aged Women in the United States." *The American Journal of Clinical Nutrition* 84, no. 3 (Sept. 2006): 587–93. doi:10.1093/ajcn/84.3.587.

33. Nagata, Chisato, Kozue Nakamura, Shino Oba, Makoto Hayashi, Noriyuki Takeda, and Keigo Yasuda. "Association of Intakes of Fat, Dietary Fibre, Soya Isoflavones and Alcohol With Uterine Fibroids in Japanese Women." *The British Journal of Nutrition* 101, no. 10 (May 2009): 1427–31.

34. Nagata, C., N. Takatsuka, N. Kawakami, and H. Shimizu. "Soy Product Intake and Hot Flashes in Japanese Women: Results From a Community-Based Prospective Study." *American Journal of Epidemiology* 153, no. 8 (Apr. 15, 2001): 790–93.

35. Wu, A. H., M. C. Yu, C. -C Tseng, and M. C. Pike. "Epidemiology of Soy Exposures and Breast Cancer Risk." *British Journal of Cancer* 98, no. 1 (Jan. 15, 2008): 9–14. doi:10.1038/sj.bjc.6604145.4

36. Herber-Gast, Gerrie-Cor M., and Gita D. Mishra. "Fruit, Mediterranean-Style, and High-Fat and -Sugar Diets Are Associated With the Risk of Night Sweats and Hot Flushes in Midlife: Results From a Prospective Cohort Study." *The American Journal of Clinical Nutrition* 97, no. 5 (May 2013): 1092–99. doi:10.3945/ajcn.112.049965.

37. Faubion, Stephanie S., Richa Sood, Jacqueline M. Thielen, and Lynne T. Shuster. "Caffeine and Menopausal Symptoms: What Is the Association?" *Menopause* 22, no. 2 (Feb. 2015): 155–58. doi:10.1097/GME.0000000000000301.

SECTION: FOR MEN

CHAPTERS 29-31

1. Kelly, D. M. and T. H. Jones. "Testosterone and Obesity." *Obesity Reviews: An Official Journal of the International Association for the Study of Obesity* 16, no. 7 (Jul, 2015): 581-606.

2. Cui, Xiangrong, Xuan Jing, Xueqing Wu, and Meiqin Yan. "Protective Effect of Resveratrol on Spermatozoa Function in Male Infertility Induced by Excess Weight and Obesity." *Molecular Medicine Reports* 14, no. 5 (Nov. 2016): 4659–65. doi:10.3892/mmr.2016.5840.

3. Forest, C. P., H. Padma-Nathan, and H. R. Liker. "Efficacy and Safety of Pomegranate Juice on Improvement of Erectile Dysfunction in Male Patients With Mild to Moderate Erectile Dysfunction: A Randomized, Placebo-Controlled, Double-Blind, Crossover Study." *International Journal of Impotence Research* 19, no. 6 (Nov.–Dec. 2007): 564–67. doi:10.1038/sj.ijir.3901570.

4. Figueroa, Arturo, Alexei Wong, Salvador J. Jaime, and Joaquin U. Gonzales. "Influence of L-Citrulline and Watermelon Supplementation on Vascular Function and Exercise Performance." *Current Opinion in Clinical Nutrition and Metabolic Care* 20, no. 1 (Jan. 2017): 92–98. doi:10.1097/MCO.0000000000000340.1

5. Souli, Einat, Marcelle Machluf, Abigail Morgenstern, Edmond Sabo, and Shmuel Yannai. "Indole-3-Carbinol (I3C) Exhibits Inhibitory and Preventive Effects on Prostate Tumors in Mice." *Food and Chemical Toxicology* 46, no. 3 (Mar. 2008): 863–70. doi:10.1016/j.fct.2007.10.026.

6. Om, A. S., and K. W. Chung. "Dietary Zinc Deficiency Alters 5 Alpha-Reduction and Aromatization of Testosterone and Androgen and Estrogen Receptors in Rat Liver." *The Journal of Nutrition* 126, no. 4 (Apr. 1996): 842–48. doi:10.1093/jn/126.4.842.

7. Oi, Y., M. Imafuku, C. Shishido, Y. Kominato, S. Nishimura, and K. Iwai. "Garlic Supplementation Increases Testicular Testosterone and Decreases Plasma Corticosterone in Rats Fed a High Protein Diet." *The Journal of Nutrition* 131, no. 8 (Aug. 2001): 2150–56. doi:10.1093/jn/131.8.2150.

8. Pilz, S., S. Frisch, H. Koertke, J. Kuhn, J. Dreier, B. Obermayer-Pietsch, E. Wehr, and A. Zittermann. "Effect of Vitamin D Supplementation on Testosterone Levels in Men." *Hormone and Metabolic Research* 43, no. 3 (Mar. 2011): 223–25. doi:10.1055/s-0030-1269854.

9. Levine, Hagai, Niels Jørgensen, Anderson Martino-Andrade, Jaime Mendiola, Dan Weksler-Derri, Irina Mindlis, Rachel Pinotti, and Shanna H. Swan. "Temporal Trends in Sperm Count: A Systematic Review and Meta-Regression Analysis." *Human Reproduction Update* 23, no. 6 (Nov. 1, 2017): 646–59. doi:10.1093/humupd/dmx022.

10. Salas-Huetos, Albert, Mònica Bulló, and Jordi Salas-Salvadó. "Dietary Patterns, Foods and Nutrients in Male Fertility Parameters and Fecundability: A Systematic Review of Observational Studies." *Human Reproduction Update* 23, no. 4 (July 1, 2017): 371–89. doi:10.1093/humupd/dmx006.

11. Torres, Marta, Ricardo Laguna-Barraza, Mireia Dalmases, Alexandra Calle, Eva Pericuesta, Josep M. Montserrat, Daniel Navajas, Alfonso Gutierrez-Adan, and Ramon Farré. "Male Fertility Is Reduced by Chronic Intermittent Hypoxia Mimicking Sleep Apnea in Mice." *Sleep* 37, no. 11 (Nov. 1, 2014): 1757–65. doi:10.5665/sleep.4166.

12. Sermondade, N., C. Faure, L. Fezeu, A. G. Shayeb, J. P. Bonde, T. K. Jensen, M. Van Wely, et al. "BMI in Relation to Sperm Count: An Updated Systematic Review and Collaborative Meta-Analysis." *Human Reproduction Update* 19, no. 3 (May–June 2013): 221–31. doi:10.1093/humupd/dms050.

13. Esmaeili, V., A. H. Shahverdi, M. H. Moghadasian, and A. R. Alizadeh. "Dietary Fatty Acids Affect Semen Quality: A Review." *Andrology* 3, no. 3 (May 2015): 450–61. doi:10.1111/andr.12024.

14. Roqueta-Rivera, Manuel, Timothy L. Abbott, Mayandi Sivaguru, Rex A. Hess, and Manabu T. Nakamura. "Deficiency in the Omega-3 Fatty Acid Pathway Results in Failure of Acrosome Biogenesis in Mice." *Biology of Reproduction* 85, no. 4 (Oct. 2011): 721–32. doi:10.1095/biolreprod.110.089524.

15. Safarinejad, M. R. "Effect of Omega-3 Polyunsaturated Fatty Acid Supplementation on Semen Profile and Enzymatic Anti-Oxidant Capacity of Seminal Plasma in Infertile Men With Idiopathic Oligoasthenoteratospermia: A Double-Blind, Placebo-Controlled, Randomised Study." *Andrologia* 43, no. 1 (Feb. 2011): 38–47. doi:10.1111/j.1439-0272.2009.01013.x.

16. Coffua, Lauren S., and Patricia A. Martin-DeLeon. "Effectiveness of a Walnut-Enriched Diet on Murine Sperm: Involvement of Reduced Peroxidative Damage." *Heliyon* 3, no. 2 (Feb. 2017): e00250. doi:10.1016/j.heliyon.2017.e00250.

17. Robbins, Wendie A., Lin Xun, Leah Z. FitzGerald, Samantha Esguerra, Susanne M. Henning, and Catherine L. Carpenter. "Walnuts Improve Semen Quality in Men Consuming a Western-Style Diet: Randomized Control Dietary Intervention Trial." *Biology of Reproduction* 87, no. 4 (Oct. 1, 2012). doi:10.1095/biolreprod.112.101634.

18. Durairajanayagam, Damayanthi, Ashok Agarwal, Chloe Ong, and Pallavi Prashast. "Lycopene and Male Infertility." *Asian Journal of Andrology* 16, no. 3 (2014): 420–25. doi:10.4103/1008-682X.126384.

Sources

19. Jensen, Tina K., Berit L. Heitmann, Martin Blomberg Jensen, Thorhallur I. Halldorsson, Anna-Maria Andersson, Niels E. Skakkebæk, Ulla N. Joensen, et al. "High Dietary Intake of Saturated Fat Is Associated With Reduced Semen Quality Among 701 Young Danish Men From the General Population." *The American Journal of Clinical Nutrition* 97, no. 2 (Feb. 1, 2013): 411–18. doi:10.3945/ajcn.112.042432.

20. Dadkhah, Hajar, Ashraf Kazemi, Mohammad-Hossien Nasr-Isfahani, and Soheila Ehsanpour. "The Relationship Between the Amount of Saturated Fat Intake and Semen Quality in Men." *Iranian Journal of Nursing and Midwifery Research* 22, no. 1 (Jan.–Feb., 2017): 46–50. doi:10.4103/1735-9066.202067.

21. Young, S. S., B. Eskenazi, F. M. Marchetti, G. Block, and A. J. Wyrobek. "The Association of Folate, Zinc and Antioxidant Intake With Sperm Aneuploidy in Healthy Non-Smoking Men." *Human Reproduction* 23, no. 5 (May 2008): 1014–22. doi:10.1093/humrep/den036.

22. Khaki, Arash, Fatemeh Fathiazad, Mohammad Nouri, Amirafshin Khaki, Navid A. Maleki, Hossein Jabbari Khamnei, and Porya Ahmadi. "Beneficial Effects of Quercetin on Sperm Parameters in Streptozotocin-Induced Diabetic Male Rats." *Phytotherapy Research* 24, no. 9 (Sept. 2010): 1285–91. doi:10.1002/ptr.3100.

23. Al-Dujaili, Emad, and Nacer Smail. "Pomegranate Juice Intake Enhances Salivary Testosterone Levels and Improves Mood and Well Being in Healthy Men and Women." *Endocrine Abstracts* 28, no. P313 (Mar. 1, 2012).

24. Roehrborn, Claus G. "Benign Prostatic Hyperplasia: An Overview." *Reviews in Urology* 7 Suppl 9 (2005): S14.

25. Epstein, Mara M., Julie L. Kasperzyk, Ove Andrén, Edward L. Giovannucci, Alicja Wolk, Niclas Håkansson, Swen-Olof Andersson, et al. "Dietary Zinc and Prostate Cancer Survival in a Swedish Cohort." *The American Journal of Clinical Nutrition* 93, no. 3 (Mar. 2011): 586–93. doi:10.3945/ajcn.110.004804.

26. Kratochvilova, Monika, Martina Raudenska, Zbynek Heger, Lukas Richtera, Natalia Cernei, Vojtech Adam, Petr Babula, et al. "Amino Acid Profiling of Zinc Resistant Prostate Cancer Cell Lines: Associations With Cancer Progression." *The Prostate* 77, no. 6 (May 2017): 604–16. doi:10.1002/pros.23304.

27. Li, Jie, and Qi-Qi Mao. "Legume Intake and Risk of Prostate Cancer: A Meta-Analysis of Prospective Cohort Studies." *Oncotarget* 8, no. 27 (July 4, 2017): 44776. doi:10.18632/oncotarget.16794.

28. Weike Wang, Meng Yang, Stacey A. Kenfield, Frank B. Hu, Meir J. Stampfer, Walter C. Willett, Charles S. Fuchs, et al. "Nut Consumption and Prostate Cancer Risk and Mortality." *The British Journal of Cancer* 115, no. 3 (July 26, 2016): 371–74. doi:10.1038/bjc.2016.181.

29. Patel, Hitendra R. H., Walid Elbakbak, Amina Bouhelal, and Stig Müller. "Does Oral Lycopene Reduce Benign Prostate Enlargement/Hyperplasia (BPE/BPH)?" *Oncology & Cancer Case Reports* 2, no. 1 (2016): 108. doi:10.4172/occrs.1000108.

30. Allott, E. H., L. Arab, L. J. Su, L. Farnan, E. T. H. Fontham, J. L. Mohler, J. T. Bensen, and S. E. Steck. "Saturated Fat Intake and Prostate Cancer Aggressiveness: Results From the Population-Based North Carolina-Louisiana Prostate Cancer Project." *Prostate Cancer and Prostatic Diseases* 20, no. 1 (Mar. 2017): 48–54. doi:10.1038/pcan.2016.39.

31. Katz, Aaron, Mitchell Efros, Jed Kaminetsky, Kelli Herrlinger, Diana Chirouzes, and Michael Ceddia. "A Green and Black Tea Extract Benefits Urological Health in Men With Lower Urinary Tract Symptoms." *Therapeutic Advances in Urology* 6, no. 3 (June 2014): 89–96. doi:10.1177/1756287214526924.

32. Beaver, Laura M., Christiane V. Löhr, John D. Clarke, Sarah T. Glasser, Greg W. Watson, Carmen P. Wong, Zhenzhen Zhang, et al. "Broccoli Sprouts Delay Prostate Cancer Formation and Decrease Prostate Cancer Severity With a Concurrent Decrease in HDAC3 Protein Expression in Transgenic Adenocarcinoma of the Mouse Prostate (TRAMP) Mice." *Current Developments in Nutrition* 2, no. 3 (Mar. 1, 2018). doi:10.1093/cdn/nzy002.

33. Paller, C. J., A. Pantuck, and M. A. Carducci. "A Review of Pomegranate in Prostate Cancer." *Prostate Cancer and Prostatic Diseases* 20, no. 3 (Sept. 2017): 265–70. doi:10.1038/pcan.2017.19.

SECTION: AT RISK

CHAPTERS 32-40

1. "Can Cancer Be Prevented?" Accessed Aug. 1, 2018. www.cancerresearchuk.org/about-cancer/causes-of-cancer/can-cancer-be-prevented.

2. Islami, Farhad, Ann Goding Sauer, Kimberly D. Miller, Rebecca L. Siegel, Stacey A. Fedewa, Eric J. Jacobs, Marjorie L. McCullough, et al. "Proportion and Number of Cancer Cases and Deaths Attributable to Potentially Modifiable Risk Factors in the United States." *CA: A Cancer Journal for Clinicians* 68, no. 1 (Jan. 2018): 31–54. doi:10.3322/caac.21440.

3. John P. Pierce, Marcia L. Stefanick, Shirley W. Flatt, Loki Natarajan, Barbara Sternfeld, Lisa Madlensky, Wael K. Al-Delaimy, et al. "Greater Survival After Breast Cancer in Physically Active Women With High Vegetable-Fruit Intake Regardless of Obesity." *Journal of Clinical Oncology* 25, no. 17 (June 10, 2007): 2345–51. doi:10.1200/JCO.2006.08.6819.

4. Aranow, Cynthia. "Vitamin D and the Immune System." *Journal of Investigative Medicine* 59, no. 6 (Aug. 2011): 881–86. doi:10.2310/JIM.0b013e31821b8755.

5. Wolfe, Kelly L., Xinmei Kang, Xiangjiu He, Mei Dong, Qingyuan Zhang, and Rui Hai Liu. "Cellular Antioxidant Activity of Common Fruits." *Journal of Agricultural and Food Chemistry* 56, no. 18 (Sept. 24, 2008): 8418–26. doi:10.1021/jf801381y.

6. World Cancer Research Fund/American Institute for Cancer Research. *Non-Alcoholic Drinks and the Risk of Cancer.* Continuous Update Project Report, 2018.

7. Sinha, Rashmi, Amanda J. Cross, Carrie R. Daniel, Barry I. Graubard, Jennifer W. Wu, Albert R. Hollenbeck, Marc J. Gunter, et al. "Caffeinated and Decaffeinated Coffee and Tea Intakes and Risk of Colorectal Cancer in a Large Prospective Study." *The American Journal of Clinical Nutrition* 96, no. 2 (Aug. 2012): 374–81. doi:10.3945/ajcn.111.031328.

8. Cassidy, Aedín, Tianyi Huang, Megan S. Rice, Eric B. Rimm, and Shelley S. Tworoger. "Intake of Dietary Flavonoids and Risk of Epithelial Ovarian Cancer." *The American Journal of Clinical Nutrition* 100, no. 5 (Nov. 2014): 1344–51. doi:10.3945/ajcn.114.088708.

9. Sugimura, Takashi, Keiji Wakabayashi, Hitoshi Nakagama, and Minako Nagao. "Heterocyclic Amines: Mutagens/Carcinogens Produced During Cooking of Meat and Fish." *Cancer Science* 95, no. 4 (Apr. 2004): 290–99.

10. Persson, E., G. Graziani, R. Ferracane, V. Fogliano, and K. Skog. "Influence of Antioxidants in Virgin Olive Oil on the Formation of Heterocyclic Amines in Fried Beefburgers." *Food and Chemical Toxicology* 41, no. 11 (Nov. 2003): 1587–97.

11. Salmon, C. P., M. G. Knize, and J. S. Felton. "Effects of Marinating on Heterocyclic Amine Carcinogen Formation in Grilled Chicken." *Food and Chemical Toxicology* 35, no. 5 (May 1997): 433–41.

12. Viegas, Olga, L. Filipe Amaro, Isabel M. P. L. V. O. Ferreira, and Olívia Pinho. "Inhibitory Effect of Antioxidant-Rich Marinades on the Formation of Heterocyclic Aromatic Amines in Pan-Fried Beef." *Journal of Agricultural and Food Chemistry* 60, no. 24 (June 20, 2012): 6235–40. doi:10.1021/jf302227b.

13. World Health Organization. "Q&A on the Carcinogenicity of the Consumption of Red Meat and Processed Meat." Accessed Aug. 1, 2018. www.who.int/features/qa/cancer-red-meat/en/.

14. Richman, Erin L., Stacey A. Kenfield, Meir J. Stampfer, Edward L. Giovannucci, and June M. Chan. "Egg, Red Meat, and Poultry Intake and Risk of Lethal Prostate Cancer in the Prostate-Specific Antigen-Era: Incidence and Survival." *Cancer Prevention Research* 4, no. 12 (Dec. 2011): 2110–21. doi:10.1158/1940-6207.CAPR-11-0354.

15. Richman, Erin L., Stacey A. Kenfield, Meir J. Stampfer, Edward L. Giovannucci, Steven H. Zeisel, Walter C. Willett, and June M. Chan. "Choline Intake and Risk of Lethal Prostate Cancer:

Sources

Incidence and Survival." *The American Journal of Clinical Nutrition* 96, no. 4 (Oct. 2012): 855–63. doi:10.3945/ajcn.112.039784.

16. Leoncini, Emanuele, Valeria Edefonti, Mia Hashibe, Maria Parpinel, Gabriella Cadoni, Monica Ferraroni, Diego Serraino, et al. "Carotenoid Intake and Head and Neck Cancer: A Pooled Analysis in the International Head and Neck Cancer Epidemiology Consortium." *European Journal of Epidemiology* 31, no. 4 (Apr. 2016): 369–83. doi:10.1007/s10654-015-0036-3.

17. Rhode, Jennifer, Sarah Fogoros, Suzanna Zick, Heather Wahl, Kent A. Griffith, Jennifer Huang, and J. Rebecca Liu. "Ginger Inhibits Cell Growth and Modulates Angiogenic Factors in Ovarian Cancer Cells." *BMC Complementary and Alternative Medicine* 7, (Dec. 20, 2007): 44. doi:10.1186/1472-6882-7-44.

18. Ishiguro, Kazuhiro, Takafumi Ando, Osamu Maeda, Naoki Ohmiya, Yasumasa Niwa, Kenji Kadomatsu, and Hidemi Goto. "Ginger Ingredients Reduce Viability of Gastric Cancer Cells Via Distinct Mechanisms." *Biochemical and Biophysical Research Communications* 362, no. 1 (Oct. 12, 2007): 218–23. doi:10.1016/j.bbrc.2007.08.012.3.

19. Kunzmann, Andrew T., Helen G. Coleman, Wen-Yi Huang, Cari M. Kitahara, Marie M. Cantwell, and Sonja I. Berndt. "Dietary Fiber Intake and Risk of Colorectal Cancer and Incident and Recurrent Adenoma in the Prostate, Lung, Colorectal, and Ovarian Cancer Screening Trial." *The American Journal of Clinical Nutrition* 102, no. 4 (Oct. 2015): 881–90. doi:10.3945/ajcn.115.113282.

20. Toledo, Estefanía, Jordi Salas-Salvadó, Carolina Donat-Vargas, Pilar Buil-Cosiales, Ramón Estruch, Emilio Ros, Dolores Corella, et al. "Mediterranean Diet and Invasive Breast Cancer Risk Among Women at High Cardiovascular Risk in the PREDIMED Trial: A Randomized Clinical Trial." *JAMA Internal Medicine* 175, no. 11 (Nov. 2015): 1752–60. doi:10.1001/jamainternmed.2015.4838.

21. Hyson, Dianne A. "A Comprehensive Review of Apples and Apple Components and Their Relationship to Human Health." *Advances in Nutrition* 2, no. 5 (Sept. 2011): 408–20. doi:10.3945/an.111.000513.

22. Chuang, Shu-Chun, Mazda Jenab, Julia E. Heck, Cristina Bosetti, Renato Talamini, Keitaro Matsuo, Xavier Castellsague, et al. "Diet and the Risk of Head and Neck Cancer: A Pooled Analysis in the INHANCE Consortium." *Cancer Causes & Control* 23, no. 1 (Jan. 1, 2012): 69–88. doi:10.1007/s10552-011-9857-x.

23. Steinmetz, K. A., L. H. Kushi, R. M. Bostick, A. R. Folsom, and J. D. Potter. "Vegetables, Fruit, and Colon Cancer in the Iowa Women's Health Study." *American Journal of Epidemiology* 139, no. 1 (Jan. 1, 1994): 1–15.

24. Hsing, Ann W., Anand P. Chokkalingam, Yu-Tang Gao, M. Patricia Madigan, Jie Deng, Gloria Gridley, and Joseph F. Fraumeni. "Allium Vegetables and Risk of Prostate Cancer: A Population-Based Study." *Journal of the National Cancer Institute* 94, no. 21 (Nov. 6, 2002): 1648–51.

25. Chan, June M., Furong Wang, and Elizabeth A. Holly. "Vegetable and Fruit Intake and Pancreatic Cancer in a Population-Based Case-Control Study in the San Francisco Bay Area." *Cancer Epidemiology, Biomarkers & Prevention* 14, no. 9 (Sept. 2005): 2093–97. doi:10.1158/1055-9965. EPI-05-0226.

26. Zhang, Cai-Xia, Suzanne C. Ho, Yu-Ming Chen, Jian-Hua Fu, Shou-Zhen Cheng, and Fang-Yu Lin. "Greater Vegetable and Fruit Intake Is Associated With a Lower Risk of Breast Cancer Among Chinese Women." *International Journal of Cancer* 125, no. 1 (July 1, 2009): 181–88. doi:10.1002/ijc.24358.

27. Vallejo, F., F. A. Tomás-Barberán, and C. García-Viguera. "Phenolic Compound Contents in Edible Parts of Broccoli Inflorescences After Domestic Cooking." *Journal of the Science of Food and Agriculture* 83, no. 14 (Nov. 1, 2003): 1511–16. doi:10.1002/jsfa.1585.

28. World Health Organization. "The Top 10 Causes of Death." Accessed Aug 2, 2018. www.who.int/news-room/fact-sheets/detail/the-top-10-causes-of-death.

29. Koeth, Robert A., Zeneng Wang, Bruce S. Levison, Jennifer A. Buffa, Elin Org, Brendan T. Sheehy, Earl B. Britt, et al. "Intestinal Microbiota Metabolism of L-Carnitine, a Nutrient in Red Meat, Promotes Atherosclerosis." *Nature Medicine* 19, no. 5 (May 2013): 576–85. doi:10.1038/nm.3145.

30. Tang, W. H. Wilson, Zeneng Wang, Bruce S. Levison, Robert A. Koeth, Earl B. Britt, Xiaoming Fu, Yuping Wu, and Stanley L. Hazen. "Intestinal Microbial Metabolism of Phosphatidylcholine and Cardiovascular Risk." *The New England Journal of Medicine* 368, no. 17 (Apr. 25, 2013): 1575–84. doi:10.1056/NEJMoa1109400.

31. Wang, Zeneng, Elizabeth Klipfell, Brian J. Bennett, Robert Koeth, Bruce S. Levison, Brandon Dugar, Ariel E. Feldstein, et al. "Gut Flora Metabolism of Phosphatidylcholine Promotes Cardiovascular Disease." *Nature* 472, no. 7341 (Apr. 7, 2011): 57–63. doi:10.1038/nature09922.

32. Estruch, Ramon, Miguel Angel Martínez-González, Dolores Corella, Jordi Salas-Salvadó, Valentina Ruiz-Gutiérrez, María Isabel Covas, Miguel Fiol, et al. "Effects of a Mediterranean-Style Diet on Cardiovascular Risk Factors: A Randomized Trial." *Annals of Internal Medicine* 145, no. 1 (July 4, 2006): 1–11.

33. Salas-Salvadó, Jordi, Monica Bulló, Nancy Babio, Miguel Ángel Martínez-González, Núria Ibarrola-Jurado, Josep Basora, Ramon Estruch, et al. "Reduction in the Incidence of Type 2 Diabetes With the Mediterranean Diet: Results of the PREDIMED-Reus Nutrition Intervention Randomized Trial." *Diabetes Care* 34, no. 1 (Jan. 2011): 14–19. doi:10.2337/dc10-1288.8

34. Estruch, Ramón, Emilio Ros, Jordi Salas-Salvadó, Maria-Isabel Covas, Dolores Corella, Fernando Arós, Enrique Gómez-Gracia, et al. "Primary Prevention of Cardiovascular Disease With a Mediterranean Diet Supplemented With Extra-Virgin Olive Oil or Nuts." *The New England Journal of Medicine* 378, no. 25 (June 21, 2018): e34. doi:10.1056/NEJMoa1800389.

35. Fung, Teresa T., Kathryn M. Rexrode, Christos S. Mantzoros, JoAnn E. Manson, Walter C. Willett, and Frank B. Hu. "Mediterranean Diet and Incidence of and Mortality from Coronary Heart Disease and Stroke in Women." *Circulation* 119, no. 8 (Mar. 3, 2009): 1093–100. doi:10.1161/CIRCULATIONAHA.108.816736.

36. Esselstyn, Caldwell B., Gina Gendy, Jonathan Doyle, Mladen Golubic, and Michael F. Roizen. "A Way to Reverse CAD?" *The Journal of Family Practice* 63, no. 7 (July 2014): 364b.

37. Ornish, D., L. W. Scherwitz, J. H. Billings, S. E. Brown, K. L. Gould, T. A. Merritt, S. Sparler, et al. "Intensive Lifestyle Changes for Reversal of Coronary Heart Disease." *JAMA* 280, no. 23 (Dec. 16, 1998): 2001–07.

38. Nilsson, A. G., D. Sundh, F. Bäckhed, and M. Lorentzon. "Lactobacillus Reuteri Reduces Bone Loss in Older Women with Low Bone Mineral Density: A Randomized, Placebo-Controlled, Double-Blind, Clinical Trial." *Journal of Internal Medicine* (Jun 21, 2018).

39. Chin, Kok-Yong, and Soelaiman Ima-Nirwana. "Olives and Bone: A Green Osteoporosis Prevention Option." *International Journal of Environmental Research and Public Health* 13, no. 8 (July 26, 2016): 755. doi:10.3390/ijerph13080755.

40. Aghajanian, Patrick, Susan Hall, Montri D. Wongworawat, and Subburaman Mohan. "The Roles and Mechanisms of Actions of Vitamin C in Bone: New Developments." *Journal of Bone and Mineral Research* 30, no. 11 (Nov. 2015): 1945–55. doi:10.1002/jbmr.2709.

41. Christiansen, Blaine A., Simrit Bhatti, Ramin Goudarzi, and Shahin Emami. "Management of Osteoarthritis With Avocado/Soybean Unsaponifiables." *Cartilage* 7, no. 1 (Jan. 2016): 114.

42. Hebert, Liesi, Jennifer Weuve, Paul Scherr, and Denis Evans. "Alzheimer Disease in the United States (2010–2050) Estimated Using the 2010 Census." *Neurology* 80, no. 19 (May 7, 2013): 1778–83. doi:10.1212/WNL.0b013e31828726f5.

43. West Health Institute/NORC at the University of Chicago. *Perceptions of Aging During Each Decade of Life After 30.* Chicago, IL: NORC at the University of Chicago and West Health Institute, 2017.

44. Cederholm, Tommy, Norman Salem, and Jan Palmblad. "Ω-3 Fatty Acids in the Prevention of Cognitive Decline in Humans." *Advances in Nutrition* 4, no. 6 (Nov. 2013): 672–76. doi:10.3945/an.113.004556.

45. Morris, Martha Clare, Yamin Wang, Lisa L. Barnes, David A. Bennett, Bess Dawson-Hughes, and Sarah L. Booth. "Nutrients and Bioactives in Green Leafy Vegetables and Cognitive Decline: Prospective Study." *Neurology* 90, no. 3 (Jan. 16, 2018): e222. doi:10.1212/WNL.0000000000004815.

46. Lukaschek, Karoline, Clemens von Schacky, Johannes Kruse, and Karl-Heinz Ladwig.

Sources

"Cognitive Impairment Is Associated With a Low Omega-3 Index in the Elderly: Results From the KORA-Age Study." *Dementia and Geriatric Cognitive Disorders* 42, no. 3–4 (2016): 236–45. doi:10.1159/000448805.

47. Muthaiyah, Balu, Musthafa Essa, Ved Chauhan, and Abha Chauhan. "Protective Effects of Walnut Extract Against Amyloid Beta Peptide-Induced Cell Death and Oxidative Stress in PC12 Cells." *Neurochemical Research* 36, no. 11 (Nov. 2011): 2096–103. doi:10.1007/s11064-011-0533-z.

48. Mattson, Mark P., Valter D. Longo, and Michelle Harvie. "Impact of Intermittent Fasting on Health and Disease Processes." *Ageing Research Reviews* 39 (Oct. 2017): 46–58. doi:10.1016/j.arr.2016.10.005.

49. Liu, Qing-Ping, Yan-Feng Wu, Hong-Yu Cheng, Tao Xia, Hong Ding, Hui Wang, Ze-Mu Wang, and Yun Xu. "Habitual Coffee Consumption and Risk of Cognitive Decline/Dementia: A Systematic Review and Meta-Analysis of Prospective Cohort Studies." *Nutrition* 32, no. 6 (June 2016): 628–36. doi:10.1016/j.nut.2015.11.015.

50. Wu, Lei, Dali Sun, and Yao He. "Coffee Intake and the Incident Risk of Cognitive Disorders: A Dose-Response Meta-Analysis of Nine Prospective Cohort Studies." *Clinical Nutrition* 36, no. 3 (June 2017): 730–36. doi:10.1016/j.clnu.2016.05.015.

51. Feng, L., M. -S. Chong, W. -S. Lim, Q. Gao, M. S. Nyunt, T. -S. Lee, S. L. Collinson, T. Tsoi, E. -H. Kua, and T. -P. Ng. "Tea Consumption Reduces the Incidence of Neurocognitive Disorders: Findings From the Singapore Longitudinal Aging Study." *The Journal of Nutrition, Health & Aging* 20, no. 10 (2016): 1002–09. doi:10.1007/s12603-016-0687-0.

52. Bowtell, Joanna L., Zainie Aboo-Bakkar, Myra E. Conway, Anna-Lynne R. Adlam, and Jonathan Fulford. "Enhanced Task-Related Brain Activation and Resting Perfusion in Healthy Older Adults After Chronic Blueberry Supplementation." *Applied Physiology, Nutrition, and Metabolism* 42, no. 7 (July 2017): 773–79. doi:10.1139/apnm-2016-0550.

53. CDC/National Center for Health Statistics. "Overweight and Obesity." FastStats, accessed Aug. 2, 2018. www.cdc.gov/nchs/fastats/obesity-overweight.htm.

54. Centers for Disease Control and Prevention. *National Diabetes Statistics Report, 2017.* Atlanta, GA: Centers for Disease Control and Prevention, US Department of Health and Human Services, 2017. Accessed Aug. 2, 2018. www.cdc.gov/diabetes/data/statistics/statistics-report.html.

55. CDC/National Center for Health Statistics. "Deaths and Mortality." FastStats, accessed Aug. 2, 2018 www.cdc.gov/nchs/fastats/deaths.htm.

56. "Long-Term Effects of Lifestyle Intervention or Metformin on Diabetes Development and Microvascular Complications Over 15-Year Follow-Up: The Diabetes Prevention Program Outcomes Study." *The Lancet. Diabetes & Endocrinology* 3, no. 11 (Nov. 2015): 866–75. doi:10.1016/S2213-8587(15)00291-0.

57. Dwyer, T., A. -L. Ponsonby, O. C. Ukoumunne, A. Pezic, A. Venn, D. Dunstan, E. Barr, et al. "Association of Change in Daily Step Count Over Five Years With Insulin Sensitivity and Adiposity: Population Based Cohort Study." *BMJ (Clinical Research Ed.)* 342, (Jan. 13, 2011): c7249.

58. Strasser, Barbara, and Dominik Pesta. "Resistance Training for Diabetes Prevention and Therapy: Experimental Findings and Molecular Mechanisms." *BioMed Research International* 2013 (2013). doi:10.1155/2013/805217.

59. Ding, Ming, Shilpa N. Bhupathiraju, Mu Chen, Rob M. van Dam, and Frank B. Hu. "Caffeinated and Decaffeinated Coffee Consumption and Risk of Type 2 Diabetes: A Systematic Review and a Dose-Response Meta-Analysis." *Diabetes Care* 37, no. 2 (Feb. 2014): 569–86. doi:10.2337/dc13-1203.

60. Costello, Rebecca B., Johanna T. Dwyer, Leila Saldanha, Regan L. Bailey, Joyce Merkel, and Edwina Wambogo. "Do Cinnamon Supplements Have a Role in Glycemic Control in Type 2 Diabetes? A Narrative Review." *Journal of the Academy of Nutrition and Dietetics* 116, no. 11 (Nov. 2016): 1794–802. doi:10.1016/j.jand.2016.07.015.

61. Risérus, Ulf, Walter C. Willett, and Frank B. Hu. "Dietary Fats and Prevention of Type 2 Diabetes." *Progress in Lipid Research* 48, no. 1 (2009): 44–51. doi:10.1016/j.plipres.2008.10.002.

62. de Munter, J. S. L, F. B. Hu, D. Spiegelman, M. Franz, and R. M. van Dam. "Whole Grain, Bran, and Germ Intake and Risk of Type 2 Diabetes: A Prospective Cohort Study and Systematic Review." *PLoS Medicine* 4, no. 8 (2007): e261. doi:10.1371/journal.pmed.0040261.

63. Zhao, Liping, Feng Zhang, Xiaoying Ding, Guojun Wu, Yan Y. Lam, Xuejiao Wang, Huaqing Fu, et al. "Gut Bacteria Selectively Promoted by Dietary Fibers Alleviate Type 2 Diabetes." *Science* 359, no. 6380 (March 9, 2018): 1151–1156.

64. Pan, An, Qi Sun, Adam M. Bernstein, Matthias B. Schulze, JoAnn E. Manson, Walter C. Willett, and Frank B. Hu. "Red Meat Consumption and Risk of Type 2 Diabetes: 3 Cohorts of US Adults and an Updated Meta-Analysis." *The American Journal of Clinical Nutrition* 94, no. 4 (Oct. 2011): 1088–96. doi:10.3945/ajcn.111.018978.

65. Kim, Hyun Min, and Jaetaek Kim. "The Effects of Green Tea on Obesity and Type 2 Diabetes." *Diabetes & Metabolism Journal* 37, no. 3 (June 2013): 173–175.

66. Bhupathiraju, Shilpa N., An Pan, JoAnn E. Manson, Walter C. Willett, Rob M. van Dam, and Frank B. Hu. "Changes in Coffee Intake and Subsequent Risk of Type 2 Diabetes: Three Large Cohorts of US Men and Women." *Diabetologia* 57, no. 7 (July 2014): 1346–1354.

67. Wilson, Emily A., and Barbara Demmig-Adams. "Antioxidant, Anti-inflammatory, and Antimicrobial Properties of Garlic and Onions." *Nutrition & Food Science* 37, no. 3 (May 29, 2007): 178–83. doi:10.1108/00346650710749071.

68. Fadus, Matthew C., Cecilia Lau, Jai Bikhchandani, and Henry T. Lynch. "Curcumin: An Age-Old Anti-Inflammatory and Anti-Neoplastic Agent." *Journal of Traditional and Complementary Medicine* 7, no. 3 (July 1, 2017): 339–46. doi:10.1016/j.jtcme.2016.08.002.

69. Elizabeth A. Townsend, Matthew E. Siviski, Yi Zhang, Carrie Xu, Bhupinder Hoonjan, and Charles W. Emala. "Effects of Ginger and Its Constituents on Airway Smooth Muscle Relaxation and Calcium Regulation." *American Journal of Respiratory Cell and Molecular Biology* 48, no. 2 (Feb. 1, 2013): 157–63. doi:10.1165/rcmb.2012-0231OC.

70. Garcia-Larsen, Vanessa, James F. Potts, Ernst Omenaas, Joachim Heinrich, Cecilie Svanes, Judith Garcia-Aymerich, Peter G. Burney, and Deborah L. Jarvis. "Dietary Antioxidants and 10-Year Lung Function Decline in Adults From the ECRHS Survey." *The European Respiratory Journal* 50, no. 6 (Dec. 2017). doi:10.1183/13993003.02286-2016.

71. Zhang, Ying, Ying Li, Can Cao, Jie Cao, Wei Chen, Yu Zhang, Cheng Wang, Jia Wang, Xin Zhang, and Xiujuan Zhao. "Dietary Flavonol and Flavone Intakes and Their Major Food Sources in Chinese Adults." *Nutrition and Cancer* 62, no. 8 (2010): 1120–27. doi:10.1080/01635581.2010.513800.

72. Mori, Nagisa, Taichi Shimazu, Shizuka Sasazuki, Miho Nozue, Michihiro Mutoh, Norie Sawada, Motoki Iwasaki, et al. "Cruciferous Vegetable Intake Is Inversely Associated With Lung Cancer Risk Among Current Nonsmoking Men in the Japan Public Health Center (JPHC) Study." *The Journal of Nutrition* 147, no. 5 (May 2017): 841–49. doi:10.3945/jn.117.247494.

73. Garcia-Larsen et al. "Dietary Antioxidants and 10-Year Lung Function Decline in Adults From the ECRHS Survey."

74. Hanson, Corrine, Elizabeth Lyden, Jeremy Furtado, Hannia Campos, David Sparrow, Pantel Vokonas, and Augusto A. Litonjua. "Serum Tocopherol Levels and Vitamin E Intake Are Associated With Lung Function in the Normative Aging Study." *Clinical Nutrition* 35, no. 1 (Feb. 2016): 169–74. doi:10.1016/j.clnu.2015.01.020.

75. Hu, G., and P. A. Cassano. "Antioxidant Nutrients and Pulmonary Function: The Third National Health and Nutrition Examination Survey (NHANES III)." *American Journal of Epidemiology* 151, no. 10 (May 15, 2000): 975–81.

76. McMillan, M., E. A. Spinks, and G. R. Fenwick. "Preliminary Observations on the Effect of Dietary Brussels Sprouts on Thyroid Function." *Human Toxicology* 5, no. 1 (Jan. 1986): 15–19.

77. Ward, Mary H., Briseis A. Kilfoy, Peter J. Weyer, Kristin E. Anderson, Aaron R. Folsom, and James R. Cerhan. "Nitrate Intake and the Risk of Thyroid Cancer and Thyroid Disease." *Epidemiology* 21, no. 3 (May 2010): 389–95. doi:10.1097/EDE.0b013e3181d6201d.

78. Messina, Mark, and Geoffrey Redmond. "Effects of Soy Protein and Soybean Isoflavones on

Sources

Thyroid Function in Healthy Adults and Hypothyroid Patients: A Review of the Relevant Literature." *Thyroid* 16, no. 3 (Mar. 2006): 249–58. doi:10.1089/thy.2006.16.249.

79. Spencer, Sarah J., and Alan Tilbrook. "The Glucocorticoid Contribution to Obesity." *Stress* 14, no. 3 (May 2011): 233–46. doi:10.3109/10253890.2010.534831.

80. Tryon, Matthew S., Kimber L. Stanhope, Elissa S. Epel, Ashley E. Mason, Rashida Brown, Valentina Medici, Peter J. Havel, and Kevin D. Laugero. "Excessive Sugar Consumption May Be a Difficult Habit to Break: A View From the Brain and Body." *The Journal of Clinical Endocrinology and Metabolism* 100, no. 6 (June 2015): 2239–47. doi:10.1210/jc.2014-4353.

81. National Institutes of Health. "Vitamin D Fact Sheet for Health Professionals." Office of Dietary Supplements, accessed Aug. 2, 2018. https://ods.od.nih.gov/factsheets/VitaminD-HealthProfessional/.

82. American Academy of Dermatology. "Position Statement on VITAMIN D." Accessed Aug. 2, 2018. www.aad.org/Forms/Policies/Uploads/PS/PS-Vitamin%20D.pdf.

83. Toledo et al., "Mediterranean Diet and Invasive Breast Cancer Risk Among Women at High Cardiovascular Risk in the PREDIMED Trial," 1752–60.

84. Yonova-Doing, Ekaterina, Zoe A. Forkin, Pirro G. Hysi, Katie M. Williams, Tim D. Spector, Clare E. Gilbert, and Christopher J. Hammond. "Genetic and Dietary Factors Influencing the Progression of Nuclear Cataract." *Ophthalmology* 123, no. 6 (June 2016): 1237–44. doi:10.1016/j.ophtha.2016.01.036.

85. Lu, Minyi, Eunyoung Cho, Allen Taylor, Susan E. Hankinson, Walter C. Willett, and Paul F. Jacques. "Prospective Study of Dietary Fat and Risk of Cataract Extraction Among US Women." *American Journal of Epidemiology* 161, no. 10 (May 15, 2005): 948–59. doi:10.1093/aje/kwi118.

86. Wang, Aimin, Jing Han, Yunxia Jiang, and Dongfeng Zhang. "Association of Vitamin A and β-Carotene With Risk for Age-Related Cataract: A Meta-Analysis." *Nutrition* 30, no. 10 (Oct. 2014): 1113–21. doi:10.1016/j.nut.2014.02.025.

87. Zhang, Yufei, Wenjie Jiang, Zhutian Xie, Wenlong Wu, and Dongfeng Zhang. "Vitamin E and Risk of Age-Related Cataract: A Meta-Analysis." *Public Health Nutrition* 18, no. 15 (Oct. 2015): 2804–14. doi:10.1017/S1368980014003115.

88. Cumming, R. G., P. Mitchell, and W. Smith. "Diet and Cataract: The Blue Mountains Eye Study." *Ophthalmology* 107, no. 3 (Mar. 2000): 450–56.

89. Weikel, Karen A., Caren Garber, Alyssa Baburins, and Allen Taylor. "Nutritional Modulation of Cataract." *Nutrition Reviews* 72, no. 1 (Jan. 2014): 30–47. doi:10.1111/nure.12077.

90. Cumming, R. G., P. Mitchell, and W. Smith. "Dietary Sodium Intake and Cataract: The Blue Mountains Eye Study." *American Journal of Epidemiology* 151, no. 6 (Mar. 15, 2000): 624–26.

91. Zhang, Y. -P., W. -Q. Li, Y. -L. Sun, R. -T. Zhu, and W. -J. Wang. "Systematic Review With Meta-Analysis: Coffee Consumption and the Risk of Gallstone Disease." *Alimentary Pharmacology & Therapeutics* 42, no. 6 (Sept. 2015): 637–48. doi:10.1111/apt.13328.

92. Wang, Jiantao, Xiaolin Duan, Bingrong Li, and Xiubo Jiang. "Alcohol Consumption and Risk of Gallstone Disease: A Meta-Analysis." *European Journal of Gastroenterology & Hepatology* 29, no. 4 (Apr. 2017): e28. doi:10.1097/MEG.0000000000000803.

93. Tsai, Chung-Jyi, Michael F. Leitzmann, Frank B. Hu, Walter C. Willett, and Edward L. Giovannucci. "A Prospective Cohort Study of Nut Consumption and the Risk of Gallstone Disease in Men." *American Journal of Epidemiology* 160, no. 10 (Nov. 15, 2004): 961–68. doi:10.1093/aje/kwh302.

94. Tsai, Chung-Jyi, Michael F. Leitzmann, Frank B. Hu, Walter C. Willett, and Edward L. Giovannucci. "Frequent Nut Consumption and Decreased Risk of Cholecystectomy in Women." *The American Journal of Clinical Nutrition* 80, no. 1 (July 2004): 76–81. doi:10.1093/ajcn/80.1.76.

95. Juraschek, Stephen P., Allan C. Gelber, Hyon K. Choi, Lawrence J. Appel, and Edgar R. Miller. "Effects of the Dietary Approaches to Stop Hypertension (DASH) Diet and Sodium Intake on Serum Uric Acid." *Arthritis & Rheumatology* 68, no. 12 (Dec. 2016): 3002–09. doi:10.1002/art.39813.

96. Rai, Sharan K., Teresa T. Fung, Na Lu, Sarah F. Keller, Gary C. Curhan, and Hyon K. Choi. "The Dietary Approaches to Stop Hypertension (DASH) Diet, Western Diet, and Risk of Gout in Men: Prospective Cohort Study." *BMJ* 357 (May 9, 2017): j1794.

97. Neogi, T., C. Chen, C. Chaisson, D. J. Hunter, and Y. Zhang. "Drinking Water Can Reduce the Risk of Recurrent Gout Attacks." Abstract. 2009 ACR/ARHP Scientific Meeting, Oct. 21, 2009.

98. Choi, Hyon K., and Gary Curhan. "Coffee, Tea, and Caffeine Consumption and Serum Uric Acid Level: The Third National Health and Nutrition Examination Survey." *Arthritis and Rheumatism* 57, no. 5 (June 15, 2007): 816–21. doi:10.1002/art.22762.

99. Zhang, Yuqing, Tuhina Neogi, Clara Chen, Christine Chaisson, David J. Hunter, and Hyon K. Choi. "Cherry Consumption and Decreased Risk of Recurrent Gout Attacks." *Arthritis and Rheumatism* 64, no. 12 (Dec. 2012): 4004–11. doi:10.1002/art.34677.

100. Choi, Hyon K., Karen Atkinson, Elizabeth W. Karlson, Walter Willett, and Gary Curhan. "Purine-Rich Foods, Dairy and Protein Intake, and the Risk of Gout in Men." *The New England Journal of Medicine* 350, no. 11 (Mar. 11, 2004): 1093–103. doi:10.1056/NEJMoa035700.

101. Kang, David, George E. Haleblian, Roger L. Sur, Nicholas J. Fitzsimons, Kristy M. Borawski, and Glenn M. Preminger. "Lemonade-Based Dietary Manipulation in Patients With Hypocitraturic Nephrolithiasis." *The Journal of Urology* 175, no. 4 (Apr. 1, 2006): 334.

102. Penniston, Kristina L., Thomas H. Steele, and Stephen Y. Nakada. "Medical Management of Calcium Oxalate Stone Formers With Lemonade Results in Therapeutic Urinary Citrate and Higher Urine Volumes Than Those on Potassium Citrate Therapy." *The Journal of Urology* 175, no. 4 (Apr. 1, 2006): 496–97. doi:10.1016/S0022-5347(18)33741-8. www.jurology.com/article/S0022-5347(18)33741-8/fulltext.

103. Seltzer, M. A., R. K. Low, M. McDonald, G. S. Shami, and M. L. Stoller. "Dietary Manipulation With Lemonade to Treat Hypocitraturic Calcium Nephrolithiasis." *The Journal of Urology* 156, no. 3 (Sept. 1996): 907–09.

104. U.S. Food and Drug Administration. "Questions and Answers About FDA's Enforcement Action Against Unapproved Quinine Products." Accessed Aug. 2, 2018. www.fda.gov/downloads/drugs/guidancecomplianceregulatoryinformation/enforcementactivitiesbyfda/selectedenforcementactionsonunapproveddrugs/ucm119653.pdf.

105. Patrick, Lyn R. "Restless Legs Syndrome: Pathophysiology and the Role of Iron and Folate." *Alternative Medicine Review* 12, no. 2 (June 2007): 101–12.

106. Hornyak, M., U. Voderholzer, F. Hohagen, M. Berger, and D. Riemann. "Magnesium Therapy for Periodic Leg Movements-Related Insomnia and Restless Legs Syndrome: An Open Pilot Study." *Sleep* 21, no. 5 (Aug. 1, 1998): 501–05.

107. McCusker, Meagen M., Khayyam Durrani, Michael J. Payette, and Jeanine Suchecki. "An Eye on Nutrition: The Role of Vitamins, Essential Fatty Acids, and Antioxidants in Age-Related Macular Degeneration, Dry Eye Syndrome, and Cataract." *Clinics in Dermatology* 34, no. 2 (Mar–Apr. 2016): 276–85. doi:10.1016/j.clindermatol.2015.11.009.

108. Tong, Haiyan, Ana G. Rappold, Melissa Caughey, Alan L. Hinderliter, Maryann Bassett, Tracey Montilla, Martin W. Case, et al. "Dietary Supplementation With Olive Oil Or Fish Oil and Vascular Effects of Concentrated Ambient Particulate Matter Exposure in Human Volunteers." *Environmental Health Perspectives* 123, no. 11 (Nov. 2015): 1173–79. doi:10.1289/ehp.1408988.

109. Tong, Haiyan, Ana G. Rappold, David Diaz-Sanchez, Susan E. Steck, Jon Berntsen, Wayne E. Cascio, Robert B. Devlin, and James M. Samet. "Omega-3 Fatty Acid Supplementation Appears to Attenuate Particulate Air Pollution-Induced Cardiac Effects and Lipid Changes in Healthy Middle-Aged Adults." *Environmental Health Perspectives* 120, no. 7 (July 2012): 952–57. doi:10.1289/ehp.1104472.

110. Whorf, R. C., and S. A. Tobet. "Expression of the Raf-1 Protein in Rat Brain during Development and its Hormonal Regulation in Hypothalamus." *Journal of Neurobiology* 23, no. 2 (Mar. 1992): 103–19. doi:10.1002/neu.480230202.

111. Shirai, Oshikazu, Takao Tsuda, Shinya Kitagawa, Ken Naitoh, Taisuke Seki, Kiyoshi Kamimura, and Masaaki Morohashi. "Alcohol Ingestion Stimulates Mosquito Attraction." *Journal of the American Mosquito Control Association* 18, no. 2 (June 2002): 91–96.

INDEX

A

Acidic foods 159, 161
Adrenal issues 290–291
Age-related cognitive ability
  265–266
Aggrecan molecules 260
Air pollution 299
Alcohol
  breast-feeding and 220
  decision-making and 172,
    191
  gallstone prevention 295
  as headache trigger 140
  holiday season 191
  insect control and 299
  as limit food 75
  PMS and period pain and
    226
  sleep and 298
  substitutions for 161, 198
Allium vegetables 248
Almond milk 75
Almonds 209, 298
Alzheimer's disease 266, 267,
  268
Amino acids 43, 135, 169
Anti-inflammatories 151–152,
  299, 319
Antioxidants 72, 209, 246–247,
  248, 264, 294–295, 319
Apples 157, 180, 246, 280
Applesauce 192
Apricots 158
Artichokes 72, 96, 263
Artificial sweeteners 141
Asparagus 72, 275
Avocado cream 97–98
Avocado oil 73, 260
Avocados 71–72, 73, 152, 216,
  250, 263, 264
"Avoid" foods 75

B

Baby formula 220
Bacon 93–94, 250
Bacteria, gut see Microbiome
Bacteria, in foods 161

Bagels and cream cheese 95
Bananas 73, 88, 157
Bean pasta 95, 97
Beans 72, 74, 134, 208, 241, 298
Beef jerky 177
Beer 198
Benign prostatic hyperplasia
  (BPH) 239–241
Berries
  as antioxidants 246, 247,
    250
  for brain health 269
  for depression 124
  for diabetes prevention 275
  as snack substitute 88
  for sperm health 238
Biological clock see Circadian
  rhythm
Black beans 208
Blackberries 248
Blanching 90
Bland foods 159, 161, 206
Bloating 160
Blood sugar level 115, 160
Blood sugar problem 45–47, 272
Blueberries 238, 248, 250, 269
Bones 260–261
BPH (benign prostatic hyper-
  plasia) 239–241
Brain 265–269
  circadian rhythm and
    26–27
  decision-making 173
  DHA for 219
  glucose for energy needs
    164
  hunger and 114–115
  mood and 124
Brain cancer 250
Braising 91
Bran cereal 250
BRAT diet 157
Bread and butter, substitutions
  for 95
Breakfast
  importance of 57–61
  before marathons 206

stereotypes 92
substitutions 93–95, 250,
  269
Breast cancer 48, 250, 294
Breast-feeding 217–221
Broccoli 72, 91, 247, 248, 263,
  280
Brown rice 75
Brussels sprouts 72, 241, 247
Buffets 181
Burgers, substitutions for 275
Butter, substitutions for 96–97,
  192, 264

C

Cabbage 72, 233, 241, 247, 280
Caffeine
  breast-feeding and 221
  for decision-making 173
  for diabetes prevention 273
  gallstone prevention 295
  headaches and 138
  hot flashes and 229
  for pain 153
  PMS and period pain and
    226
  prostate health and 241
  sleep and 135, 298
  for test-taking 164–165
  see also Coffee; Tea
Calcium 226, 262–263
Cancer 243–250
  food as medicine 16, 233,
    246–247, 294
  visceral fat and 48
Candy, substitutions for 88, 280
Caraway 161
Carbohydrates
  avoiding 167–168
  blood sugar and 45, 47, 160
  in breast milk 218
  inflammation and 152
  nutrition basics 39–41
  slow-digesting 160
  see also Complex carbohy-
    drates; Simple
    carbohydrates

Carbonated drinks *see* Soda
Cardiovascular diseases *see*
　Heart health
Carrots 72, 248, 250
Cartilage 260
Cataracts 294–295
Cauliflower 72, 247, 248, 280
Celery 72, 201, 225, 280
Cereal 93, 250, 269
Cheese, limiting 74, 75, 209,
　264
Cherries 153, 296
Chia seeds 147
Chicken 74, 134, 135, 198, 207,
　250
Chicken soup 146
Chicken tenders, substitutions
　for 198
Chickpeas 116, 241
Chips, substitutions for 87, 118,
　209, 216, 238, 275, 307–308
Chocolate 141
　see also Dark chocolate;
　Milk chocolate
Cholesterol 319
　see also LDL cholesterol
Chronic pain 149–150
Chrononutrition, defined 54,
　319
Cinnamon 161, 273
Circadian rhythm
　basics 25–28
　defined 319
　food clock and 28–32,
　　55–56, 59, 311
　microbiome and 32–34
Citrus fruits 247, 264, 284, 297
Coconut oil 75
Coffee
　for bone health 263
　for brain health 269
　for cancer-fighting 248
　for decision-making 173
　for diabetes prevention
　　273, 275
　at events 180–181
　for fatigue 121
　gallstone prevention 295
　for gout 296
　for hanger 118
　hot flashes and 229
　for job interviews 169
　for memory 169
　for pain 153

substitutions for 221, 226,
　241
　for test-taking 164–165
　see also Caffeine
Cognitive decline 265–268
Colon 156
Colon cancer 248, 250
Colostrum 218
Complex carbohydrates 40–41,
　122, 124, 141, 160, 206, 215
Consistency, food clock guide-
　lines 62–63
Constipation 158–159
Convenience foods 175–177
Cookies, substitutions for 88,
　238
Cooking techniques 90–92
Corn 74, 198, 238, 241, 280
Cortisol 290
Cotton candy and Cracker
　Jacks 198
Crackers, substitutions for 87,
　250
Cramps, leg 297–298
Cramps, menstrual 223–225
Cranberries 158
CRAP diet 158
Croutons, substitutions for 226
Cruciferous vegetables 233,
　241, 247, 248, 250, 289
Cucumbers 72, 250

D

Dairy products 75, 161, 215, 237,
　262
Dark chocolate 88, 153, 200,
　209, 225–226, 275
Dating, first-date food 199–201
Daytime, food clock guidelines
　55–57, 311
Decision fatigue 127–128
Decision-making 171–173
Dementia 266
Depression 123–125
Desserts
　avoiding 117
　fruit for 81, 135
　holiday favorites 192
　substitutions 88, 135, 226,
　　275, 308
Diabetes
　breakfast and 58, 60
　glucose and 44
　heart disease and 253

insulin and 29
prevention 16, 271–276
related health problems 45
risk factors 47
visceral fat and 48
Diarrhea 157–158
Diet soda 153
Digestive problems 155–161,
　295–296
Digestive process 44, 156
Dinner 64–65, 78–81, 99, 134
Doughnuts, substitutions for
　117

E

Eggs 74–75, 93–94, 135, 140,
　208, 249, 252
Endometrial cancer 248
Energy drinks, substitutions
　for 221
Erectile dysfunction *see* Tes-
　tosterone boost
Esophagus 44, 156, 159
Esselstyn, Caldwell 256
Events, eating at 179–181,
　195–198
Exercise
　benefits 106, 203, 245, 273
　on vacation 185–186
　what to eat 203–209
　when to eat 204–205
Extra-virgin olive oil 73, 152,
　264, 299

F

Farro 74, 95
Fasting 66–67, 141, 205
Fat (body fat) 47–48, 205
Fat (macronutrient) 41–43, 218
Fatigue fighters 119–122
Fatty liver disease 46
Fertility 211–216, 235–238
Fiber
　for bloating 160
　cancer-fighting properties
　　250
　for constipation 158
　in fruit 72
　gallstone prevention
　　295–296
　for inflammation 284–285
　for sleep 134
Fibroids 224
Figs, for bone health 263

Index

First dates 199–201
Fish
  for cancer-fighting 250
  high-mercury fish 214, 215
  inflammation reduction
    152, 285, 299
  pregnancy and 214, 215, 216
  for sleep 134
  for thyroid health 290
  see also Ocean trout;
    Salmon
Flax 168
Flaxseed 224, 269
Folate 238, 298
Folic acid 237
Food clock *see* When to eat
Formula, infant 220
Free radicals 246
Freezing vegetables 91–92
Fried foods 75, 279
Fries, substitutions for 198, 275
Frittatas 93–94
Fruit
  added sugar 153
  cancer-fighting 245,
    246–247
  for depression 125
  for fatigue 122
  for on the go 176
  before holiday meals 190
  inflammation reduction
    284
  monthly plan 72
  for PMS and period pain
    226
  for testosterone boost
    232–233
  on vacation 186

G

Gallstones 295–296
Garlic 146, 200–201, 233, 247,
  248, 279
Ginger 146, 152, 161, 226, 250,
  279
Glucose
  avoiding 165
  blood sugar problem
    45–46, 48, 272
  defined 319
  as energy 30, 39–40, 164,
    204
Glycemic index, defined 319
Glycogen 39–40, 46, 204, 319

Gout 296
Granola bars 177
Grapefruit 280
Grapes 232
Gravy 193
Greek yogurt 75, 93, 177, 285,
  308
Green bananas 73, 88
Green tea 125, 229, 241, 275
Greens 72, 135, 139–140, 263,
  268, 292, 298
Grief 127–129
Gut bacteria *see* Microbiome

H

Hamburgers, substitutions for
  275
Headaches 137–141
Healthy fats 71–72, 73, 121,
  273–274, 285
Heart health 16, 48, 251–257
High-glycemic foods 47, 319
Holidays 189–193
Hormones
  adrenal issues 290–291
  circadian rhythm and 26,
    56
  hormonal issues 287–292
  skin issues 291–292
  thyroid issues 288–290
  see also Hot flashes; Tes-
    tosterone boost
Hot dogs, substitutions for 198
Hot flashes 227–229
Hummus 177, 221, 225
Hunger
  brain and 114–115
  circadian rhythm and 59
  focus on satisfied, not full
    103–104
  food clock 28–32, 59
  instincts 34–35
Hydration drinks 158
  see also Sports drinks;
    Water
Hyperthyroidism 289
Hypothyroidism 289–290

I

Icelandic yogurt 93, 285
Illness *see* Sickness
Immune system 245–246, 278,
  282–283
Infant formula 220

Infertility 212–213, 215
Inflammation 281–285
  defined 319
  heart disease and 255
  pain and 151–152
  saturated fats and 41
  spices for 279
Insect control 299
Insomnia 131–135
Insulin 29–30, 39, 45–47, 160,
  272, 319
Insulin resistance
  consistent meals and 63
  defined 320
  exercise for 273
  health implications 46–47
  saturated fats and 41
  time of day and 47, 56, 59
  timing of eating and 29–32
  visceral fat and 48
Insulin sensitivity 29–32, 320
Intermittent fasting 66–67
Iodine 289, 290
Iron 224, 298

J

Jackson, James Caleb 58
Jet lag 33–34
Job interviews 167–169
Joints 259, 261–262, 264, 296
Juice, substitutions for 147,
  241, 264

K

Kale 263, 280, 299
Kellogg, John Harvey 58
Kidney beans, for prostate
  function 241
Kidney stones 296–297
Kiwi 135, 246

L

Lactation 217–221
LDL (bad) cholesterol 41, 46,
  58, 60, 63, 253, 255
Leftovers, substitutions for 118
Legumes 74, 219, 241
Lentils 238, 298
Libido 201, 231–232
Lima beans, for prostate func-
  tion 241
"Limit" foods 74–75
Liver, glycogen storage 46
Liver cancer 248

Longo, Valter 66–67
Lunch, importance of 58
Lung health 277–280, 299
Lycopene 237, 241, 247, 248

M

Macronutrients 38–43, 218, 320
  see also Carbohydrates;
  Fat; Protein
Magnesium 134–135, 140, 226,
  263, 298
Marathons 206–207
Marinara sauce 200
Mashed potatoes 192
Meditation 291
Mediterranean diet 151–152,
  228, 250, 255–256, 294
Melatonin 135
Memory 163–165, 169, 265–269
Menopause 227–229
Menstruation 223–226
Mercury, in fish 214, 215, 219
Metabolic syndrome 60, 62,
  102, 320
Microbiome 32–34, 156–157,
  284–285, 320
Micronutrients 38, 320
Milk 93, 220, 238
Milk chocolate, substitutions
  for 192, 209
Mindful eating 101–107,
  308–309
Monounsaturated fats 42
Morning sickness 214
Mornings, food clock guide-
  lines 57–61
Mosquitoes 299
Mourning 127–129
Mushrooms 73, 146, 247

N

Nachos, substitutions for 198
Neck cancer 250
Neurons 266–267
Night, snacking at 60, 82, 135
Night shift 27–28
Night vision 299
Nitrates 249, 290
Non-starchy vegetables 71,
  72–73
Nursing mothers 217–221
Nut milks 75
Nutrition basics 37–49
  carbohydrates 39–41

fat 41–43
  macronutrients 38–43
  protein 43
  trans fats 42
  why food matters 43–49
Nuts
  for brain health 268
  diabetes prevention 274
  as exercise food 209
  fertility and 216
  gallstone prevention 295
  for on the go 176
  for headaches 140
  as healthy fat 71, 73
  inflammation reduction
    285
  for job interviews 169
  monthly plan 86
  for prostate function 241
  snacking on 86, 87
  for sperm health 237
  for stadium events 197

O

Oats and oatmeal 74, 93, 117,
  285
Obesity, and timing of eating
  60
Ocean trout 74, 125, 141, 147,
  219, 237, 267
Okra 73, 263
Olive oil 73, 152, 221, 250, 264,
  269, 299
Olives 71
Omega-3 fats
  as anti-inflammatory 152
  for brain health 42–43,
    268
  for decision-making 173
  for depression 125
  fertility and 214
  for headaches 141
  for heart health 42
  sources 71–72
  for sperm health 237
On-the-go eating 175–177
Onions 73, 248, 279
Oral rehydration solution
  (ORS) 158
Orange juice, substitutions for
  147, 241
Oranges 147, 209, 280, 299
Ornish, Dean 256
Osteoarthritis 261–262

Osteoporosis 260–261
Ovarian cancer 249
Oven roasting 91

P

Pain 149–153, 223–226
Palm oil 75
Partially hydrogenated oils 192
Pasta, white 95, 97
Pasta, whole grain 71, 74, 95
Pastries, substitutions for 88
Peanuts 125, 197, 198, 241
Period pain 223–226
Phytoestrogens 224, 228
Phytonutrients 264, 320
Pizza 198, 275
Plaques 252–253
PMS (premenstrual syndrome)
  223–226
Pollution 299
Polyphenols 248, 263
Polyunsaturated fats 42, 241,
  273–274, 294
Pomegranates and juice 232,
  238, 241, 248
Popcorn 74, 87, 117, 198
Pork 74
Potassium 263
Potato chips see Chips
Potatoes, sweet 73, 192, 208,
  263
Potatoes, white 73, 75, 192, 216,
  263, 275
Prebiotic fiber 284–285
Prediabetes 47
Pregnancy 211–216, 220
Premenstrual syndrome (PMS)
  223–226
Preparation techniques 89–92
Pretzels, substitutions for 87,
  198, 280
Probiotics 263
Processed foods 75, 86–88, 274
Processed meats 74, 177, 216,
  224, 249, 250, 274
Prostate, shrinking of 239–241
Prostate cancer 48, 233, 240,
  249
Protein
  for breakfast 61
  in breast milk 218
  for fatigue 121
  monthly plan 72, 74
  nutrition basics 43

Index

pre-date meal 201
red meat 94
for runners 207
Prunes 158
Pumpkin seeds 135, 226, 233, 238, 241
Purposeful eating 106–107

Q
Quercetin 238, 280
Quinine 298

R
Raisins 104, 158
Raspberries 248
Red meat
  cancer and 249
  diabetes and 274
  heart disease and 252
  limiting 74, 94, 224
  sperm health and 237
  substitutions for 141, 250
Red wine 140, 275
Reflux 159
Resistant starch vegetables 73
Restaurants 184–185, 186
Restless leg syndrome 297–298
Restricted eating 66–67
Resveratrol 232
Rice 75, 97, 157, 215
Roasting 91
Running 206–207

S
Sadness 123–125
Salad 73, 81, 200, 268
Salad dressing 96–97, 200, 250
Salmon
  as anti-inflammatory 152, 299
  for bone health 263, 264
  for brain health 267
  for breast-feeding moms 219
  for cataracts 295
  defined 320
  for depression 125
  for diabetes prevention 275
  for headaches 141
  as healthy fat 42–43, 71
  pregnancy and 214
  for sickness 147
  for sperm health 237

for testosterone boost 233
vitamin D in 292
as yes food 74
Salt 221
Sardines 264
Saturated fats 41, 94, 192, 237, 241, 256, 285
Sautéing 90
Seafood 74, 298
Seeds 73, 140, 241
Selenium 207, 237, 247, 248
Sesame seeds 226, 241
Sex drive 201, 231–232
Shift workers 27–28
Shortening, substitutions for 192
Shrimp, substitutions for 264
Sickness 143–147
  see also specific conditions
Simple carbohydrates 40–41, 167–168, 285, 295
Skeleton fortification 259–264
Skin issues 291–292
Sleep 27, 30, 172
Sleeplessness 131–135
Small intestine 44, 156
Smell, sense of 105–106
Smoking 253, 277
Snacks 81, 82, 116, 117
Social functions 179–181, 195–198
Soda, substitutions for 153, 198, 269, 275, 280
Sodium 160
Soup 98, 146
Soy, thyroid medication and 290
Soy sauce, substitutions for 141
Soybeans 135, 228, 260
Sperm health 232, 235–237
Spices 107, 152, 276, 279, 307–308
Spicy foods, substitutions for 161
Spinach 135, 139–140, 240, 263, 295, 298, 299
Sporting events 195–198
Sports drinks 206–207
Sprouts 73, 247
Stadiums, eating at 195–198
Starchy vegetables 71, 75
Steaming 91
Stereotyping food 63–65, 92–95, 312
Stomach 44, 156, 159

Stressed and hangry 113–118, 290–291
Sugar
  avoiding 75, 117, 165
  brain health and 269
  cancer and 250
  carbohydrates as 39
  diabetes and 274–275
  inflammation and 152, 285
  substitutions 250
  wreaking biological havoc 40
Suprachiasmatic nucleus 26, 29, 320
Sushi 147, 198
Sweet potatoes 73, 192, 208, 263
Syrups 75

T
Tart cherry juice 135, 153
Taste, sense of 17–18, 105
Tea
  for brain health 269
  for cancer-fighting 248–249
  for decision-making 173
  for fatigue 121
  green tea 125, 229, 241, 275
  for hanger 118
  sweeteners 250
  for test-taking 164–165
  while breast-feeding 221
  see also Caffeine
Television 196
Temptation, managing 303–309
  10 Commandments 311–312
Test-taking 163–165
Testosterone boost 231–233, 238
Thanksgiving 134, 193
31-day plan *see* When Way diet
Thyroid issues 288–290
Tiredness *see* Fatigue fighters
Toast 157
Tomatoes 73, 237, 241, 247, 248, 263, 279
Tonic water 298
Trans fats 42, 192, 285
Triglycerides 46, 283
Trout 74, 125, 141, 147, 219, 237, 267
Tryptophan 125, 134–135, 168

Turkey 74, 134, 193, 198
Turmeric 152, 279
Type 2 diabetes
   breakfast and 58, 60
   heart disease and 253
   prevention of 271–276
   risk factors 47
   visceral fat and 48

U
Unsaturated fats 41–42
Uterine fibroids 224

V
Vacations, eating on 183–187
Vegetable cream 96–97
Vegetable oil, substitutions for 269
Vegetables, non-starchy
   for bone health 263
   cancer-fighting 245, 246–247, 248
   as chips substitute 118, 307–308
   for depression 125
   for diabetes prevention 275
   for fibroids 224
   freezing 91–92
   for holidays 191
   inflammation reduction 284
   list of 72–73
   preparation techniques 89–92
   at stadium events 196
   31-day plan 71, 81
   on vacation 186
Vegetables, resistant starch 73
Veggie burgers 275
Visceral fat 42, 48–49
Vitamin C 144, 237, 264, 294–295
Vitamin D 245–246, 263, 291–292
Vitamin E 237, 294–295
Vitamins, prenatal 213
Vomiting 157–158

W
Walnut milk 75
Walnuts
   health benefits 152, 237, 263, 268, 285

as healthy fats 71–72
snacking on 86, 87, 141
Water
   breast-feeding and 221
   for digestive problems 159, 161
   at events 180–181
   for fatigue 120–121
   for on the go 176
   for gout 296
   for holidays 190–191
   increasing sense of smell 106
   for job interviews 169
   for kidney stones 297
   for lung health 278–279
   before marathons 206
   for PMS and period pain 225
   for sleeplessness 135
   as snack substitute 87
   for sperm health 238
   at stadium events 198
   substitutions for 118, 221
   10 commandments 312
   on vacation 186–187
Water retention 160
Watermelon 232–233
Weight loss 48, 232, 236
When to eat
   circadian rhythm and food clock 28–32, 55–56, 59, 311–312
   circadian rhythm basics 25–28
   day-to-day consistency 62–63
   for decision-making 173
   eat early 34–35
   eat more in the morning and less later on 57–61, 78–83
   eat when the sun shines 55–57, 84
   food clock guidelines 53–67
   intermittent fasting 66–67
   introduction 17, 18, 23–24
   microbiome's circadian rhythm 32–34
   science behind 23–35
   stop stereotyping food 63–65, 92–95, 312

When Way diet
   avoid foods 75
   baseline 76–77
   daily plan 78–99
   goal 70–72
   guidelines 54–65
   for heart health 255–256
   hybrid plan 257
   introduction 19
   limit foods 74–75
   nuts 86
   plus plan 256–257
   10 Commandments 311–312
   31-day plan 69–99
   yes foods 72–74
White pasta, substitutions for 95, 97
White potatoes 73, 75, 192, 216, 263, 275
White rice 75, 97, 157, 215
Whole grains
   for depression 124
   diabetes prevention 273–274
   for fatigue 122
   before holiday meals 190
   list of 73–74
   monthly plan 71, 73–74, 95
   for restless leg syndrome 298
   as snack substitute 87
   for test-taking 165
Wild rice 74, 97
Willpower 305
Wine 140, 275
Working out see Exercise

Y
Yams 216
"Yes" foods 72–74
Yogurt 75, 93, 177, 285

Z
Zinc-rich foods
   for breast-feeding moms 219
   for colds 144
   fertility and 216
   for prostate function 240
   sense of smell and 106
   for sperm health 237, 238
   as testosterone booster 233
Zinc supplements 144, 146

ABOUT THE
AUTHORS

Dr. Michael Roizen is chief wellness officer of the Cleveland Clinic, and served as founding chair of its Wellness Institute from 2007 to 2017. Certified in internal medicine and anesthesiology, he is a Phi Beta Kappa graduate of Williams College and Alpha Omega Alpha honor society from University of California, San Francisco School of Medicine, and served 16 years on U.S. Food and Drug Administration advisory committees. He has written more than 188 peer-reviewed scientific publications, four *New York Times* #1 best sellers, and nine overall best sellers. A recipient of an Emmy, an Ellie, and the Paul G. Rogers best medical communicator award from the National Library of Medicine, Dr. Roizen is devoted to helping people live younger. Follow him @DrMikeRoizen.

Dr. Michael Crupain is a multiple Emmy Award–winning producer and the medical unit chief of staff at *The Dr. Oz Show*. He is board certified in preventive medicine and a fellow of the American College of Preventive Medicine. He completed his residency and master's in public health at the Johns Hopkins Bloomberg School of Public Health, where he is a member of the faculty. A graduate of New York Medical College and Duke University, he previously ran the food safety testing program at Consumer Reports and is passionate about creating a healthier world through policy and culture change. He cooks every day. Follow him @DrCrupain.

Ted Spiker is the author or co-author of more than 20 books, including multiple *New York Times* best sellers. A former articles editor at *Men's Health*, he has had hundreds of stories published in various publications, many focusing on health and fitness. A professor at the University of Florida since 2001, Spiker was named the university's Teacher of the Year (representing more than 3,000 faculty) in 2016–17. Follow him @ ProfSpiker.

WHAT TO EAT WHEN: YOU ASK, WE ANSWER

Have a question about What to Eat When? Want more help deciding what foods and timing can work for you? Let us know. We're happy to answer questions that may not be addressed in the book. Please reach out to us at questions@whenway.com.